RATIONAL FAITH

Library of Religious Philosophy

THOMAS V. MORRIS, General Editor

Volume 10

Rational Faith

CATHOLIC RESPONSES TO REFORMED EPISTEMOLOGY

Edited by
Linda Zagzebski

UNIVERSITY OF NOTRE DAME PRESS
NOTRE DAME, INDIANA

Copyright © 1993
University of Notre Dame Press
Notre Dame, Indiana 46556
All Rights Reserved
Manufactured in the United States of America

Library of Congress Cataloging-in-Publication Data

Rational faith : Catholic responses to Reformed epistemology / edited
by Linda Zagzebski.
    p.   cm.—(Library of religious philosophy ; v. 10)
    Includes bibliographical references
    ISBN 0-268-01643-7 (alk. paper)
    1. Reformed epistemology.   2. Faith and reason.   3. Natural
theology.   4. Christianity—Philosophy.   I. Zagzebski, Linda
Trinkaus, 1946– .   II. Series.
    BL51.R288   1992
    210—dc20   92-53742
                                                              CIP

∞ *The paper used in this publication meets the minimum requirements*
of the American National Standard for Information Sciences—Permanence of Paper
for Printed Library Materials, ANSI Z39.48-1984.

Contents

Contributors

John Greco, Assistant Professor of Philosophy, Fordham University

Patrick Lee, Associate Professor of Philosophy, Franciscan University of Steubenville, Ohio

Ralph McInerny, Michael P. Grace Professor of Philosophy, University of Notre Dame

Hugo Meynell, Professor of Religious Studies, University of Calgary, Alberta, Canada

Philip L. Quinn, John A. O'Brien Professor of Philosophy, University of Notre Dame

James Ross, Professor of Philosophy, University of Pennsylvania

Thomas D. Sullivan, Aquinas Chair in Philosophy and Theology, University of St. Thomas, St. Paul, Minnesota

Linda Zagzebski, Professor of Philosophy, Loyola Marymount University, Los Angeles

John Zeis, Associate Professor of Philosophy, Canisius College, Buffalo, New York

vi

Introduction

Linda Zagzebski

1. The search for a new account of the rationality of religious belief is currently one of the major interests of Anglo-
American philosophy of religion. To some viewers of the
philosophical scene this is merely an *ad hoc* reaction to religious
skepticism, but it is, in fact, part of a widespread desire to re-
examine the nature of rationality—a desire found among
philosophers in such diverse fields as moral and political
philosophy, philosophy of science, and philosophy of mind,
and arising from scholars who have been influenced primarily
by continental Europe as well as from those who have been an-
alytically trained. An important line of inquiry in this area
comes from Alvin Plantinga and other Calvinist philosophers,
notably Nicholas Wolterstorff, George Mavrodes, and Kenneth
Konyndyk. The work of these thinkers is both strong and original, and it has been responsible for giving religious philosophers a much-needed sense of pride. Because of its Calvinist
origin, this approach to religious knowledge and belief has
been called "Reformed Epistemology."

Plantinga's best-known claims are that religious belief can
be rational without propositional evidence or any support
by argument, that natural theology is unnecessary for the
epistemic respectability of religion, and that Christian philosophers ought to take Christian doctrines for granted in at least
some of their philosophical research. Most of these claims have
also been strongly defended by Mavrodes and Wolterstorff.

1

Connected with the first claim is Plantinga's view that no one has demonstrated that theistic belief cannot be "properly basic," or rationally held without being based on other beliefs. In the beginning, most of the literature on Reformed Epistemology focused on this claim and the related attack on classical foundationalism and evidentialism. Continuing discussion of these topics in this volume has been taken up by Philip L. Quinn, John Zeis, Hugo Meynell, Thomas D. Sullivan, and Patrick Lee. Strong defenses of the need for natural theology are given in the papers by John Greco, Philip Quinn, and John Zeis; a discussion of Plantinga's notion of Christian philosophy is presented in the paper by Ralph McInerny.

In Plantinga's most recent work an original theory of knowledge has emerged. Briefly, he proposes that knowledge is true, warranted belief, where a belief B has warrant for S just in case B is produced in S by S's epistemic faculties working properly in the appropriate environment, according to a design plan successfully aimed at truth.[1] Armed with this new account of warrant, Plantinga now has the resources to defend the positive position that religious beliefs have warrant and, when true, constitute knowledge. This is obviously much stronger than the earlier claim that no one has shown it to be irrational to hold theistic belief in the basic way. A discussion of this view in this volume is taken up in my own paper, the papers by Patrick Lee, John Greco, and Thomas D. Sullivan, and more briefly by James Ross.

The purpose of *Rational Faith* is to present critical reflections on Reformed Epistemology by Catholic philosophers who appreciate the theories in question but who also have a special interest in, and understanding of, Catholic philosophy, both traditional and contemporary. The papers are by no means wholly polemical. Several accept Plantinga's most important claims but urge that they be extended or revised in certain ways. Other papers have deeper criticisms, but even then, they are offered in the spirit of appreciation for the importance of Plantinga's work for theistic philosophy. Objections are based on a combination of philosophical and religious interests, and separating the two is often difficult. Each paper also makes proposals that reflect the personal philosophical projects of its author and so is Catholic only in the sense that that term applies to the author.

The authors of this volume have a few characteristics that distinguish them from the Reformers. First, almost all of them have a very high regard for the powers of human reason, although it is doubtful they could be called rationalists, at least not in the sense that term has been used since the Enlightenment. A deep respect for natural theology is, of course, an important part of the Catholic tradition, and the efficacy of natural reason in obtaining religious knowledge has been forcefully and repeatedly stated in official documents of the Catholic church.[2] Furthermore, Catholic scholarship long accepted the idea that revealed theology rests on natural theology, which is to say, the work of philosophers, and the preeminent philosophy was that of Aquinas. This was officially recognized in the encyclical *Aeterni Patris* (1879), in which Pope Leo XIII called special attention to the importance of Thomistic philosophy and declared it to be the basis of ecclesiastical theology. Now, although Thomism no longer enjoys a privileged position in the church, Catholic philosophers generally retain the philosophical confidence of scholastic philosophy—at least that is indicated in the papers collected here. This inheritance of Catholic philosophers distinguishes them from their Calvinist colleagues, and the resulting difference in attitude is expressed well in Plantinga's paper, "The Reformed Objection to Natural Theology."[3] Still, some Calvinists are as hopeful for the prospects of natural theology as are the contributors to this volume, and, in fact, Plantinga himself has enthusiastically proposed arguments for theism, notably in his recent "Two Dozen (Or So) Arguments for the Existence of God."[4]

In my paper in this volume I suggest that the difference between Catholic and Calvinist attitudes towards natural theology is connected with the difference between Catholic and Calvinist views on the Fall. Although both traditions agree that natural human faculties have suffered damage as a result of original sin, Catholic theology has commonly maintained that the will suffered more than the intellect, and that our powers of reasoning can still hope to achieve much that points the way to

Christian belief. Catholic philosophy also has a long tradition of natural law, which implies that our reason is a potent source of knowledge about moral matters. The extension to matters metaphysical is relatively easy. The idea is that both moral and metaphysical knowledge have important underpinnings in the knowledge of human nature, and the knowledge of human nature is within the reach of ordinary human reason.

The combination of a strict criterion of rationality and the idea that we are blameworthy if we form beliefs in a way that violates this criterion forms the view now called *evidentialism.* From the beginning this set of ideas has been the primary object of attack by Reformed philosophers. The most extreme statement of evidentialism was given by W. K. Clifford, who famously said, "It is wrong always, everywhere, and for anyone to believe anything upon insufficient evidence."[5] Less extreme forms of evidentialism, while less interesting, are also more plausible, and much has been written on this subject. Interestingly, although evidentialism is no part of Catholic doctrine, some Catholic philosophers are evidentialists. They claim that religious beliefs—even, some say, revealed truths, are adequately justified by evidence.[6] The evidentialist position is represented in this volume by Hugo Meynell.

A second way in which the contributors to this volume differ from the Reformers is that most of the authors support some degree of cognitive voluntarism, whereas Plantinga and Mavrodes are clearly on the other side. The reasons for this difference are complex. I suggest that it is in part connected with differences in views about the nature of faith, with the Catholic view historically dominated by Thomas's philosophy. Both traditions say that salvific faith is a gift from God, but the history of doctrinal conflict shows that Catholics have generally assigned a higher degree of voluntary control over belief and the processes leading to belief than have Protestants. In particular, Aquinas assigns to the will the function of leading the believer to form a belief when the belief is not fully supported by reason. We can see this stance in a quote from Aquinas in the paper by Thomas Sullivan: "The will, influenced by the movement of the good contained in the divine promise, proposes as worthy of assent something not apparent to natural understanding."[7] The suggestion here is that the belief-forming mechanisms of human beings do allow a function for the will. What's more, Aquinas suggests that the ground of the *certitude* of revelatory beliefs is the will, not the intellect, which in turn suggests that Aquinas was not an evidentialist.

Some of the strongest statements of cognitive voluntarism can be found in the writings of John Henry Newman, whose influence on several of the contributors to this collection is evident. I quote Sullivan quoting Newman:

> Faith then is not a conclusion from premises, but the result of an act of the *will*, following upon a *conviction* that to believe is a *duty*. The simple question you have to ask yourself is, "Have I a *conviction* that I *ought* to accept the (Roman) Catholic Faith as God's word . . . ?" For directly you have a conviction that you *ought* to believe, reason has done its part, and what is wanted for faith, is, not proof, but *will*.[8]

Related to cognitive voluntarism is internalism. The internalist/externalist distinction has become important in recent epistemology. Briefly, a theory is internalist to the extent that the conditions for justification (warrant) are accessible to the consciousness of the believer; a theory is externalist to the extent that the conditions are not so accessible. Plantinga's criterion for warrant is basically externalist, although it is vague enough to cover a multitude of theories and the externalism is not explicit in his statement of the criterion alone. Plantinga's examples and applications suggest that the fact that one's belief-forming faculties are working properly is not something typically accessible to the believer's consciousness, although nothing in the criterion *excludes* such accessibility. The difference between Plantinga and those who want to see a stronger internalist element in the account of warrant is probably less a matter of dispute about the question of whether a warranted belief involves properly functioning faculties than it is a dispute about the extent to which the properly functioning believer is self-reflective. In this collection, objections to the externalist aspect of Plantinga's theory are given in the papers by Lee, Greco, Ross, and Quinn, as well as in my paper.

We have just sketched the most noticeable features of the papers in this volume that set them apart from Reformed Epistemology: a high regard for reason and natural theology, and a tendency towards cognitive voluntarism and internalism. Less marked, but worth mentioning, is characteristic of several papers that may reflect at least a difference in tendency between Catholic and Calvinist approaches to epistemology. Some of the papers take a more social view of rationality than is found in the work of the Reformers; a social approach is explicitly discussed by John Greco, James Ross, and myself, while John Zeis hints at it. It is tempting to speculate that the reason for this difference can be traced to a difference in ecclesiology. If Catholics are more communitarian and Calvinists more individualistic, this difference might extend to ideas about the nature of rationality. Who or what is it that, properly speaking, is the possessor of rationality? Is it the individual or the community? This matter deserves investigation.

2. An important early response to Reformed Epistemology was Philip Quinn's paper, "In Search of the Foundations of Theism."[9] In his reply, Plantinga raised four sets of problems. The first of the nine papers in this volume is Quinn's rejoinder; in it, the discussion of each of the problems continues. First, Quinn discusses the particularistic quasi-inductive method of justifying epistemic criteria recommended by Plantinga. Second, he considers the question of whether the criterion for proper basicality proposed by the classical foundationalist could be justified by means of this method. Third, Quinn explores the issue of whether properly basic beliefs can also, without loss of justification, be properly based on other beliefs. Finally, he returns to the question of whether belief in God can be properly basic for intellectually sophisticated adult theists in our culture. The first two sets of questions involve substantial disagreement between Quinn and Plantinga, but Quinn believes progress can be made towards resolving them. The third and fourth questions, though, involve such deep disagreement that Quinn thinks it unlikely that they can be resolved in a mutually satisfactory way.

John Zeis carries on the discussion of proper basicality in his paper, "Natural Theology: Reformed?" Here Zeis uses William Alston's papers that relate religious beliefs to perceptual beliefs along with Wittgenstein's notion of a criterion, in an attempt to establish three points: (1) there is a single criterion of proper basicality that perceptual beliefs, memory beliefs, and beliefs about other minds share; (2) manifestation beliefs (such as the belief *God is speaking to me now*) lack this feature, but they can be construed as properly basic in a special way, namely, by being truth-warranted in a way analogous to privileged access beliefs; (3) even though manifestation beliefs can be properly basic, natural theology is epistemically viable and necessary for the attainment of certain important epistemic ends.

Both foundationalism and evidentialism are strongly defended in the paper by Hugo Meynell, "Faith, Foundationalism, and Nicholas Wolterstorff." Meynell supports a type of foundationalism based on the work of the Jesuit philosopher-theologian Bernard Lonergan, in which the foundations of a rational cognitive structure are certain cognitive operations rather than certain beliefs. Briefly, the foundational operations are these: the cognizer is *attentive* insofar as she takes into account the relevant evidence in experience; the cognizer is *intelligent* insofar as she envisages the range of possible ways in which the evidence might be explained; and she is *reasonable* insofar as she judges to be so that possibility which does best explain the evidence. Meynell then defends classical foundationalism against the attack found in the work of Wolterstorff and argues that Wolterstorff's arguments against classical foundationalism do not work against Meynell's version of foundationalism. Further, Meynell argues that Plantinga and Wolterstorff have not successfully refuted charges that their epistemology permits absurdities in the foundations, such as that arising from the famous Great Pumpkin objection. The epistemology of the Reformers ends up supporting a kind of relativism that Meynell's own version of foundationalism avoids.

Thomas D. Sullivan has a more moderate disagreement with the Reformers in his paper, "Resolute Belief and the

Problem of Objectivity." Sullivan agrees with Plantinga that believers are right to refuse to pare down confidence in a putative
revelation in the face of unanswered objections. But his justification for such resolute belief is different from Plantinga's. The
attempt to justify absolute conviction cannot be made successfully on the basis of Plantinga's account of warrant, Sullivan argues, but must instead be justified by reference to certain
functions of the will that make belief in revelation both reasonable and objective. Sullivan answers objections from the rationalist and the evidentialist in the course of defending a position
similar to John Henry Newman's.

Patrick Lee's paper, "Evidentialism, Plantinga, and Faith
and Reason," also takes on Plantinga's account of warrant and
argues that warranted belief must have an internalist and voluntarist aspect. With a stricter criterion of epistemic warrant,
Lee argues that we should grant that Christian belief does not
have epistemic warrant, although it is not irrational either. Instead, the warrant of Christian belief is moral rather than
epistemic. Not only is it morally warranted to believe in Christianity, but such belief has certitude because it is morally
proper to believe partly for the sake of a good other than the
possession of truth. Next, Lee argues that to be morally justified, the religious belief of reflective believers must have evidence or reasons, for only then does such an act of belief have
the morally required regard for the basic good of the possession of truth. Finally, Lee argues that the function that reasons
or evidence play in a reasonable act of faith is to make it clear
to oneself that one's act of belief is a morally responsible act or
that one morally ought to believe. This paper also owes much
to Newman.

In his paper, "Is Natural Theology Necessary for Theistic
Knowledge?" John Greco considers the conditions for epistemic justification and warrant defended by Plantinga and
Wolterstorff and finds them both to be too weak. When they
are appropriately strengthened (with an internalist element), it
becomes plausible that natural theology is required for theistic
knowledge. Specifically, the use of natural reason is necessary
to provide the kind of coherence required for knowledge in
epistemically hostile conditions. The required coherence in-

cludes coherence among one's beliefs and experiences, coherence among one's various cognitive faculties, and coherence with one's epistemic community.

In "Religious Knowledge and the Virtues of the Mind" I identify three features of Reformed Epistemology that I find objectionable, and I briefly propose a theory of the normative element in knowledge that does not have these features. First, I object to the fact that in Plantinga's theory the element that converts true belief into knowledge (what Plantinga calls "warrant") is taken to be a property of the belief itself. This feature of the theory has nothing to do with its Calvinist origin but is common to almost all contemporary theories. Second, I object to the fact that Reformed Epistemology is externalist and nonvoluntarist, a feature that *is* related to the Calvinist background of the theory and that is discussed by other contributors to this volume. Third, I object to the fact that the criteria for justification or warrant are not socially or communally based; Reformed Epistemology is individualistic. This point also, I think, is related to the Calvinist origin of the theory and is discussed in John Greco's paper as well. Next, I propose that the element that converts true belief into knowledge is epistemic virtue—an enduring quality of a person rather than a temporally limited property of an individual belief. The analysis of epistemic virtue as an analogue of moral virtue in an Aristotelian moral theory shows epistemic virtue to be more internalist, voluntarist, and communitarian than Reformed concepts of justification and warrant.

In "Cognitive Finality" James Ross agrees with the Reformed attack on evidentialism and classical foundationalism but takes exception to Plantinga's positive doctrines. Although accepting Plantinga's claim that religious belief does not need evidence, Ross argues that Plantinga's psychology of cognition is defective, so he gets the right results for the wrong reasons. In particular, Plantinga has no better explanation of the role of the will in belief than the people he is opposing, and the result is that he ends up much closer to his opponents than he intends. Ross proposes an entirely different account of the role of the will and the feelings in cognition. The most common mechanism by which assent is produced in the absence of compelling evidence is rational reliance, which includes reliance on other people. Since compelling evidence is rare, commitment becomes important in most areas of human knowledge, and commitment is caused by the will and the feelings. Ross goes on to argue for an analogy between the community of believers and a community of craftsmen or musicians. One needs to be an expert "craftsman" to evaluate the rationality of the commitments of such a community, and the same can be said for the Christian community. Plantinga's account of rationality cannot account for this. Finally, Ross argues that Plantinga has got himself into an epistemic circle, analogous to the Cartesian circle. Plantinga argues that belief in God can be warranted without an evidential base on the grounds that warranted beliefs are those produced by faculties working properly according to design. But he could not know this without knowing that the system as designed by God does not need an evidential base. Further, the Calvinist doctrine of total depravity should prevent Plantinga from having assurance that what seems to be proper functioning in our fallen state actually is what it seems. Ross claims that it can, however, be explained by his own doctrine of rational reliance.

The nature and possibility of Christian philosophy is the focus of Ralph McInerny's paper, "Reflections on Christian Philosophy." McInerny begins with a good review of the fascinating debate among French Thomists in the early 1930s on the question of whether there is a Christian philosophy. All parties to the dispute agreed on the formal difference between knowledge and faith and derivatively between philosophy and theology, although some affirmed and some denied that there is a distinctively Christian philosophy. McInerny then turns to Plantinga's recent Stob Lectures, delivered at Calvin College 1989–1990 on the nature of Christian scholarship. While agreeing with Plantinga's point that it is a mistake to think that philosophy uninfluenced by Christian belief is influenced by nothing at all, McInerny takes exception to Plantinga's move to reconcile the Augustinian and the Thomistic views on the relation between faith and reason. While the Thomist distinguishes between theology and philosophy, the Augustinian is in favor of using all that we know, including what we know by faith and revelation, in our research and not bothering about labels distinguishing one science from another. Plantinga sides with the Augustinians on this matter but offers a proposal to reconcile the two viewpoints. McInerny objects to the attempted reconciliation. Where F stands for the Christian motivation of a research project and S stands for a result assessible by criteria other than faith, Plantinga argues that Christian philosophical discourse is characterized by the formula "If F, then FS," whereas McInerny suggests that it is best characterized by "If F then S," a formula that permits his desired distinction between philosophy and theology.

3. There is much more interaction between Catholic and Protestant philosophers than ever before in this century, but more needs to be done, and I hope that this book will be a useful contribution towards that end. Due to the contingencies of history, the waning of the influence of Thomism had the result that Catholic philosophy in this country was predominantly influenced by continental schools of thought while Protestant philosophy was primarily analytic. The fact that there was insufficient interaction among Christian philosophers, then, was due more to philosophical than to religious differences. Fortunately, there now seems to be a growing recognition that Christian philosophers have both philosophical and religious interests in common, and the Society of Christian Philosophers, founded in 1978, has been an important stimulant for philosophical exchange within the Christian community. Interestingly, Thomistic scholarship is enjoying a renaissance both inside and outside Catholic milieux. Further, there is evidence that differences between the analytic and continental traditions are breaking down. This development is not only important for Christianity, it is important for philosophy. The fact that sometimes the contributors to this volume and the Reformers are acquainted with a different philosophical literature can be helpful to both groups. Christianity and philosophy do not meet only at a single point, the point of any given Christian philosopher's favorite philosophy, and it is important that religious philosophers not be philosophically insular. It is

important, in fact, that *philosophers* not be insular, and there is much in this volume of interest to contemporary epistemologists, Christian or not.

The papers in this collection are partly original contributions on the methodology of epistemology and the analysis of basic epistemic concepts, and partly contributions to applied epistemology that focus on the epistemology of religion. To consider the question of which comes first, basic or applied epistemology, is interesting, and I do not think the answer is obvious. In ethics I accept the position that we should not think of the foundations of moral theory as *a priori*, or as close to being *a priori* as we can get, with applied ethics a routine deduction from basic principles together with empirical facts. Our confidence in our knowledge of certain particular moral truths sometimes outstrips our confidence in the principles. If this is right, perhaps the same point applies to epistemology. Our confidence in any suggested account of the criteria for justification or warrant or rationality can be outstripped by our confidence that we are rational or justified or warranted in certain particular beliefs. The fact that some of these beliefs are religious may be no objection. This, I think, is one of Plantinga's most important points—and I find it persuasive.

NOTES

1. The latest definition appears in Alvin Plantinga's forthcoming book, *Warrant and Proper Function* (Oxford: Oxford University Press, 1992). Earlier and similar definitions appear in his "The Prospects for Natural Theology," in *Philosophical Perspectives* 5: *Philosophy of Religion*, ed. James Tomberlin (Atascadero, Calif.: Ridgeview Press); and his "Positive Epistemic Status and Proper Function," *Philosophical Perspectives* 2: *Epistemology*, ed. James Tomberlin (Atascadero, Calif.: Ridgeview Press, 1988), p. 34. In the latter the *definiendum* is "positive epistemic status" rather than "warrant." As Plantinga now uses these terms, "warrant" applies to whatever it is that converts true belief into knowledge, while "justification" is a term for the deontological concept of doing one's epistemic duty. He argues in *Warrant and Proper Function* that justification is neither necessary nor sufficient for warrant.

2. See especially the Vatican I dogmatic constitution *Dei Filius, On the Catholic Faith,* 3004.

3. *Proceedings of the American Catholic Philosophical Association* 54 (1980), pp. 49–62.

4. This paper is part of Plantinga's Gifford Lectures.

5. W. K. Clifford, *Lectures and Essays* (London: Macmillan, 1879).

6. This position is argued by Thomas Russman in "A Faith of True Proportions: Reply to Sullivan," *Thomistic Papers V,* ed. Thomas Russman (Houston: Center for Thomistic Studies, 1990), pp. 81–91. Sullivan gives a reply in the same volume.

7. *Disputed Questions on Truth* q. 14. art 2.

8. Letter to Mrs. William Froude, 27 June 1848, in *Letters and Diaries,* vol. 12, p. 227. Quoted below by Thomas D. Sullivan in his paper in this volume, "Resolute Belief and the Problem of Objectivity," n. 21.

9. *Faith and Philosophy* 2/4 (October 1985), pp. 468–486. Plantinga's response appears in *Faith and Philosophy* 3/3 (July 1986).

1. The Foundations of Theism Again: A Rejoinder to Plantinga

Philip L. Quinn

During the past dozen years Alvin Plantinga has published an impressive series of papers in which he advocates a point of view on questions of religious epistemology that has, on account of its Calvinian inspiration, come to be called "Reformed Epistemology."[1] A few years ago I tried my hand at criticizing some of the characteristic claims and arguments of Reformed Epistemology and succeeded in provoking a forceful reply by Plantinga.[2] I have recently been persuaded that some philosophical progress might be made if my discussion with Plantinga were continued. So I have returned to the issues raised by Plantinga's reply and have thought my way through them again. This rejoinder is a product of that effort.

Before I turn to those issues, let me note two limits on what I hope to achieve in this paper. First, in order to keep the paper within reasonable bounds of length, I restrict my attention to just the four sets of problems that Plantinga raised in his reply to my earlier paper. Much ink has already been spilled over Reformed Epistemology, and doubtless more is to come. But I make no attempt here to treat other philosophers whose work, published and unpublished, has stimulated my thinking on this topic.[3] Second, I make no attempt to bring the discussion to closure, but only to advance it a step or two. I have no doubt that there will remain plenty more for Plantinga to say if he, in turn, decides there would be some profit in carrying the discussion beyond where I leave off at the end of this paper. But I do hope to narrow the gap between us by indicating points on which I think we are already close to agreement and by acknowledging points on which he has persuaded me to change my mind. And I also aim to sharpen the focus on the remaining disagreements by explaining why I find some of his arguments unpersuasive and by presenting objections to some of the things he says in his reply.

The paper is divided into four parts. In the first, I discuss the particularistic, quasi-inductive method of justifying epistemic criteria that Plantinga recommends. In the second, I consider the question of whether the criterion for proper basicality proposed by the Classical Foundationalist could be justified by means of this method. These sections of the paper cover terrain on which lie substantial disagreements between us, but I think there are opportunities for progress toward resolving them. In the third part, I explore the issue of whether properly basic beliefs can also, without loss of justification, be properly based on other beliefs. And, finally, I return in the last part to the vexed question of whether belief in God, or theistic beliefs that self-evidently entail the existence of God, can be or are properly basic for intellectually sophisticated adult theists in our culture. In these last two sections of the paper I treat issues on which, as I see it, such deep disagreements are to be found between us that we have almost no hope of achieving a mutually satisfactory resolution. But even on these topics there is room, I think, to make some progress in the direction of achieving greater clarity about the issues.

1. JUSTIFYING EPISTEMIC CRITERIA

Following Chisholm, Plantinga endorses a particularistic and broadly inductive method of arguing for epistemic criteria. Applied to the case of criteria for proper basicality, the claim is this:

> We must assemble examples of beliefs and conditions such that the former are obviously properly basic in the latter, and examples of beliefs and conditions such that the former are obviously not properly basic in the latter. We must then frame

hypotheses as to the necessary and sufficient conditions of proper basicality and test these hypotheses by reference to those examples. (RBG, p. 76)

So we are to begin with examples that serve as data for the induction. They can be expressed as instances of the following two schemata:

> (1)   The belief that p is properly basic in conditions C.

And

> (2)   The belief that p' is not properly basic in conditions C'.

Let the set of examples thus assembled be the initial set. The next step is to frame hypotheses that specify necessary, sufficient, or necessary and sufficient conditions for proper basicality. They can be expressed as instances of the following three schemata:

> (3)   A belief is properly basic only if it is P.

> (4)   A belief is properly basic if it is Q.

And

> (5)   A belief is properly basic if and only if it is R.

And then, according to Plantinga, we are to test these hypotheses against those examples.

There is, of course, no guarantee that there will be a perfect fit between the first hypotheses we frame and the data in the initial set. Neither our first hypotheses nor the examples in the initial set of data are immune from revision. It might, as I pointed out, turn out that the initial set itself is inconsistent or otherwise incoherent, in which case "perhaps we should be allowed to throw data out of the initial set should we discover that it is in some fashion incoherent" (p. 472). More generally, as Plantinga observes, the initial set "should be revisable in the light of theory and under the pressure of argument" (RBG, p. 76). In short, the initial set of examples is not an Archimedean fixed point that has to remain unchanged throughout the process of making revisions.

Plantinga also notes that applications of this method are constrained in other ways. Thus, "various constraints on such criteria may indeed be self-evident; more important, there are theoretical constraints arising from one's general philosophical views as to what sorts of beings human beings are" (FT, p. 313). One theoretical constraint needs to be made explicit because it will be important in the subsequent discussion. The constraint is required to insure the coherence of our final hypotheses with the examples in our final set of data. If the instances of (1) and (2) that wind up in the final set of data are basic beliefs, they must at least satisfy any necessary conditions for proper basicality specified by instances of (3) and (5) among the final hypotheses. And if such instances of (1) and (2) are not basic beliefs, then there must be a path from them in the inquirer's noetic structure to other beliefs that are basic and at least satisfy any such necessary conditions for proper basicality.

There is a lot more that could be said about this method. One might, for example, discuss the similarities it bears to the procedure for getting to narrow reflective equilibrium that has been debated in recent moral epistemology.[4] But I do not have the space to say such things here. So let me just acknowledge that, as thus far characterized, it is a perfectly legitimate method of arriving at, and justifying, epistemic criteria.

In fact, I even think the method could be employed in constructing a rationally persuasive argument for the conclusion that theistic beliefs which self-evidently entail the existence of God can be properly basic. Imagine someone who starts out by being genuinely puzzled and uncertain about whether such theistic beliefs can be properly basic. Not being firmly convinced they cannot be, she is willing to let further inquiry settle the matter for her. Since it is not obvious to her that there are any conditions in which such theistic beliefs are properly basic, she includes no instance of (1) involving such a theistic belief among the examples in her initial set of data. Assume that these two things do not change in the course of the inquiry and that it terminates successfully with a final set of data that includes no instance of (1) involving a theistic belief and final hypotheses that have among them an instance of (4), all appropriate constraints on the process having been satisfied. Now our inquirer notices that there are circumstances in which a theistic belief satisfies the sufficient condition for proper basicality specified by the instance of (4) among her final hypotheses and concludes that this theistic belief is in those circumstances properly basic. She is in a position at this point to argue inductively from the examples in her final set of data to a criterion for proper basicality and from that criterion to the conclusion that some theistic beliefs are, and hence can be, properly basic. Because there are no theistic beliefs in her final set of data, this argument is not circular and does not beg the question. I can see no reason for thinking that such an argument would not be rationally persuasive for our inquirer. She had been disposed to let the outcome of her inquiry settle the matter, and it has done so.

No argument of this sort appears in Plantinga's papers. He does not actually try to justify any criteria for proper basicality by putting the quasi-inductive method to work; indeed, he does not even frame any hypotheses about the necessary and sufficient conditions of proper basicality. Instead, he assumes that the Reformed Epistemologist will include instances of (1) involving theistic beliefs in his initial set of data. Why not? After all, Plantinga insists

> . . . there is no reason to assume, in advance, that everyone will agree on the examples. The Christian will of course suppose that belief in God is entirely proper and rational; if he does not accept this belief on the basis of other propositions, he will conclude that it is basic for him and quite properly so. Followers of Bertrand Russell and Madelyn Murray O'Hare [sic] may disagree; but how is that relevant? Must my criteria, or those of the Christian community, conform to their examples? Surely not. The Christian community is responsible to its set of examples, not to theirs. (RBG, p. 77)

In response to these claims, I had said: "The difficulty is, of course, that this is a game any number can play. Followers of Muhammad, followers of Buddha, and even followers of the Reverend Moon can join in the fun" (p. 473). In his reply, Plantinga interpreted these remarks as an allegation that the method is defective. This interpretation is not utterly unreasonable because I had said that "Plantinga's sketch of the first stage of a procedure for justifying criteria of proper basicality is nonetheless well enough developed to permit us to see that it confronts at the outset at least one important difficulty" (p. 473).

Plantinga's response to the allegation that the method is defective is right on target:

> It is indeed true that if people start with different beliefs as to which propositions are properly basic in various circumstances, then following the method I sketched, they may well come to different conclusions. But why think this is a defect in the proposed method? If it is, it is a defect this method shares with such paragons of propriety as deductive reasoning. (FT, p. 303)

I agree that a flawless method can yield different outputs for different inputs. That was not the aspect of Plantinga's procedure which bothered me. He himself comes very close to expressing my concern in the following passage:

> And hence criteria for proper basicality arrived at in this particularistic way may not be polemically useful. If you and I start from different examples—if my set of examples includes a pair <B, C> (where B is, say, belief in God and C is some condition) and your set of examples does not include <B, C>—then we may very well arrive at different criteria for proper basicality. Furthermore I cannot sensibly use my criterion to try to convince you that B is in fact properly basic in C, for you will point out, quite properly, that my criterion is based upon a set of examples that, as you see it, *erroneously* includes <B, C> as an example of a belief and condition such that the former is properly basic in the latter. You will thus be quite within your rights in claiming that my criterion is mistaken, although of course you may concede that, given my set of examples, I followed correct procedure in arriving at it. (RBG, pp. 77–78)

There are, however, two rather different reasons why I might have decided to exclude the pair <B, C> from my initial set of examples. I might be antecedently convinced that it is an example of a belief and condition such that the former is *not* properly basic in the latter. If that were the case, I would indeed conclude that the Reformed Epistemologist's criterion is mistaken, and quite properly so. It would therefore be polemically useless in a dispute with me. But, like the puzzled and uncertain inquirer previously described, I might begin by being unconvinced that it is an example of a belief and condition such that the former is properly basic in the latter but be open to being persuaded that it is. If that were the case, I would not necessarily conclude that the Reformed Epistemologist's criterion is mistaken, for I might well consider it an open question whether it could be properly based on other examples. So I would object to how the Reformed Epistemologist applies the particularistic method because I find his procedure philosophically unhelpful in the extreme. Here I am, like the inquirer of my example, open to being persuaded that B is properly basic in C if the particularistic method is applied in a way that generates a good argument for this conclusion, and the Reformed Epistemologist tells me that the way he applies the method involves assuming at the outset the very thing I need an argument for. Hence all I can expect from his application of the method is an argument that begs the question by my lights.

Plantinga urges the Christian community to be responsible to its set of examples. The trouble is that not all Christians who have considered the matter agree with the Reformed Epistemologist's claim that pairs like $<B, C>$ belong in that set. It does not follow that such Christians are not open to being persuaded that belief in God is properly basic. Some, like the inquirer of my example, might welcome an argument to that effect and even be willing to apply the particularistic method in way that could give rise to one. But the Reformed Epistemologist's use of the particularistic method is not likely to be helpful to such people, for it appears to be committed to assuming without argument that belief in God is properly basic.

Moreover, even if it is granted that the Reformed Epistemologist is within his epistemic rights in including instances of (1) involving theistic beliefs which self-evidently entail the existence of God in his initial set of data, this is not enough to guarantee that application of the quasi-inductive method will ultimately vindicate the claim that those theistic beliefs are properly basic in the conditions specified. Suppose the Reformed Epistemologist stumbles across an hypothesis that is an instance of (3) which satisfies the following condition: (i) all the nontheistic beliefs in the initial examples that are said to be properly basic possess the feature the hypothesis claims is a necessary condition for proper basicality; (ii) all the nontheistic beliefs in the initial examples that are said not to be properly basic lack the feature the hypothesis claims is a necessary condition for proper basicality; and (iii) all the theistic beliefs in the initial examples, both those that are said to be properly basic and those that are said not to be properly basic, lack the feature the hypothesis claims is a necessary condition for proper basicality. I do not see how this possibility could be ruled out in advance. Indeed, being properly basic and nontheistic is trivially a feature of the required kind. But even if we make the supposition interesting by resolving not to appeal to such trivial features, I still do not see how to rule out the possibility in question. Nor do I see how to rule out in advance the possibility that the simplest thing to do in such circumstances would be to revise the initial set of data by deleting from it the instances of (1) involving theistic beliefs. And, of course, if this were done, subsequent inquiry might terminate with criteria for proper basicality according to which no theistic beliefs are properly basic. To be sure, the Reformed Epistemologist has another option open to him at this point; to reject the hypothesis in question and continue the search for criteria of proper basicality. But, in that case, I do not see how to rule out in advance the possibility that the search goes on interminably without coming up with anything as good as the rejected hypothesis. Nor do I see how to rule out in advance the possibility that the instances of (1) involving theistic beliefs that were at the outset among the Reformed Epistemologist's basic beliefs and go into his initial set on that account will themselves fail to satisfy the necessary conditions for proper basicality specified by all the otherwise plausible instances of (3) and (5) he manages to generate in the course of his search for hypotheses.

So it should not be taken for granted that once the Reformed Epistemologist gets down to business and puts the particularistic method to work, he is bound to succeed in justifying criteria for proper basicality according to which theistic beliefs are properly basic. We should pass judgment on the success of this enterprise only after it has been completed.

2. CLASSICAL FOUNDATIONALISM REVISITED

Plantinga's energies have not been devoted to this enterprise in his papers on Reformed Epistemology. Instead he has concentrated them on attacking the criterion for proper basicality of Classical Foundationalism. It may be put as follows:

(6)   A proposition p is properly basic for a person S if and only if p is either self-evident to S or incorrigible for S or evident to the senses for S. (RBG, p. 59)

Since theistic beliefs that self-evidently entail the existence of God are neither self-evident, nor incorrigible, nor evident to the senses, such beliefs will not be properly basic if this criterion is correct. So it must be discredited in order to clear the ground for Reformed Epistemology.

The main thrust of Plantinga's attack on Classical Foundationalism is an attempt to show that it is, or at least is likely to be, self-referentially incoherent. What does the charge of self-reverential incoherence amount to in this case? Consider, by way of contrast, the following proposal for a criterion of truth:

(7)   An English sentence is true if and only if it contains fewer than ten English words.

Now (7) itself is an English sentence that contains more than ten English words. So if we assume that it is true, it follows that it is not true. In short, (7) is self-refuting. But (6) is not like (7) in this respect. Plantinga and I agree that it is neither self-evident, nor incorrigible, nor evident to the senses for the Classical Foundationalist. So if we assume that (6) is true, what follows is that it is not properly basic for her. But this does not suffice to refute (6) or even to show that the Classical Foundationalist is irrational in accepting it. For all that has been said so far, it could be that (6) is both true and rationally acceptable for her because it is properly based on beliefs that are for her self-evident, incorrigible, or evident to the senses.

After acknowledging that it could be the case that (6) is properly based on beliefs that are for the Classical Foundationalist self-evident, incorrigible, or evident to the senses, Plantinga goes on to contend that this seems unlikely (RBG, p. 62).

Maybe so. But even if we suppose that (6) is initially not thus properly based for the Classical Foundationalist, fairness demands that we give her a chance to conduct an inquiry designed to find out whether her noetic structure can be transformed in such a way that by inquiry's end (6) has come to be properly based on beliefs that satisfy the conditions for proper basicality it itself lays down. And, of course, she is entitled to make use of the particularistic method described above, though it cannot be guaranteed in advance that the method will yield an inductive justification of (6) if it is correctly applied. As for the Reformed Epistemologist, so too for the Classical Foundationalist: we should await the results and only then evaluate the success of the enterprise.

Trying to lend a hand to the Classical Foundationalist in getting this project started, I had suggested a couple of examples she might want to put in her initial set of data.[5] Thus, I imagined her contemplating believing that she is being appeared to redly in conditions optimal for visual experience in which she is being appeared to redly. My claim was this: "Surely she can plausibly say that it is self-evident to her that the belief would be properly basic for her in those conditions" (p. 474). So my suggestion was that the following instance of (1) could go into her initial set of data:

(8)   The belief that I am being appeared to redly is properly basic in conditions optimal for visual experience in which I am being appeared to redly.

Similarly, I had imagined her contemplating believing that Jove is expressing disapproval in conditions optimal for auditory experience in which she is being appeared to thunderously. And so I had suggested that the following instance of (2) could also be put in her initial set:

(9)   The belief that Jove is expressing disapproval is not properly basic in conditions optimal for auditory experience in which I am being appeared to thunderously.

My proposal was that the Classical Foundationalist proceed to build up a large and rich set of data by ringing the changes on thought experiments such as these.

In his reply, Plantinga argues that this proposal does not have much real promise. If such things as (8) and (9) are basic beliefs for the Classical Foundationalist, they must satisfy her criterion for proper basicality in order to be rationally acceptable. Clearly neither of them is incorrigible or evident to the senses for anyone. Could they be self-evident? Plantinga is prepared to grant, if only for the sake of argument, that (8) can be self-evident, but he insists that (9) is not. The argument goes as follows:

> But if it is self-evident that this belief is not properly basic in those circumstances, then it must be self-evident that a person who accepted it in those circumstances would either be going contrary to an epistemic duty or be displaying a cognitive defect or malfunction in accepting it in those circumstances. It seems to me entirely clear that neither of these nor their disjunction could be self-evident to a human being. Obviously a person need not be going contrary to his epistemic duties in accepting the relevant proposition. Indeed, it may be *impossible* for him not to accept the proposition on an occasion when he does accept it; our beliefs are not for the most part within our direct control. And how could it be just *self-evident* that in accepting such a proposition one would be displaying some cognitive malfunction? It is not self-evidently false that there is such a person as Jove; and not self-evidently false that he has created us in just such a way as to be aware of his disapproval upon being appeared to thunderously. (FT, pp. 301–302)

I am persuaded by this argument that (9) is not self-evident.

But I do not think this suffices to show that my proposal lacks promise. By Plantinga's own admission, the initial set of data can be revised under the pressure of argument. So the next move for the Classical Foundationalist is to revise (9) in such a way that Plantinga's objection to its being self-evident is no longer telling. One such revision yields the following result:

(10)   The belief that Jove is expressing disapproval is not properly basic in conditions optimal for auditory experience in which I am being appeared to thunderously and I can refrain from believing that Jove is expressing disapproval.

Plantinga's stated reason for considering it obvious that one need not be going contrary to epistemic duty in accepting the proposition in question is that it may be impossible for one not to accept it. By the ought–implies–can principle, if this is impossible, one does nothing contrary to duty in accepting it. But since it is not impossible in the conditions specified in (10), Plantinga has given us no reason to think that one need not be going contrary to epistemic duty in accepting that proposition in those conditions. Hence Plantinga's argument does not put intolerable pressure on the claim that (10) is self-evident. Of course he might be able to come up with another argument that does put such pressure on that claim. If he did, the Classical Foundationalist could try to revise (10) in such a way as to relieve that pressure, and I see no way to guarantee in advance that she could not succeed.

Thus, for example, suppose I could have been born and raised in ancient Rome where worship of Jove was common. On this supposition, belief that Jove is expressing disapproval could have been properly basic for me in the conditions specified in (10); if I had been a Roman youth, my situation would have been much like that of the Christian youth in one of Plantinga's examples for whom belief in God is properly basic. Of course, the Classical Foundationalist might want to reject the supposition on the Kripkean grounds that our biological origins are essential to us. But she might also respond with a successor to (10) that adds further conditions to those explicitly stated in it. Perhaps such conditions would include my living in a society in which Jove is not worshiped and children are taught in grade school courses that cover mythology that the deities of the Roman pantheon do not exist. The Classical Foundationalist is, after all, entitled to respond to challenges to her examples as they come up, one by one, either by attacking some assumption of the challenge or by making additional revisions in the example.

So I believe it remains open to the Classical Foundationalist to claim that (10) or some successor to it is self-evident.[6] Suppose she does. Speaking for myself, I think (10) is not self-evident, and I doubt that I will be persuaded that any of its successors is self-evident; on this point I am in agreement with

Plantinga's position. If we are right on this score, she is mistaken. But I have no proof that we are right. And if she is right, it is we who are mistaken. This is just another instance of disagreement about the examples, which does not differ in kind from the disagreement between the Reformed Epistemologist and someone who is firmly convinced that theistic beliefs that self-evidently entail the existence of God cannot be properly basic. In both disputes one party is mistaken, but in neither dispute is it obvious which party that is.

Plantinga challenges another instance of (1) that he supposes the Classical Foundationalist may wish to include in her initial set of data. He puts it this way:

(11)   The belief that $2 + 1 = 3$ is properly basic in circumstances C. (FT, p. 301)

According to Plantinga, if she assumes that (11) is self-evident,

she must accordingly suppose that it is self-evident that in those circumstances her intellectual and cognitive equipment is functioning properly in producing such beliefs in her. It would therefore have to be self-evident to her that, for example, her accepting those beliefs is not due to the malevolent activity of a Cartesian evil demon. (FT, p. 301)

Clearly it is not self-evident to the Classical Foundationalist that she is not being deceived by a Cartesian demon. But whether or not this would have to be self-evident to her in order for (11) to be self-evident to her cannot be determined in the absence of a specification of the circumstances referred to in (11). Suppose they are spelled out in the following way:

(12)   The belief that $2 + 1 = 3$ is properly basic in conditions optimal for grasping mathematical truths in which that proposition is clearly and distinctly conceived.

If one is being deceived by a Cartesian demon, one is not in conditions optimal for grasping mathematical truths. But even though it is not self-evident to the Classical Foundationalist that she is, in fact, in such conditions, it could, I think, be self-evident to her that the belief that $2 + 1 = 3$ would be properly basic if she were in such conditions and conceived that proposition clearly and distinctly. And I also think it could be self-evident to her that her intellectual and cognitive equipment would be functioning properly in producing this belief in her if she were in the circumstances specified in (12). In other words, if (12) is construed hypothetically, as I think it may be, then Plantinga's argument does not prove that it could not be self-evident to the Classical Foundationalist.

I conclude that the arguments of Plantinga's reply do not demonstrate that the Classical Foundationalist is bound to fail in justifying her criterion for proper basicality if she makes use of the particularistic method. Responses to the objections he brings to bear on the examples are available to her. Of course it does not follow that she is bound to succeed in this enterprise. So I must confess I was excessively optimistic when I wrote that, after assembling an initial set of examples, the Classical Foundationalist "is then in a position to claim, and properly so, that his or her criterion, though not itself properly basic, is properly based, in accord with what Plantinga has told us about proper procedures for justifying criteria for proper basicality, on beliefs that are properly basic by its own lights" (p. 474). As I now see, the Classical Foundationalist has a lot more work to do before she will be in a position to make any such claim with propriety. She must defend her examples against objections of the sort Plantinga has set forth or revise them under the pressure of such arguments. And I see no way to guarantee in advance that she will ultimately be able to assemble and defend a sufficiently large and varied stock of examples to justify her criterion inductively, for it could turn out that the examples in her final set are so few that the weak inductive support they give to her criterion is insufficient to provide a proper basis for it. But the Reformed Epistemologist is in the same boat. He, too, has a lot more work to do before he can properly make such a claim; after all, he has not yet framed any hypotheses about the necessary and sufficient conditions for proper basicality. Nor can it be guaranteed in advance that he will succeed in justifying his criterion inductively once he tells us what it is. If we judge by what has been done so far by the contending parties in this dispute to apply the particularistic method, I think we should conclude that neither party has yet done enough to give us a good reason to adopt its criterion for proper basicality. Hence I am of the opinion that we thus far have no better reason for adopting criteria according to which some beliefs that self-evidently entail the existence of God can be properly basic than for adopting criteria according to which no such beliefs can be properly basic.

3. JUSTIFYING THEISTIC BELIEFS

For Plantinga properly basic beliefs are not groundless. Upon having an experience of a certain sort, I form the belief:

(13)   I see a tree before me.

My having the experience of being appeared to treely plays a crucial role in justifying that belief. According to Plantinga, "my being appeared to in this characteristic way (together with other circumstances) is what confers on me the right to hold the belief in question; this is what justifies me in accepting it" (RBG, p. 79).[7] We may say that this experience is the ground of my justification and, by extension, the ground of the belief itself. There is, then, one sense in which properly basic beliefs are not supported by evidence. Since they are basic, they are not based on other beliefs and so are not supported by doxastic or propositional evidence. But there is another sense in which properly basic beliefs are supported by evidence. Because they are grounded in experience, they are supported by nonpropositional experiential evidence. In the case of perceptual beliefs such as (13), the experiential evidence in question is often spoken of as the evidence of one's senses. And, on Plantinga's view, properly basic memorial beliefs and beliefs ascribing mental states to other persons are similarly grounded in experience and hence supported by experiential evidence.

Something analogous appears to be at work in the case of theistic beliefs that self-evidently entail the existence of God. Plantinga supposes there are conditions in which such beliefs as the following are properly basic:

(14)   God is speaking to me.

(15)   God disapproves of what I have done.

And

(16)   God forgives me for what I have done.

He offers a partial description of such conditions in the following passage:

> Upon reading the Bible, one may be impressed with a deep sense that God is speaking to him. Upon having done what I know is cheap, or wrong, or wicked, I may feel guilty in God's sight and form the belief *God disapproves of what I have done.* Upon confession and repentance I may feel forgiven, forming the belief *God forgives me for what I have done.* (RBG, p. 80)

These conditions all include an experiential component, and, indeed, Plantinga speaks of exploring their phenomenology. So it seems fair to attribute to him the assumption that such beliefs as (14)–(16) are, when properly basic, grounded in such experiences, which, together with other circumstances, justify one in accepting them. And, if this is correct, the experiences in which such theistic beliefs are grounded are nonpropositional evidential support for them.

According to the argument of the previous sections of this paper, Plantinga's supposition that such theistic beliefs are properly basic in such conditions has not yet been established by means of the particularistic method. But it seems to me to be *prima facie* plausible in its own right. So I am prepared to grant it for the sake of argument and to explore the consequences of adopting it.

Plantinga and I disagree rather sharply about what the consequences are. Suppose the belief in (13) is properly basic for me in conditions that include my being appeared to treely. On that assumption, my experience of being appeared to treely grounds the belief and is nonpropositional evidence for it, and the belief is justified for me in those conditions. Assume next that, after reflecting upon my experience, I form this belief, which I had not previously had:

(17)   I am being appeared to treely.

Suppose further that I then proceed to change my noetic structure in such a way that (13) comes to be based on (17). And assume, finally, that there are no other changes in the conditions in which (13) was properly basic for me. Now (17) is properly basic for me. My experience of being appeared to treely grounds it and is nonpropositional evidence for it, and it is justified for me in these circumstances. But what of (13)? Though it is no longer basic for me, my claim is that it is now properly based on (17) and is now no less justified for me than it was when it was properly basic for me. The reason I gave for this claim in my earlier paper goes as follows:

> Since, by hypothesis, my visual experience in those conditions suffices to confer a certain degree of justification on the proposition expressed by (13), the amount of justification that reaches the proposition expressed by (13) from that experience will not be less in those conditions if it passes by way of the proposition expressed by (17) than if it is transmitted directly without intermediary. (P. 478)[8]

After quoting a passage that includes this sentence, Plantinga charges that I am mistaken here.

What, he asks, is the reason for the "Since" in the quoted sentence? This query suggests that Plantinga means to challenge the claim that visual experience is strong evidence or, perhaps, is evidence at all for (13). Such a challenge is implicit in what he says next:

> Thus what justified me in believing the corresponding conditional of *Modus Ponens*, say, is my having a certain sort of experience; and no doubt *Modus Ponens* has a great deal of warrant for me. It does not follow, however, that my having that sort of experience is much by way of *evidence* for *Modus Ponens;* that I am appeared to in a certain way is weak evidence indeed, if it is evidence at all, for the truth of *Modus Ponens.* (FT, p. 306)

I think it is Plantinga who is mistaken here.

Perhaps he is right in saying that experience does not provide much by way of evidence for simple logical truths. So maybe my being appeared to in a certain way is weak evidence, if evidence at all, for the corresponding conditional of *Modus Ponens.* It does not follow that visual experience does not provide much by way of evidence for certain perceptual truths. In other words, it does not follow that my being appeared to treely in certain circumstances is, in those circumstances, weak evidence, if evidence at all, for (13). Moreover, if Plantinga is right in saying that my having a certain sort of experience is weak evidence, if evidence at all, for the conditional corresponding to *Modus Ponens*, then he is wrong in saying that what justifies me in believing that conditional is my having that sort of experience. If I nonetheless do come to be justified in believing that conditional in circumstances in which I have that sort of experience, what does the justifying is not the experience in question but something else about those circumstances. And if what justifies me in believing that conditional is my having a certain sort of experience, my having that sort of experience is evidence strong enough to justify me in believing it rather than weak evidence, if evidence at all. Or, at any rate, so it seems me.

Plantinga's reply suggests another line of argument that might succeed without leading to a denial of the truism that sensory experience is good evidence for perceptual beliefs. It aims to show that such beliefs as (17) are not good evidence for such beliefs as (13), not that such experiences as my being appeared to treely are not good evidence for such beliefs as (13). According to Plantinga, the whole development of modern philosophy from Descartes to Hume and Reid shows that Reid was correct "in agreeing with Hume (as he understood him) that such beliefs as (17) do not in fact constitute much by way of (non-circular) *evidence* for such propositions as (13)" (FT, p. 305). But why does he think Reid was right about this? The only remark he makes that even hints at an answer is this: "It is exceedingly hard to see how to construct a cogent argument—deductive, inductive, abductive or whatever—from experiential beliefs (beliefs like (17)) to propositions which, like (13), entail the existence of such material objects as tables, houses, and horses" (FT, p. 305).[9] I agree with this remark. But how is this difficulty relevant to the issue of whether (17) is good evidence for (13)? Plantinga does not say.

So at this point I can only conjecture about how he might flesh out the argument. Perhaps he would say something like this:

(18)   (17) is good evidence for (13) only if someone has constructed a cogent argument from (17) to (13).

I am prepared to admit that no one has constructed such an argument. Hence if I were to accept (18), I would have to conclude that (17) is not good evidence for (13). But what reason is there for me to accept (18)? It is not obviously true. The only such reason I can think of is that (18) is a deductive consequence of some general principle that is itself inductively supported by other examples. One principle worth looking at in this connection is the following:

(19)   For all p and q, p is good evidence for q only if someone has constructed a cogent argument from p to q.

Is (19) an acceptable principle?

I think not. It seems to me there are counterexamples to (19). Suppose that, as I look out over my class, I observe a fidgety student. Upon noticing this, I form the following belief:

(20)   That student is moving restlessly about.

I also form this belief:

(21)   That student feels uncomfortable.

Now it is exceedingly hard to see how to construct a cogent argument from (20) to (21), as anyone who has studied Plantinga's *God and Other Minds* must admit.[10] If the problem of other minds is as yet unsolved, as I think it is, no one has constructed such an argument. But (20) is good evidence for (21), and so (19) is false. It follows that the valid deductive argument from (19) to (18) is unsound. Hence it does not give me any reason to accept (18). Since I can think of no other reason for me to accept (18), I conclude that I am within my epistemic rights in not accepting it. And because I can think of no better way to flesh out Plantinga's argument for the conclusion that (17) is not good evidence for (13), I also conclude that I am within my epistemic rights in affirming that (17) is good evidence for (13).

Where does this leave us? My claim is that if (13) is properly basic for me in conditions in which I am being appeared to treely, then it can in those conditions also be properly based on (17) without loss of justification. I am in agreement with Plantinga that my claim is true only if (17) is good evidence for (13), and I have argued that I am within my epistemic rights in affirming this consequence of my claim. Plantinga, of course, may be within his epistemic rights in denying what I affirm even if he has as yet offered no argument that should convince me to change my mind. I am prepared to grant that he is, and so I do not think either of us fails in doing his epistemic duty when we differ about what are, after all, difficult and contested philosophical issues. And clearly one of us is mistaken. He thinks it is I, but I continue to think it is he.

The disagreement carries over from perceptual beliefs grounded in sensory experience to experientially grounded theistic beliefs. Suppose I base the belief in (14) on the following belief:

(22)   It seems to me that God is speaking to me.

The claim I made about this case goes as follows: "If the proposition expressed by (14) were indirectly justified for me by being properly based on the proposition expressed by (22), its justification would be no better, and no worse, than if it were properly basic and directly justified for me by being directly grounded in my experiential sense that God is speaking to me, other things remaining the same" (pp. 478–479). I do not think that anything Plantinga has said in his reply shows that this claim is indefensible. No doubt in this case Plantinga and I will disagree about whether (22) is good evidence for (14). As in the previous case, though one of us is mistaken, neither of us need be undutiful or irrational from an epistemic point of view when we thus differ. And at present I do not see how to resolve such disagreements or even how to advance the discussion of them.

Fortunately, I do not need to resolve our disagreements about examples of this kind in order to make the point with which I am going to conclude this section of the paper. Following Plantinga, let us call the property such that enough of it turns true belief into knowledge "warrant." Warrant comes in degrees. When a belief is properly basic, it has a certain amount of warrant at minimum, but it need not then have the highest degree it is capable of acquiring or enough to make it knowledge. So there will be cases in which beliefs have more warrant when they are properly based on other beliefs than when they are properly basic. Here, I think, is one such case. When I was a senior in high school an older friend, who was then a college sophomore, told me that there are infinite sets larger than the set of all natural numbers but teasingly refused to show me a proof. I took his word for it and formed the belief that there are such sets. It was then among my basic beliefs. I did not reason to it as follows: "Tony tells me that there are infinite sets larger than the set of all natural numbers, and most of what he tells me is true; so probably there are indeed such sets." Suppose that it then was, as I tend to think, properly basic but not knowledge. Later on, when I was a college sophomore, I was exposed to Cantor's Diagonal Argument, studied it and came to understand it. I thereby came to base my belief that there are infinite sets larger than the set of all natural numbers on the premises of that argument. As a result my belief that there are such sets acquired additional warrant, enough of it, I would say, to make it knowledge.

There are conditions, let us suppose, in which theistic beliefs that self-evidently entail the existence of God have, when properly basic, enough warrant to make them knowledge. But there are also conditions in which such beliefs, when properly basic, do not have enough warrant to make them knowledge. If I were initially in conditions of the second sort and discovered a deductive argument for the existence of God whose premises were known to me and whose validity was self-evident to me, I could improve the epistemic status of my belief in God by basing it on the premises of that argument. If I did so base it, it would become knowledge, which it had not previously been, and would have more warrant than it had when it was properly basic. So there is a way in which a successful piece of natural theology could improve the epistemic status of belief in God even for some theists who do not, if Plantinga is right, need it in order to be within their epistemic rights in believing in God. And, of course, as Plantinga notes, "natural theology could be useful in helping someone move from unbelief to belief" (RBG, p. 73).

4. DEFEATING THEISTIC BELIEFS

The intellectually sophisticated adult theist in our culture is an ideal type I constructed in my earlier paper for the purpose of making vivid certain questions about the defeasibility of theistic beliefs such as (14)–(16). Such a person is supposed to know a good deal about standard objections to belief in God. These objections include various versions of the problem of evil as well as the tradition of explaining theistic belief projectively that stems from Feuerbach and comes down to us through Freud and Durkheim. Can such theistic beliefs as (14)–(16) be properly basic for the intellectually sophisticated adult theist in our culture? If so, under what conditions?

The answer I proposed to the latter question was framed in terms of the following principle:

> (23) Conditions are right for propositions like (14)–(16) to be properly basic for me "only if (i) either I have no sufficiently substantial reason to think that any of their potential defeaters is true, or I do have some such reason, but for each such reason I have, I have an even better reason for thinking the potential defeater in question is false, and (ii) in either case any situation involves no epistemic negligence on my part." (P. 483)

Plantinga's reply contains an attack on this principle; he thinks it is pretty clearly false and can be shown to be so. Suppose, he says, an atheologian gives me an initially convincing argument for thinking that

> (24) God exists and is omniscient, omnipotent, and wholly good

is extremely improbable on

> (25) There are 10^{13} turps of evil.[11]

Plantinga's analysis of the situation proceeds as follows:

> Upon grasping this argument, perhaps I have a substantial reason for accepting a defeater of theistic belief, namely that (24) is extremely improbable on (25). But in order to defeat this

potential defeater, I need not know or have very good reason to think that it is *false* that (24) is improbable on (25); it would suffice to show that the atheologian's argument (for the claim that (24) is improbable on (25)) is unsuccessful. To defeat this potential defeater, all I need to do is refute this argument; I am not obliged to go further and produce an argument for the denial of its conclusion. (FT, p. 309)

There are, he reminds us in terminology borrowed from John Pollock, undercutting defeater-defeaters as well as rebutting defeater-defeaters.

But does this show that (23) is false? I think not. Suppose that the only potential defeater of theistic belief I need to worry about is

(26)   (24) is extremely improbable on (25),

and assume also that the only reason I have for accepting (26) is the argument the atheologian gives me. On these assumptions, if I do show that the atheologian's argument is unsuccessful by refuting it, then I have no sufficiently substantial reason to think that any potential defeater of theistic belief is true, for surely an argument I know to be unsuccessful because I myself have refuted it gives me no reason to accept its conclusion. So it is not a consequence of (23) that, once I encounter the atheologian's argument, theistic belief ceases to be properly basic for me unless I have a good reason for thinking that (26) is false. Even if I have no argument for the denial of (26), I can satisfy both (ii) and the first disjunct of (i) in the consequent of (23) by showing that the atheologian's argument fails. Hence even if I lack a good reason for the falsity of (26), (23) does not preclude theistic belief from being properly basic for me both before I am given the atheologian's argument and after I have refuted it. It seems to me that Plantinga has failed to notice the fact that, although the atheologian's argument is a substantial reason for accepting a defeater or theistic belief if it is undefeated, it is not a substantial reason for accepting such a defeater if it has been undercut by a successful refutation. Therefore I am not persuaded that he has shown (23) to be false by means of this line of argument.

Nor am I persuaded by the possibility of there being intrinsic defeater-defeaters, though I must admit that this possibility had not occurred to me before Plantinga pointed it out. An intrinsic defeater-defeater is a basic belief that has more by way of warrant than some of its potential defeaters. Suppose that one of my basic theistic beliefs has so much warrant that it remains properly basic for me even after I have acquired a substantial reason for thinking one of its potential defeaters is true because that reason, though substantial, confers less warrant on the defeater in question than my basic theistic belief has in its own right. On this assumption, the antecedent of (23) is satisfied. But if I am not epistemically negligent, the consequent of (23) holds as well because the second disjunct of condition (i) is satisfied. Though I do have a substantial reason for thinking that a potential defeater of my basic theistic belief is true, for the only such reason I have, I have an even better reason, namely, my basic theistic belief itself, for thinking the potential defeater in question is false. The existence of intrinsic defeater-defeaters would falsify (23) if it were read in such a way that my reason for thinking the defeater in question is false has to be an extrinsic defeater-defeater. But since, as I have acknowledged, I did not have the distinction between extrinsic and intrinsic defeater-defeaters in mind when I formulated (23), it was certainly not my intention that it be so understood. Nor need it be read in that way.

But are there such things as intrinsic defeater-defeaters? The example Plantinga gives convinces me that there are. A letter that could embarrass me disappears from my department chair's office under mysterious circumstances. I had motive, means, and opportunity to steal it, and a reliable member of the department testifies to having seen me furtively entering the office around the time the letter must have disappeared. I have been known to steal things in the past. This circumstantial evidence persuades my colleagues, who are fair-minded people, that I am guilty, and I have all the evidence they do. Yet the fact of the matter is that I spent the whole afternoon in question on a solitary walk in the woods, and I clearly remember having done so. It is one of my basic beliefs that

(27)   I was alone in the woods all that afternoon, and I
          did not steal the letter.

The evidence I share with my colleagues gives me a substantial
reason to believe a defeater of (27), but the warrant (27) has
for me in virtue of my memory is greater than that conferred
on this defeater by that evidence. Hence (27) is an intrinsic
defeater-defeater.

It is worth noting that the power of this example to per-
suade depends critically on what we may assume about the
case. One such assumption is quite explicit; it is said that my
memory of the walk in the woods is clear. If it were not clear,
the warrant (27) has for me in virtue of my memory might well
be less than that conferred on its defeater by the circumstantial
evidence I share with my colleagues. But there are also some
tacit assumptions. Thus, for example, I suppose (27) would
not have much, if any, warrant for me if I suffered from certain
sorts of memory disorder or even had a sufficiently substantial
reason to consider myself thus afflicted and no reason to think
otherwise.

And, of course, from the fact that some basic memorial beliefs are intrinsic defeater-defeaters, it does not follow without
further ado that basic theistic beliefs are ever intrinsic defeater-
defeaters. Nonetheless I am willing to grant that some basic
theistic beliefs are or, at least, could be intrinsic defeater-
defeaters. Another example Plantinga gives illustrates the
point. He remarks, with what I take to be some asperity:
"When God spoke to Moses out of the burning bush, the belief
that God was speaking to him, I daresay, had more by way of
warrant for him than would have been provided for its denial
by an early Freudian who strolled by and proposed the thesis
that belief in God is merely a matter of neurotic wish fulfillment" (FT, p. 312). But having the experience of being spoken
to out of a burning bush is one thing; having a deep sense that
God is speaking to one upon reading the Bible is quite another.
Even if the former experience is part of a condition in which
(14) has more warrant for Moses than would have been provided for its denial by the casual proposal of an early Freudian,
it does not follow that the latter experience is part of a condi-

tion in which (14) has more warrant for a contemporary theist than is provided for its denial by the results of current psychoanalytic inquiry. So from the assumption that (14) is an intrinsic defeater-defeater for Moses it does not follow that it is also an intrinsic defeater-defeater for the intellectually sophisticated adult theist in our culture. It may be; but, then again, it may not. For all that has been said so far, when contemporary theists form the belief that God is speaking to them upon reading the Bible, that basic theistic belief has less warrant for them than at least some of its potential defeaters and so is not a defeater of all its defeaters. And perhaps basic theistic beliefs such as (14)–(16) do not have enough warrant in the circumstances described by Plantinga, in which the believer reads the Bible, feels guilty or feels forgiven, to defeat any potential defeaters of theism but those the believer has only relatively insubstantial reasons to think true.

If basic theistic beliefs such as (14)–(16) do not in such circumstances have enough warrant to serve as intrinsic defeater-defeaters of all the potential defeaters of theism, natural theology might come to the theist's rescue. Suppose there is a sound deductive argument for the existence of God. If the theist comes to see that it is valid and to know its premises and bases belief in God on those premises, belief in God will come to have a great deal of warrant for the theist. The increment in warrant might well be sufficiently large that belief in God comes to have more warrant for the theist than all its potential defeaters. So this is another way in which natural theology might improve the theist's epistemic situation. Its fate, then, may turn out to be no small matter even if it is conceded to the Reformed Epistemologist that belief in God can be properly basic in certain special conditions.

Whether or not basic theistic beliefs such as (14–(16) are intrinsic defeater-defeaters depends both on how much warrant they have and on how much warrant potential defeaters of theistic belief have. How much warrant do basic theistic beliefs have? It is not easy to say. For what it is worth, my view is that they do not have a great deal of warrant except in extraordinary conditions such as those we may imagine to be present in Plantinga's Moses example. As I see it, such basic theistic beliefs as (14)–(16) have only modest amounts of warrant in conditions in which the theist reads the Bible, feels guilt, or feels forgiven. Plantinga says: "It could be that your belief, even though accepted as basic, has more warrant than the proposed defeater and thus constitutes an intrinsic defeater-defeater" (FT, p. 312). It could indeed; this might even be the case for all proposed defeaters, not just for one. I accept this weak modal claim because I think the Moses example establishes it. But I have never been spoken to out of a burning bush. Nor, I daresay, have many other contemporary theists been thus addressed. Of course, even if I am right in thinking that basic theistic beliefs such as (14)–(16) have only modest amounts of warrant in ordinary conditions, they would still be intrinsic defeater-defeaters if the potential defeaters of theistic belief had even less warrant.

How much warrant do potential defeaters of theistic belief have? Much needs to be said on this topic, and I have space here to say only a little bit of it. I think both the evidential problem of evil and projective explanations of theistic belief provide substantial reasons for thinking the following defeater of theistic belief is true:

(28)   God does not exist.

In his reply Plantinga argues that these reasons for rejecting theism warrant a good deal of skepticism. I do not find his arguments convincing for reasons I shall briefly explain.

My claim about evil is this: "What I know, partly from experience and partly from testimony, about the amount and variety of non-moral evil in the universe confirms highly for me the proposition expressed by (28)" (p. 481). It is worth bearing in mind that this claim is consistent with (28) being highly disconfirmed by my total evidence. Plantinga's counterclaim is this: "So far as I can see, no atheologian has given a successful or cogent way of working out or developing a probabilistic atheological argument from evil; and I believe there are good reasons for thinking that it can't be done" (FT, p. 309).[12] But even if it is the case that it cannot be shown that (28) is highly probable given the amount and variety of non-moral evil in the universe, it does not follow that it cannot be shown that (28) is highly confirmed by that evil unless it is also assumed that confirmation is to be understood probabilistically. I do not accept this additional assumption. It seems to me that the failure of philosophers of science in the Carnapian tradition to work out a satisfactory probabilistic confirmation theory gives me reason enough not to accept it. I do not for a minute doubt that in science, observation statements sometimes confirm theoretical hypotheses. I take intuitively clear cases of scientific confirmation and disconfirmation as data against which philosophical accounts of confirmation are to be tested. Such data have an epistemic presumption in their favor, as I see it, and so should be rejected only for good reasons. And I am inclined to think that the claim the (28) is highly confirmed by the nonmoral evil in the universe is another such datum for confirmation theory.

The treatment of projection theories in Plantinga's reply is very harsh. He dismisses them with this remark: "Freud's jejune speculations as to the psychological origin of religion and Marx's careless claims about its social role can't sensibly be taken as providing argument or reason for (28), i.e., for the nonexistence of God; so taken they present textbook cases (which in fact are pretty rare) of the genetic fallacy" (FT, p. 308). There are, I admit, some textbook cases of the genetic fallacy in Freud's writings; I enjoy seeing students discover this in class discussions of *The Future of an Illusion*. But to construe Freud's contribution to our understanding of religion as nothing but jejune speculation and bad argument strikes me as uncharitable in the extreme. There is, I suggest, a great deal more to his legacy than that, and things get even more complicated when we take into account sociological projection theories such as Durkheim's.

I believe it is useful to think of projection theories of religious belief as constituting a research program in the human sciences.[13] This research program has not and is not likely to come up with a theory having the explanatory power of Newtonian mechanics, but that is probably too much to hope for in any research in the human sciences. The unifying idea of the research program is that there is in us a mechanism of belief formation and maintenance that involves projecting attributes of individual humans or their societies outwards and postulating entities in which the projected attributes are instantiated. The existence of the postulated entities is supposed to play no role in explaining the formation or persistence of belief in the postulates. The various theories that make up this research program attempt to specify in some detail the workings of the projection mechanism; typically they consist of hypotheses about its inputs and outputs. If such hypotheses can explain religious beliefs in a wide variety of circumstances, leaving unexplained no more anomalies than other good theories, then appeal to some principle of economy such as Ockham's razor can be made to justify the conclusion that the entities whose existence is postulated as a result of the operation of the projection mechanism do not exist because they are explanatorily idle. To the extent that such hypotheses have explained religious beliefs, that conclusion has warrant. I believe that projection hypotheses have so far achieved a real, but limited, success in explaining religious beliefs of some sorts, and I think this success does give the intellectually sophisticated adult theist in our culture a substantial reason for thinking that (28) is true.

This is another point at which natural theology might perform useful services. Suppose the natural theologian presented us with an abductive argument for the existence of God according to which divine activity is the best explanation of a wide variety of phenomena, including, but not restricted to, theistic beliefs. The successes of the projection theorist's research program would undercut this argument to some extent, but they would leave untouched the claim that divine activity is the best explanation of phenomena other than theistic beliefs. Though the strength of the abductive argument would be diminished, it might retain enough force to confer a good deal of warrant on belief in the existence of God. If that were so, theists could accept the successes of projection theories with equanimity, for they could view the projection mechanisms discovered by the human sciences as secondary causes divinely ordained to serve as generators of theistic belief.

Of course the research program of the projection theorists is open to being criticized in the same ways that other scientific research programs are criticized by scientists and philosophers of science. Thus, for example, it might be argued that although the program was progressive back around the beginning of the century, when Freud and Durkheim were making contributions to it, it has more recently been degenerating and ought now to be abandoned. Or it might be argued that projection hypotheses explain only religious beliefs that are "primitive" or "pathological" and that the best explanation of the religious beliefs of mature theists involves the truth of theism and the existence of God. I myself am inclined to believe that an argument for the conclusion that the truth of theism is part of the best explanation of theistic belief might well be, when all is said and done, the best way for theists to reply to projection theorists. But I think it is a mistake to ignore the explanatory successes of projection theories and the warrant they confer on a potential defeater of theistic belief such as (28). Dismissing the work of projection theorists as a combination of jejune speculation and bad argument would not do justice to their real accomplishments.

So I am convinced that defeaters of theistic belief have a good deal of warrant. It seems to me they have enough to insure that, for the intellectually sophisticated adult theist in our culture, basic theistic beliefs such as (14)–(16) are not intrinsic defeater-defeaters unless such a theist is in extraordinary circumstances of the sort that are assumed in Plantinga's Moses example. If such a theist is not thus circumstanced, then theistic beliefs such as (14)–(16) will be properly basic only if the theist has extrinsic defeater-defeaters for defeaters of theism like (28).

For simplicity's sake, I have up to this point been conducting the discussion in terms of the idealized figure of the intellectually sophisticated adult theist in our culture. How should my conclusions be applied to actual adult theists? In considering this question I wish to proceed more cautiously than I did in my previous paper. An answer to this question is bound to be speculative unless it is based on empirical knowledge of the doxastic situations of adult theists.

Imagine a large research project whose first phase aims at finding out how many adult theists there are in the United States who both have propositions such as those expressed by

(14)–(16) among their basic beliefs and know a good deal about non-moral evil and projective theories of religious belief. A follow-up phase of the project is designed to learn more about such people in order to subdivide them into three groups. In the first group will be people in conditions in which their basic theistic beliefs are intrinsic defeater-defeaters of the defeaters of theism that derive warrant from what they know of non-moral evil and projective theories. In the second group will be people who have extrinsic defeater-defeaters of such defeaters of theism. Anyone who satisfies both these conditions will be arbitrarily placed in the first group. Those who satisfy neither conditions will be placed in the third group; they are people whose basic theistic beliefs are not properly basic and who are to some extent irrational. In determining the membership of the second group, a generous communitarian account of what it is to have the requisite defeater-defeaters is to be adopted. That one know exactly how to solve the evidential problem of evil or to respond on behalf of theism to projection theorists is not necessary. It would suffice to have it on the authority of a reliable informant that the experts had reached consensus on these matters, the trouble of course being that, as things actually stand at present, it is well known that there is no such expert consensus and so testimony to that effect could hardly come from a reliable informant.

Now it strikes me as rather silly to try to predict, in advance of doing the imagined research, the actual numbers of people who would wind up in each of the three groups. But, given his views, I would expect Plantinga to predict that a very large percentage of the total will be in the first or second groups, leaving the third group sparsely populated. So it is understandable that he should think little of importance hangs on the fate of natural theology, since few people need it in order to escape from irrationality in theistic belief. Given my views, however, I am willing to predict that a large percentage of the total will be in the third group, rendering it thickly populated. Therefore I believe a great deal hangs on the fate of natural theology, for it seems to me that many people need it, or, at least, need assurances that the experts of the relevant community have it, if their theistic beliefs are to avoid irrationality. My hunch is that this is the issue on which Plantinga and I disagree most deeply, and the prospects of progress toward agreement do not seem to me good.

But I wish to conclude by paying tribute to Plantinga's achievement. I think he has succeeded in identifying a view of theistic belief that, though it may be inchoately present in the Calvinian theological tradition, has never before been seriously discussed by analytic philosophers of religion. And I think he has by this time said enough about the view to show that it has real promise of developing coherently into a religious epistemology worthy of respect. What he has not shown, in my opinion, is that it is superior to alternatives that display similar promise of coherent development.[14]

NOTES

1. Alvin Plantinga, "Is Belief in God Rational?" *Rationality and Religious Belief,* ed. C. F. Delaney (Notre Dame: University of Notre Dame Press, 1979); Alvin Plantinga, "Is Belief in God Properly Basic?" *Nous* 15 (1981); Alvin Plantinga, "Rationality and Religious Belief," *Contemporary Philosophy of Religion,* ed. Steven M. Cahn and David Shatz (New York: Oxford University Press, 1982); Alvin Plantinga, "Reason and Belief in God" (hereafter RBG), *Faith and Rationality,* ed. Alvin Plantinga and Nicholas Wolterstorff (Notre Dame: University of Notre Dame Press, 1983); Alvin Plantinga, "Coherentism and the Evidentialist Objection to Belief in God," *Rationality, Religious Belief, and Moral Commitment,* ed. Robert Audi and William J. Wainwright (Ithaca: Cornell University Press, 1986); and Alvin Plantinga, "Justification and Theism," *Faith and Philosophy* 4 (1987). I include page references to RBG parenthetically in the body of my text.
2. Philip L. Quinn, "In Search of the Foundations of Theism," *Faith and Philosophy* 2 (1985); Alvin Plantinga, "The Foundations of Theism: A Reply" (hereafter FT), *Faith and Philosophy* 3 (1986). I include page references to this paper of mine and to FT parenthetically in the text.
3. I do however need to acknowledge the work I have found especially helpful, including the following published papers: William P. Alston, "Plantinga's Epistemology of Religious Belief," *Alvin Plantinga,* ed. James Tomberlin and Peter van Inwagen (Dordrecht: D.

46   PHILIP L. QUINN

Reidel, 1985); Robert Audi, "Direct Justification, Evidential Dependence, and Theistic Belief," *Rationality, Religious Belief, and Moral Commitment*, ed. Robert Audi and William J. Wainwright (Ithaca: Cornell University Press, 1986); and Stephen J. Wykstra, "Toward a Sensible Evidentialism: On the Notion of 'Needing Evidence'," *Philosophy of Religion: Selected Readings*, 2d ed., ed. William L. Rowe and William J. Wainwright (New York: Harcourt Brace Jovanovitch, 1989). I have also found helpful unpublished work by Anthony Kenny, Norman Kretzmann, James F. Sennet, Stephen J. Wykstra, and Linda Zagzebski.

4. See, for example, John Rawls, *A Theory of Justice* (Cambridge: Harvard University Press, 1971), pp. 19–21, 48–51; and Norman Daniels, "Wide Reflective Equilibrium and Theory Acceptance in Ethics," *Journal of Philosophy* 76 (1979).

5. It is important to bear in mind that I took these examples to involve thought experiments about hypothetical situations.

6. When I say that this option remains open to her, I do not mean to deny that she may have to bite the bullet in exercising it. The situation here seems to be on a par with an example that Plantinga discusses. Though my memorial belief that I had lunch this noon is neither self-evident nor evident to the senses nor incorrigible for me, it is basic for me. Will this putative counterexample convince the Classical Foundationalist to abandon (6)? According to Plantinga, perhaps she "will bite the bullet and maintain that if I really *do* take it as basic, then the fact is I *am*, so far forth, irrational" (RBG, p. 60).

7. According to Plantinga, a belief is justified for a person at a time "if (a) he is violating no epistemic duties and is within his epistemic rights in accepting it then and (b) his noetic structure is not defective by virtue of his then accepting it" (RBG, p. 79).

8. I change numerals within this and some subsequent quotations in order to produce conformity with the numbering system of the present paper. Also, I used a different example in my earlier paper. In order to allude to G. E. Moore I there spoke of seeing a hand and seeming to see a hand.

9. Even if (17) is good evidence for (13), an argument for (13) whose only premise is (17) will not effectively refute a kind of Humean skepticism about the external world and so will lack the sort of cogency I assume Plantinga has in mind.

10. Alvin Plantinga, *God and Other Minds: A Study of the Rational Justification of Belief in God*. (Ithaca: Cornell University Press, 1967). Even if (20) is good evidence for (21), an argument for (21) whose

only premise is (20) will not effectively refute skepticism about other minds and so will not solve the philosopher's problem of other minds.

11. A turp is $1/10^{13}$ times all the evil there is in the actual world.

12. In a footnote Plantinga refers the reader who is interested in finding out what those reasons are to Alvin Plantinga, "The Probabilistic Argument from Evil," *Philosophical Studies* 35 (1979).

13. In this paragraph and the next I make use of ideas derived from Imre Lakatos, "Falsification and the Methodology of Scientific Research Programmes," *Criticism and the Growth of Knowledge,* ed. Imre Lakatos and Alan Musgrave (Cambridge: Cambridge University Press, 1970). Those who doubt that there are such things as human *sciences* could, I believe, translate my talk about research programs into talk about traditions of inquiry of the sort contained in Alasdair MacIntyre's recent writings. See Alasdair MacIntyre, *Whose Justice? Which Rationality?* (Notre Dame: University of Notre Dame Press, 1988); and Alasdair MacIntyre, *Three Rival Versions of Moral Enquiry* (Notre Dame: University of Notre Dame Press, 1990).

14. I am grateful to Alvin Plantinga for spending most of an afternoon discussing a draft of this paper with me. It takes a rare kind of generosity to help one's critics improve their arguments.

2. Natural Theology: Reformed?

John Zeis

INTRODUCTION

What constitutes a belief as properly basic? Is belief in God a properly basic belief? What are the implications for natural theology as traditionally conceived in a broadly Thomistic sense? These are the questions I wish to raise and the answers to which I hope to provide some insight in this essay. The development of the tradition of what has become known as "Reformed Epistemology" challenges theists to re-tool and re-evaluate their assumptions about the nature and function of natural theology and its relation to faith. The general tenor of this paper is one of reconciliation. Many of the central theses of Reformed Epistemology will be incorporated into the proposal for religious epistemology, and the modifications suggested do not, I think, upset the foundations of Reformed Epistemology. What is here proposed is, rather, a synthesis of the Reformist position of Alvin Plantinga with the epistemological views of William Alston and the traditional conception of natural theology. In this spirit of reconciliation, I will henceforth refer to the position as "theological foundationalism" rather than as "Reformed Epistemology," removing the possible connotation that this position is an apologetic arm of one particular Christian sect, whereas it is in fact a proposed epistemology for theism as such.

I wish to make clear as an initial caveat what sort of version of theological foundationalism Thomistic natural theology can be reconciled to. Some theological foundationalists seem to hold that belief in God *must* be properly basic because there is something intrinsically defective about the method of natural theology.[1] Under this radical interpretation, natural theology has no role in providing a justified belief in God's existence. In the moderate view of theological foundationalism, the sort that I interpret Plantinga[2] and Alston[3] as espousing, the position is that belief in God *can* be properly basic and that this does not pre-empt natural theology from playing some sort of role in the justification of religious belief. After all, as far as I know, Plantinga has not recanted positions he defended in *God and Other Minds, God, Freedom, and Evil, The Nature of Necessity*, etc., works in which natural theology abounds. Theological foundationalists have provided no compelling argument for the demise of natural theology; at best their arguments establish that the methods of natural theology are *not necessary* for rational belief. Hence I reject radical theological foundationalism out of hand and will only consider the relative merits and limitations of moderate theological foundationalism.

Although I will not argue from a position of classical foundationalism,[4] I do agree that there is something epistemologically satisfying about the classical strategy of deriving theological propositions from propositions which are non-theological in nature. Insofar as a particular system of beliefs is insulated from beliefs of other noetic systems, there seems to be an element of arbitrariness associated with that particular system of beliefs. This is one of the points that seems to make a person uncomfortable about theological foundationalism. If belief in God is properly basic and the rest of theology is founded upon it, there would be the appearance of a sort of epistemological independence of theology from non-theologically based noetic systems.[5] Descartes's grand skyscraper has been supplanted by a skyline of independently grounded skyscrapers of distinct architectural design, where we can neither see nor find any overall rational plan which unifies the different structures. One of the significant tasks of natural theology, whether or not theological foundationalism is true, is to provide the overall rational perspective in which distinct noetic sub-systems, possibly with their own foundations, are conjoined to form one unified, coherent, conceptual system. I propose to start with the following list of theses.

1. Perceptual beliefs, memory beliefs, and beliefs about other minds, in certain circumstances, are paradigmatic examples of properly basic beliefs.[6]

2. Manifestation beliefs (M-beliefs), like "God is speaking to me now," or "God has forgiven me for such-and-such," in certain circumstances are rationally justified without being based on other beliefs as evidential grounds.[7]

3. Belief in God's existence is not properly basic.[8]

4. Properly basic beliefs are *prima facie* justified and are subject to mediate justification.[9]

5. One of the essential tasks of natural theology is to provide a mediate justification of belief in God's existence.

6. There is a distinction between the state of being epistemologically justified and the process of providing a justification.[10]

In the rest of my essay I will attempt to defend a conception of religious epistemology which is consistent with the six theses listed above.

As I see it, clarification and further support is needed for two fundamental axioms of the position of theological foundationalism. The first is that there are properly basic beliefs and that the criterion for proper basicality is to be discerned by broadly inductive procedures. The second principle is that beliefs about God's actions and properties can function as epistemically basic and as such are immediately justified.

According to the theological foundationalist, there are many kinds of beliefs which can function as properly basic. As such they need not be based on the evidence of other propositions. These properly basic beliefs are grounded, and hence justified, not by other propositions which serve as evidence but by experience of a certain sort.[11] Examples of the kinds of belief which can be properly basic are perceptual beliefs, beliefs based on memory, and beliefs about the mental states of other persons. The classical foundationalist's dogmatic adherence to the strategy of deriving God's existence from a set of founda-

tional beliefs, none of which are theological in nature, is defective because of self-referentially inconsistent or question-
begging evidentialist presuppositions about what can count
as a basic belief.[12] But even if natural theology fails in its task
and theological beliefs cannot be derived from a set of non-
theological beliefs, this does not show that religious belief is unjustified. The theological foundationalist's strategy is based on
the argument that some beliefs about God's action and attributes can function as properly basic beliefs, and since these
beliefs entail God's existence, theism is thereby justified. Simply put, if perceptual beliefs, etc., can be properly basic, so can
beliefs about God's action and attributes.[13]

That some beliefs are properly basic does not entail that
those beliefs are indefeasible or that a justification which appeals to other propositions as evidence *cannot* be given. All that
is entailed is that these beliefs are initially credible because they
are grounded by experience of a certain sort and as such are
prima facie justified.[14] For example, if I am having the appropriate kind of experience, say looking at a tree, the belief that
"There is a tree" is properly basic. In order to be justified, the
belief need not be inferred from other beliefs that I have at the
time; the belief is immediately justified. I may, if pressed, provide evidence or reasons for my belief that there is a tree and as
such provide a mediate justification for the belief, but the validity of the immediate justification is not contingent on my
producing—or even on my ability to produce—a mediate justification of the belief in question.[15]

One may object that it can not be the experience as such
which grounds the belief, but rather appropriate *beliefs about*
the experience. This, however, is a line of criticism which questions the entire notion of proper basicality and is beyond the
scope of the issues I wish to raise here.[16] At this point I wish to
grant the theological foundationalist the premise that certain
kinds of beliefs, like perceptual beliefs, can be properly basic
and as such are grounded and hence justified by experience of
a relevant sort. Can, then, certain beliefs which entail God's existence be considered as properly basic?

Theological foundationalism has come under a great deal
of criticism for equating the epistemic status of beliefs about

God with perceptual beliefs, memory beliefs, and beliefs about other minds. Grigg, Quinn, Audi, and McKim[17] have focused on dissimilarities between theological beliefs and the paradigmatic set of properly basic beliefs in questioning the legitimacy of the proper basicality of religious beliefs. There are two basic strategies of attack. One is to propose a criterion for proper basicality which is shared by beliefs in the paradigmatic set but that theological beliefs lack, thereby denying them status as properly basic. The other strategy is to argue that if beliefs about God are properly basic for the theist, then the same ought to apply to religious beliefs held by others, including sufficiently silly (and I suppose also *dangerous*) ones. I believe that there are some merits to the criticisms raised by the anti-theological foundationalists,[18] but I do not wish to pursue them or the counterarguments here. My intention is rather to propose a view which I think is more sympathetic to theological foundationalism but nonetheless includes concessions concerning the value of the two lines of criticism outlined above.

A CRITERION OF PROPER BASICALITY

In "Reason and Belief in God," Plantinga proposed a method for determining necessary and sufficient conditions for proper basicality, about which much ink has already been spilled.

> And hence the proper way to arrive at such a criterion is, broadly speaking, *inductive*. We must assemble examples of beliefs and conditions such that the former are obviously basic in the latter, and examples of beliefs and conditions such that the former are obviously *not* properly basic in the latter. We must then frame hypotheses as to the necessary and sufficient conditions of proper basicality and test these hypotheses by reference to those examples.[19]

Alston has taken the lead in the development of epistemic principles consistent with epistemological foundationalism and his recent contributions provide us with some hints as to the grounds of properly basic beliefs. In "A 'Doxastic Practice' Approach to Epistemology" Alston proposes that beliefs which are grounded in socially established doxastic practices are justified. A doxastic practice is a "system or constellation of *dispositions* or habits, or, to use a currently fashionable term, *mechanisms*, each of which yields a belief as output that is related in a certain way to an 'input.'"[20] Each doxastic practice has its own "conditions of justification," and "its own fundamental beliefs." "There is no one unique source of justification or knowledge, such as Descartes and many others have dreamed of."[21] And in "Christian Experience and Christian Belief" Alston has argued that there is no good reason for thinking that Christian doxastic practice has any less of a claim to reliability than perceptual practice. Presumably, each socially established doxastic practice has its own set of properly basic beliefs, but Alston does not directly pursue the question as to the criterion for those beliefs. Given his warnings above about the differences of doxastic practices, the search for a generic criterion for proper basicality may very well be wrongheaded; I shall nevertheless make an attempt to apply Plantinga's inductive procedure in order to do just that.

Like Alston, I think there is an interesting parallel between how the new foundationalists treat properly basic beliefs and Wittgenstein's critique of traditional epistemology.[22] Wittgenstein, like the new foundationalists, had no truck with the skeptical demands to provide arguments based on evidence for such claims as "S in pain." As Alston himself suggests in "A 'Doxastic Approach,'" Wittgenstein's "language games" can be construed as reliable doxastic practices.[23] I suggest that we can even enlist Wittgenstein further in the support of proper basicality for beliefs of the same kind which the new foundationalists, whether theological or anti-theological, use as their paradigms, and I wish to develop the suggestion here.

Essential to the Wittgensteinian position is the connection between beliefs like "S is in pain" and criteria for their application.[24] The criteria for the application of a claim are meaning-relevant *experiential* features, but the experience itself is not sufficient for establishing the criteria. What is also required is that the criteria be shared or at least shareable by a linguistic community. We have clear criteria for claims like "S is in pain" and "There is a tree" not only because of a particular sort of experience which prompts the belief, but also because a convention is established in the linguistic community for the appropriate assertion of such claims. This accords with what Alston asserts is a necessary condition for an established doxastic practice in "A 'Doxastic Approach.'"

For Wittgenstein, criteria govern the use of linguistic expressions which a speaker could in principle justify. They are established by convention in a language and contribute to the meaning of the expressions for which they serve as a criterion. Criteria are part of the public domain of language. Speakers learn the appropriate circumstances for the assertion of justifiable expressions in a language by knowing their criteria. In the case of expressions like "There is a tree," the most common criterion for the use of that expression is a sense experience of a tree. But suitable substitutes may function as criteria when the object is unavailable. We can teach a child the appropriate use of the expression "There's an elephant" without traveling to a zoo or a circus; a picture and accompanying explanation will do. In the case of sensations, like pain, the criterion is neither the object in question nor even a representation of it, but the typical behavior associated with the sensation. The connection between an expression and its criterion is not one of simple inference nor a matter of evidence. We cannot infer on the basis of pain behavior that the person is actually in pain. The subject may be playacting. It is not a question of evidence because the criterion is the means by which we identify the object or state of affairs. Appealing to evidence for a claim implies that such an identification has already been settled.

Although not functioning as evidential, a case can be made for appeals to criteria functioning as justifying *grounds*. If the circumstances are appropriate, e.g., if I am having the right kind of tree-like appearance, my belief that "There is a tree" may be said to be justified on the basis that this is just the sort of experience which serves as the criterion for the expression. Given the fundamental semantic connection between the expression and its criterion in the linguistic community, no appeal to further beliefs or evidence need be made. This is where language and experience meet; the criterion serves as adequate ground, for in appealing to the criterion, we have reached the bedrock of our linguistic conventions, or, in Alston's sense, the doxastic practice. We can, if we wish, question or even alter these conventions, and this would require the adoption of a new criterion. But we cannot go without the use of criteria for *some* expressions, for then none of our claims would be warranted. Here Wittgenstein's position parallels the foundationalists' argument for the necessity of foundational beliefs *somewhere* within the noetic structure.

Wittgenstein may have held that all justifiable claims in a language must have a criterion associated with their use,[25] but I think we need not go that far. Although we may agree that some expressions must be connected with criteria in order to have adequate grounds, other expressions may lack a clear criterion but be derivable through some form of inference or analogy from expressions that do have criteria. I would suggest that this is so for beliefs which have theoretical content or are of an explanatory nature which are not so easily identified by clear experiential features. What would be the criteria for expressions like "Water is H_2O"? It seems to me plausible that the use of the expression "This is water" is learned via a connection with an observable circumstance established through linguistic convention as the criterion. And if water *is* H_2O, then "This is H_2O" is true if and only if "This is water" is true, so the same phenomenon which serves as a criterion for the use of the one might be thought to serve as the criterion for the use of the other. But "Water is H_2O" is synthetic, not analytic, and so the criteria for what is water and what is H_2O should differ. Using Wittgenstein's distinction between criteria and symptoms,[26] I think it is better if we view the matter this way. Once the meaning of the expression "This is water" is established (partly via the connection to a criterion), claims about a substance's being or not being water are justified. Water can be identified for further investigation, and then symptoms associated with water can be discovered (e.g., its being H_2O).

What contribution, if any, can be derived from an application of the Wittgensteinian notion of criteria to the dispute at hand? The terminology of the theological foundationalists differs: what Plantinga calls "properly basic beliefs," Alston calls "immediately justified beliefs," but the beliefs' function as epistemologically foundational appears to be the same. As I noted above, one of the oft-mentioned difficulties associated with the position is the explanation (or lack thereof) of why some kinds of beliefs may be foundational and not others. Some clues, however, can be derived from the paradigmatic examples and the properties associated with such beliefs. Perceptual beliefs, beliefs from memory, and beliefs about other minds are proposed examples of beliefs which can be properly basic and as such they need not be based on reasons or evidence, are grounded by experience, and are *prima facie* justified.

The clues seem to me to point to an explanation of properly basic beliefs via the notion of Wittgensteinian criteria. Perceptual beliefs, beliefs from memory, and beliefs about other minds have clear criteria associated with their use. For each kind there are observable circumstances which can serve a linguistic community in the establishment of conventions for their use. The criteria establish *prima facie grounds of justification* for the expressions, for the observable circumstances function as their grounds. The immediate and spontaneous assertability of such expressions under certain conditions is explained by the connection between those conditions (the criterion) and the expression in the history of the individual and the speech community's use of the expression in question. The use of the expression under such circumstances is *immediately justified* because we come face-to-face with just those conditions which stipulate assertability conditions for the meaning of the expression. Under certain conditions "This is a tree" is justified because those are just the circumstances about which we mean that "This is a tree." However, since there are no entailment relations between the criterion and the truth of the claim, we may be wrong; the claim is *only prima facie justified and can be overridden.* Imagine, for example, that someone is deliberately feigning pain behavior to fool us. But as we have seen, these are the same kinds of properties theological foundationalists associate with properly basic beliefs.

What I propose then is that we take properly basic or immediately justified beliefs to be those which have a criterion associated with them. The criteria are Wittgensteinian in the sense of being publicly observable circumstances which stipulate part of the meaning of a linguistic expression and so satisfy conditions of *prima facie* justification for the expression.

But although this proposal accommodates perceptual beliefs, beliefs from memory, and beliefs about other minds, it spells trouble for the consideration of beliefs about God's actions or attributes being properly basic. If I have a belief that "God is speaking to me now," this belief is based on private experience. There is no publicly observable circumstance which can serve as a criterion. Wittgenstein's objection to private criteria is that in the absence of public criteria which stipulate the use of the expression, we can make no sense of the distinction between my thinking that something is so, and its being so. Whatever impresses us as right must then be taken to be right; but in the absence of public criteria there can be no distinction between a right and wrong use of the expression. If "*S* is in pain" has public criteria, then "I am in pain" can refer to a private object; but if "God is speaking to *S* now" has no public criterion, then "God is speaking to me now" cannot similarly refer.

Wittgenstein's attack on private criteria is not, of course, universally accepted, and so to appeal to it for the critique of theologically basic beliefs may seem highly suspect. I will return to this objection below. But I think that the worry about private criteria is somewhat substantiated by considering the doubts concerning beliefs about religious experience that seem to be very difficult to resolve. If I believe that "God is speaking to me now," how am I to tell whether the experience which prompts my belief is the *right* sort of experience which justifies my claim and hence makes my belief properly basic? In the case of perceptual beliefs, the experience of a tree which grounds the properly basic belief that "There is a tree" is shareable and established by linguistic convention. And this is just as true for beliefs about someone else's being in pain and basic memory beliefs. The pain behavior of the person is the ground which justifies my basic belief and that experience is shareable as well. The breakfast I had plus my assertion later that I had it serve in a similar fashion as justifying conditions which are publicly observable. If we imagine the lack of those publicly observable conditions in connection with any of those types of claims, would we still wish to consider the beliefs properly basic? If you assert "There is a tree" in the absence of any shareable tree-like experience, or "Tom is in pain" in the absence of any publicly observable pain behavior on Tom's part, or "I had coffee this morning" when I remember serving you tea because I had no coffee, surely none of these beliefs would be accepted *by others* as immediately justified. Could they still, however, be properly basic for you? They might be, but I think only if you could in principle point out some feature of shareable experience which grounds the belief. It would be one thing if you said, "Tom gets bad headaches and whenever he does, he rubs his temples like that," and another if instead you said, "I just have this feeling that he is." What could serve as a suitable criterion for expressions like "God is speaking to me now" besides my having the feeling that God is?

There are surely criteria for expressions like "Tom is speaking to me now." I think we can even extend this by analogy to strange occurrences of hearing voices when no one is present and described as "Tom is speaking to me now." The extension of the claim to the inner voice does not seem to me objectionable in cases like this; enough of a connection to the criteria for the normal use of the expression seems to be preserved in this instance. I am not sure about what to say concerning claims like "Caesar is speaking to me now," said of an inner voice, when we have no criterion for the typical use of that expression. But one thing seems clear: such claims could not be properly basic. The claim that "God is speaking to me now" seems to be in at least as much jeopardy as "Caesar is speaking to me now." In the case of the latter, at least there is a clear criterion for the functional expression "*x* is speaking to me now" when *x* refers to some individual similar in kind to Caesar. Whether extension by analogy to God's speaking to me works seems questionable. And even then, without suitable criteria for "This is God," the connection between the expression "God is speaking now" and criteria for its use would have to be so tenuous that immediate justification would be out of the question.

Again, I wish to stress that my use of the notion of criteria is distinct from Wittgenstein's in that I do not think that criteria are required for the use of *every* justifiable expression in a language, but only for those we ought to consider as immediately justified. The contribution to 'meaning' is merely the establishment of *prima facie* justifying conditions in order for language to get a foothold in experience. For those that lack a criterion for their use, a mediate justification is still a possible option. This then is my view about claims about God's actions and attributes. Since they lack a clear criterion for their use, they cannot be properly basic for the reasons that perceptual beliefs, memory beliefs, or beliefs about other minds are properly basic. Consequently, from what I have argued here, it would follow that they are in need of a mediate justification in order to be justified.

Two more points ought to be added in defense of the position that proper basicality be construed as applying only to expressions for which there exists a criterion for their use. In this section, I have argued that properly basic beliefs, if there be such things, are justified by their relation to criteria and that these criteria be circumstances which are in principle observable by other members of a linguistic community. As such, these criteria function, like the deductive rules of inference, by providing rules which are intersubjectively verified. And once such rules are reached, whether in a proof or in the assertion of a claim, we have reached acceptable foundations of justification.

I also believe that the notion of criteria developed above coincides fairly well with the Aristotelian–Thomistic view that "all knowledge begins with the senses." This view has been very influential in the epistemology of natural theology, and I remarked earlier how there was something appealing about the attempt to justify religious beliefs from a foundation which includes no theologically loaded beliefs. If we accept the suggestion that only those expressions which have criteria can serve as expressions of properly basic beliefs, we will obtain a class of beliefs "evident to the senses" in a traditional, Aristotelian sense. Aristotelians have never been bothered about the justification conditions for beliefs like "S is in pain" or "I had coffee this morning," and I think that is because they would consider them to be, epistemically, of the same degree of warrant as "This is a tree," for which there was also no puzzle concerning its justification. My discussion of criteria provides a ground for this position, for these beliefs *are* of the same sort in the sense that, although none are beliefs *about* sense experience, sense experience provides the non-linguistic portion of the criteria for their use. And since the criteria function as grounds, it seems quite plausible to say that these beliefs are "evident to the senses."

If my analysis is correct, the sorts of beliefs on which natural theology has traditionally rested are properly basic, while M-beliefs are not. I will now consider the theological foundationalists' probable rejoinder to my use of Wittgensteinian criteria as a ground for proper basicality.

MANIFESTATION-BELIEFS AND PROPER BASICALITY

In "Christian Experience and Christian Belief," Alston considers four salient features of perceptual practice which may be said to "manifest or betoken reliability,"[27] and argues that even though Christian practice lacks all four of these features, this is not an adequate reason for regarding Christian practice as unreliable.[28] He then proceeds to argue that since "the reality CP (Christian practice) claims to put us in touch with is conceived to be vastly different from the physical environment,"[29] it is not at all surprising, but ought to be expected, that the sorts of procedures which "put us in effective cognitive touch with this reality be equally different."[30] And in a later publication, "Religious Diversity and Perceptual Knowledge of God," he reaffirms this position:

> I have in previous writings examined a number of objections to this thesis, e.g., that there are no objective intersubjective tests of particular M-beliefs, that the experience involved can be adequately explained in terms of natural factors, and that many people claim to have no such perceptions. I have argued that all these objections, and others as well, are based either on epistemic chauvinism . . . or on arbitrarily holding different practices subject to different requirements (the double standard).[31]

If Alston's argument is sound, then the argument I presented in the last section of this paper merely begs the question. By restricting my selection of properly basic beliefs to those within the paradigmatic set, I have simply violated the canons of induction for the formation and confirmation of suitable hypotheses. Plantinga has made it clear that this is what is to be expected from those who are anti-theological foundationalists.[32] The selection of what sorts of beliefs are going to be included in the data set is critical to what sorts of hypotheses will be confirmed when applied to the data in turn. Although it is obvious to *me* that if there are properly basic beliefs, then perceptual beliefs and beliefs about other minds are such, it is *not obvious* to me that manifestation beliefs are. And what is it to me that the Cartesian foundationalist begins with a much more restrictive class of beliefs? Am I bound to adjust my data to fit hers? Clearly not, for that is precisely how classical foundationalism and logical positivism got their deadly grips on us in the first place. The theological foundationalist argues that there is, similarly, no reason for them to restrict their data set to mine. That manifestation beliefs are properly basic *is obvious* to them, and consequently ought to belong to the data set.

The most reasonable explanation for this difference of opinion is that *both* are true. Although *I* have never had an experience which would justify a claim like "God is speaking to me now" in any properly basic way, it would be sheer arrogance for me to insist that the same is true about Abraham, Moses, St. Paul, St. Theresa, or Plantinga and Alston for that matter. A theist who is an anti-theological foundationalist seems to me to be in an awkward position. The prophets, authoritative apostles, and mystics of theism who claimed personal divine guidance were not natural theologians and the central doctrines of the faith are such that they *cannot* be derived from non-theological propositions. Unless the theist is willing to grant their irrationality, what could the status of their epistemic warrant be?

I wish now to take this presumed objection to my analysis in the last section to heart and attempt to articulate the position on the proper basicality of M-beliefs from another perspective. Although perceptual beliefs, memory beliefs, and beliefs about other minds form the paradigmatic set of properly basic beliefs in most discussions of proper basicality, there is a limiting set of cases of properly basic beliefs which I did not consider in the last section. This set consists of those beliefs to which one has privileged access. In the rest of this section, I would like to explore the extension of the notion of proper basicality suggested by Alston's position on such beliefs. My proposal is that beliefs to which we have privileged access (hereafter PA-beliefs) are better analogues for M-beliefs when it comes to the question as to their proper basicality.

In "Self-Warrant: A Neglected Form of Privileged Access," Alston argues for the position that PA-beliefs are justified by their being self-warranted. According to Alston, a belief, b, is self-warranted if and only if "b is warranted just by virtue of being b (being b is sufficient for b's being warranted)."[33] Self-warranted beliefs are a limiting case of properly basic beliefs for, unlike beliefs in the paradigmatic set, there is nothing distinct from the belief itself which serves as its ground. In "Concepts of Epistemic Justification," Alston considers self-evident beliefs and beliefs about one's conscious states:

> But where are the adequate grounds on which my belief is based? It is not that there are grounds here about whose adequacy we might have doubts; it is rather that there seems to be nothing identifiable as grounds. There is nothing here that is distinguished from my belief and the proposition involved, in the way evidence or reasons are distinct from that for which they are evidence or reasons, or in the way my sensory experience is distinct from the beliefs about the physical world that are based on it. A similar problem can be raised for normal beliefs about one's own conscious states. What is the ground for a typical belief that one feels sleepy? If one replies "One's consciousness of one's feeling of sleepiness," then it may be insisted, with some show of plausibility, that where one is consciously feeling sleepy, there is no difference between one's feeling sleepy and one's being conscious that one is feeling sleepy.[34]

Self-warranted beliefs, although properly basic, are such that they have no independent ground for their justification.

In developing the concept of epistemic justification in essays after "Privileged Access," Alston has insisted that no belief is justified unless it is based on adequate grounds.[35] This has led him to reject the main thesis of self-warrant defended in "Privileged Access." That the grounds of PA-beliefs are "not distinguished from the fact that makes them true," . . . "support[s] a diagnosis of truth-warrant, rather than of self-warrant."[36] The principle of truth-warrant I would assume he has in mind would be some such version of what he considers and then rejects in "Privileged Access," viz., "A B is warranted if and only if it is true."[37] And since adequate grounds for a belief in Alston's sense are what the belief is based on,[38] PA-beliefs are adequately grounded if and only if they are based on the truth of the belief.

Extending Alston's diagnosis of truth-warrant for PA-beliefs, I propose that we take M-beliefs as an extraordinary species of PA-beliefs. Like beliefs about one's own mental states, properly basic M-beliefs are such that the agent has privileged access. The agent is in a cognitive state which gives him a privileged position in relation to its justifying conditions, and whatever justifies the agent's believing M, no one else can have the same justification. M-beliefs are properly basic because they are truth-warranted: an M-belief is warranted if and only if it is based on its truth. What would justify *my* believing that "God is speaking to me now" is its being grounded in the truth that God is speaking to me now; but its being true that God is speaking to me now *cannot* function as a warrant for anyone else's believing that God is speaking to me now. Construed in this way, M-beliefs, like other PA-beliefs, are self-presenting[39] and are a limiting case of properly basic beliefs.

That properly basic M-beliefs are truth-warranted by being PA-beliefs of an extraordinary character I think coincides with how we view the nature of M-beliefs. Abraham, Moses, St. Paul, St. Theresa, and the many anonymous believers who have had M-beliefs have a degree of warrant for God's presence which surpasses the degree of warrant possessed by beliefs formed by *any* other doxastic practice.[40] As Plantinga has argued, we ought not to conceive of properly basic M-beliefs as in need of strengthening or support via mediate justification. Properly basic M-beliefs have a degree of certitude which is not shared by any other sorts of belief. This is reflected in the resolve of the believer under even *very* difficult circumstances. Abraham had no doubts that God wanted him to sacrifice Isaac and Mary no doubt that she would conceive, even though the "defeaters" of such beliefs seem to be overwhelming. So, properly basic M-beliefs are not just *prima facie* justified, they are unqualifiedly justified.[41]

M-beliefs are an *extraordinary* type of PA-beliefs. It is not typical that humans would form such beliefs in a reliable way, and there is no natural mechanism or doxastic practice which converts the input to output.[42] Properly basic M-beliefs are formed through a *super*natural doxastic practice. God's grace elevates the intellect of the person to whom God presents God's self, and God's manifestation to us is possible only through a supernatural alteration of the cognitive powers of the human intellect. As a result, most of us, most of the time, do not have the capacity to form properly basic M-beliefs; and it is quite possible that *some* of us never have the capacity to form properly basic M-beliefs. As the congenitally blind person has no reliable perceptual mechanism for the formation of properly basic color beliefs, the person (believer or non-believer), to whom God does not graciously manifest God's self in this self-presenting way, has no reliable cognitive mechanism and cannot form properly basic M-beliefs. And lacking such a cognitive mechanism, it would be unimaginable to such a person how such basic beliefs are formed. I cannot imagine what kind of experience would justify my belief that God has commanded me to sacrifice my son; whatever I conceive of seems subject to conclusive doubt or deception.

Although properly basic M-beliefs are warranted to such a high degree, one must keep in mind that under my proposal, such beliefs are warranted if and only if they are *true*. This is another distinguishing mark from properly basic beliefs which are not of the PA sort. "There is a tree," or "Tom is in pain" may be warranted in a properly basic way, even in circumstances where the beliefs are false, and *not* warranted in circumstances where the beliefs are true. But if I am right, truth is both a necessary and sufficient condition for the grounding of properly basic M-beliefs. Although this condition may open the way for claims of indubitability, incorrigibility, and omniscience for properly basic M-beliefs, M-beliefs as such are not infallibly justified.[43] If someone has an M-belief and it is not true, such a belief is then unjustified. Mary's belief that she will conceive, Abraham's that he sacrifice his son, are properly basic beliefs and warranted if and *only if* those beliefs are true.

This condition allows theists to dispose of the worries about Great Pumpkinites[44] and others who have a false faith being justified in their holding M-beliefs. But of course the Great Pumpkinites who claim revelations from the Great Pumpkin *think* that their claims are justified because they are true, and under my view they can (they think) similarly dispose of the claims of Christians, Jews, and Muslims on the basis that they are false. Although the truth-warranting thesis I am defending entails that if M-beliefs are justified, then they are true, and if they are true, they are justified, of course anyone who holds M-beliefs will think that they have satisfied the truth-warrant condition.

As a species of PA-beliefs, M-beliefs are essentially subjectively justified. I would presume that any adequate construal of the justification conditions for M-beliefs would entail this feature. This is the most obvious difference between the justification conditions for beliefs in the paradigmatic set and M-beliefs. It is also the feature on which anti-theological foundationalists commonly focus in their critiques of theological foundationalism. If my analysis here is correct, these critiques miss the mark. M-beliefs can be properly basic, even though the conditions which would make them properly basic are dramatically different from the conditions which make beliefs in the paradigmatic set properly basic. I now wish to turn to a consideration of the implications for natural theology.

NATURAL THEOLOGY: REFORMED?

Before tackling the problem head-on, I will first present a synopsis of some of Alston's views on justification which seem to be not only necessary for the plausibility of epistemological foundationalism in general, but are also critically relevant to the issue of the function of natural theology in the face of the proper basicality of M-beliefs.

According to Alston, although properly basic beliefs are immediately justified, they are open to the possibility of mediate justification. As he expresses it: "It is very plausible to suppose that *any* belief, however it arose, can be evaluated for truth, justification, or rationality by reference to reasons or evidence. . . . There is even some plausibility in holding that it is always, in principle, possible to find such reasons."[45] In Alston's view, IJBs (immediately justified beliefs) are properly basic in the sense that they are immediately justified, and as such they do not *require* other beliefs or reasons as their ground. But IJBs are potential subjects of mediate justification as well.

In the second section of this paper, I defended a foundationalist interpretation of perceptual beliefs, memory beliefs, and beliefs about other minds on the basis of a Wittgensteinian notion of criteria. Expressions which have criteria are experientially grounded by their criteria and as such seem to be plausible candidates for IJBs. But since there is no entailment relation between a belief and its criteria, the belief is subject to mediate justification as well.

The fact that IJBs can be mediately justified ought not to impugn their status as properly basic. Alston argues that thinking that it does involves a fundamental epistemological confusion between a belief's *being* justified and the activity of *showing* a belief to be justified. Alston claims that the confusion is pervasive in epistemology, and he seems to think that it is at the heart of the coherentist position on justification, particularly in their attack upon the given. The coherentist objection that the 'given' is something which is itself subject to mediate justification does not show, according to Alston, that these beliefs are not justified. That there are contexts and circumstances in which giving reasons for IJBs may very well be appropriate, and that IJBs are dependent on the knowledge of a whole range of concepts, Alston is willing and able to admit. But what he is *not* willing to grant is that the production of reasons for these beliefs or an articulation of concepts are necessary conditions for IJBs being grounded. A pre-reflective child or a non-reflecting adult can have a justified belief that there is a tree in front of them "just by virtue of forming that belief by normal perceptual processes in normal circumstances."[46] Their inability to produce a mediate justification for these beliefs does not entail that these beliefs are not immediately justified.

And if we push Alston to tell us where the process of mediate justification ends, he will respond that it has no end. According to Alston, we cannot be fully reflectively justified. The impossibility of fully reflective justification is developed in Alston's discussion of the reliability of belief-forming processes like perception. Since the adequacy of grounds for IJBs can be satisfied only if perception is reliable, one might be tempted to consider whether we are justified in believing in the reliability of perception. In order to obtain critical assurance, we then might engage in the process of attempting to justify this belief. But "when the attempt to show that one is justified in supposing a basic belief source to be reliable is pressed in the way that S has been doing, the attempt will founder on *logical* circularity. At some point back along the way, and not so very back at that, one will be appealing to the very reliability thesis one is seeking to justify."[47] Fully reflective justification is obtained only when the beliefs which are employed in the justification of a belief are themselves shown to be justified. And this, because of the inevitability of circularity, cannot be attained.

Now although this would be a very disturbing consequence for foundationalists of a Cartesian bent, this negative conclusion does not disturb the new foundationalist, for it in fact bolsters the crucial distinction between being justified and the activity of justifying. As Alston expresses it:

> Let us recur to the point that it is by appreciating the distinction between *justifying* and *being justified* that we can see the (relative) innocuousness of epistemic circularity. We have finally found some negative consequence thereof, but *only by washing out that distinction*. The quest for FRJ (fully reflective justification) is undertaken just when we ignore, or lose interest in merely being justified.[48]

Alston believes that the state of being justified, rather than the activity of justifying, is what the theory of epistemic justification ought to focus on. If we lose this focus, we are then caught in the trap of attempting to provide fully reflective justification, which is bound to fail.

The distinction between being justified and the activity or process of justification is, I think, a plausible one. And this distinction is crucial to the foundationalist's position on properly basic beliefs being immediately justified but nonetheless being subject to further (mediate) justification. And the long, frustrating history of epistemology seems to confirm the thesis that a fully reflective justification is not attainable. But what I think is relevant for the perspective of the natural theologian is that the epistemology of theological foundationalism, when viewed in its totality rather than as a singular focus on what is properly basic, actually entails what I take to be a re-affirmation of the significance of traditional natural theology.

As I argued in the previous section, it seems quite plausible, or at least pointless to dispute, that there are beliefs about religious experience that are properly basic for some believers, but not for others. If this is so, then for those believers who have basic religious beliefs, there is no need of a mediate justification in order to *be justified* in these beliefs. But for those believers who do not have immediately justified religious beliefs, some other avenue of justification is necessary in order to *be justified* in their belief, either mediate justification or reliable testimony. And even for those believers who have properly basic M-beliefs or have reliable testimonial evidence and are thereby justified in their beliefs, there is still the desideratum of *showing* that religious belief is justified. If M-beliefs are justified because they are truth-warranted, this attains further significance, but I will consider this below. Here it is sufficient to note that even though Alston may be right about the superior epistemological value of being justified over the process of demonstrating justification, there is still of course significant epistemological value in showing that one is justified. And for theologically relevant propositions, this service of demonstrating justification is provided by natural theology.

The above reasoning applies to all sorts of properly basic beliefs, but the desirability of demonstrating justification for religious beliefs seems even more important than for perceptual beliefs or PA-beliefs which are not theologically loaded. As construed in the last section, properly basic M-beliefs are essentially subjective (similar to other PA-beliefs), but they also lack the universality of PA-beliefs. According to my view, and in agreement with Alston, this does not entail that they are unjustified, but I think it does make reflective justification more significant for religious beliefs than for properly basic beliefs of other sorts where either objective criteria, universality, or both apply.

Second, although this seems to be treated in the literature as epistemologically insignificant, I think it is quite important to emphasize that beliefs like "God exists" are not properly basic. Although properly basic M-beliefs like "God is speaking to me now," "God has forgiven me for such-and-such," or "God is presenting himself to me as loving Father" manifest God's presence and insofar as they are manifestations of God's presence, are also manifestations of God's existence, there is plenty of room for degrees and aspects of manifestation.[49] When a person manifests herself to us, there is always the question of how much of the person's being is made manifest, and under what aspects she is made manifest. If you are speaking to me on the phone, your existence is in some way made evident to me, but only under a very restrictive aspect of your being. Unless properly basic M-beliefs are all formed as the result of a beatific vision of God in God's completeness, properly basic M-beliefs *do not* necessarily make evident the proposition that God exists, as articulated and understood in, let us say, an Anselmian way as entailing the existence of that than which nothing greater can be conceived, or in a Thomistic way as the existence of that being for which essence entails existence. Even if Moses had a properly basic M-belief encountering God's presence in "I am who am," this does not entail that he had a recognition or knowledge, nor surely an articulation of the metaphysical implications of God's manifestation; for this a Thomas is required.[50]

The mediate justifications which natural theology produce however, do not apply directly to properly basic M-beliefs, which are particular, referring to a subject here and now. But such beliefs carry general assumptions about God's existence and nature, albeit opaquely. And those general assumptions of M-beliefs are still within the special province of natural theology. Natural theology and the dogmas of the church can provide a context and a meaning for M-beliefs, supplying a general conceptual underpinning to the more individual claims of M-beliefs. Even more intrinsically, natural theology and dogma may supply the instruments of articulation for the expression of M-beliefs themselves. But as to whether or not particular M-beliefs are true, I think natural theology has very little to contribute in the way of confirmation. Its role would seem to be more significant for refutation. If a Christian claims to have had an M-belief that is contrary to dogma and natural theology, then skepticism, relative to the level of contrariety, seems to be the appropriate response. There are likely exceptions, e.g., Abraham's belief that God commanded him to sacrifice Isaac. But again, I think it is crucial here to defer to the distinction between being *justified* and the process or activity of *justifying*. Even in the absence of the support of dogma and natural theology, and its apparent contrariety, if my position is correct, Abraham's M-belief is nonetheless justified as long as it is true.

One may also have warranted M-beliefs which are not properly basic. A discernment of the truth of certain M-beliefs may require a gradual contemplation which includes the consideration of evidence of other propositions as part of their grounds. In any case, I would still insist that for M-beliefs which are not properly basic, a necessary condition for their being warranted is their truth.[51]

Third, and maybe most significantly, according to the view presented in the last section of this paper, basic M-beliefs are justified *only if* they are true. And although if true, they are evident to the subject, M-beliefs can *seem* evidently true and consequently properly basic, even when they are not true. In short, since we are not infallible in our identification of true M-beliefs, even though someone may be immediately justified in believing certain M-beliefs, their emphatic claims are no reason for someone else's taking them as justified. And if truth is what justifies, since truth is an externalist property of the proposition believed, there is nothing intrinsic about the subject's cognitive state which would allow us (or him, if he is wrong), to determine its status as warranted. Only those who have *true* M-beliefs are warranted, and since claims about M-beliefs commonly conflict, we need to find some other way to approach the question of the plausible truth of such claims: the other way is of course through natural theology.

Some may consider it objectionable that, in the view which I am proposing, there is no way to identify properly basic M-beliefs from "the inside"; there is no phenomenological characteristic which distinguishes a genuine M-belief from a spurious one. George Mavrodes has considered this issue in his article "Enthusiasm," and concludes that probably the best response is no response, that there is very little in the way of validation that is applicable to M-beliefs.[52]

The first response I wish to make is that, for all *I* know, there *may* be a phenomenological characteristic of genuine M-beliefs which spurious M-beliefs lack. But don't ask me what this property might be, for I am here like the congenitally blind man being asked to describe the phenomenology of color perception. Secondly, even if there is a phenomenological mark of properly basic M-beliefs, it is not something which is articulated by those who seem to have them. As St. Theresa recounted, "I did not know how I knew it. . . . There are no words to explain."[53] In another work, Mavrodes suggests that these experiences are basic, and that like other basic actions or experiences, we just do them or have them, and there is nothing of note to articulate about them.[54] So even if there is a phenomenological or psychological mark of properly basic M-beliefs which causes a valid cognition in the subject, if this experience cannot be communicated by genuine mystics, spurious manifestation experiences would still be problematic. It may be that there is a phenomenological mark which distinguishes properly basic M-beliefs, but that it is identifiable only by those who have had them before, and those who have not can be genuinely mistaken about having them.

So, the first reason for my rejection of theological foundationalism as a displacement of natural theology is that either there are or there are not properly basic theological beliefs. If there are not, the need for mediate justification is evident. If there are, they are still subject to mediate justification, and their lack of intersubjective grounds common to other types of properly basic beliefs makes mediate justification more pressing. And even if theological beliefs may be properly basic for some people, then it still seems highly questionable that beliefs about religious experience are properly basic for *all* believers. If beliefs about religious experience are not *universally* properly basic and there is an absence of reliable testimony, there is still the need for a mediate justification of theism for some beliefs to have any justification whatsoever, which is precisely what natural theology is supposed to provide. I do not believe that the theological foundationalists can plausibly maintain that all theologically loaded beliefs *must* be properly basic; the most that theological foundationalists can want to claim is that such beliefs *can* be properly basic. They then ought to have no objection, and ought to support, the project of providing mediate justification of theism via natural theology. And even if fully reflective justification is not possible, a mediate justification of religious beliefs which rests on a foundation of properly basic beliefs in the paradigmatic set ought to be attainable.

Second, natural theology is primarily the product of engaging in a process of justification. The epistemic value of natural theology should not be construed as a thesis about the state of being justified *vis-à-vis* religious beliefs. The theological foundationalist may be exactly right in claiming that religious beliefs are immediately justified. Others, less philosophically inclined, or just not philosophically inclined toward epistemological foundationalism, may be precisely correct in claiming that faith as an assent to authority on the basis of testimony is what justifies religious belief. Natural theology in no way conflicts with these positions, for these are positions about the *state* of being justified. Natural theology should not be interpreted as a description or explanation of what it is to *have* justified theistic belief. It is an articulation of a *process* of justifying religious belief. If successful, natural theology of course enhances the state of being justified in believing theism but is not meant to be productive or a replacement, or even necessarily a strengthening of that state.

Finally, natural theology is indispensable for the adjudication of the truth, and consequently the warrant, of general religious claims even if there are properly basic M-beliefs. Natural theology may not have a history of great actual success in this regard, but it is our *only* possible instrument of success.

One last word is necessary. Aquinas has been charged with evidentialism, namely, the view that "belief in God is rationally acceptable only if there is evidence for it—only if, that is, it is probable with respect to some body of propositions which constitutes the evidence."[55] But I see no reason to charge Aquinas with a version of evidentialism which entails a strict implication between the rationality of belief and evidence for the individual believer. Aquinas certainly holds that in order for belief in the proposition that God exists to be rational, the *proposition* that God exists must be supportable and even supported by evidence. But this does not entail that a believer is irrational in *believing* the proposition even without the evidence. Aquinas clearly affirms that some accept God's existence without the support of natural theology, but he also insists that this is a *knowledge* (*cognitio*) that the believer has, and in fact it is a knowledge which is superior to the sort provided through natural theology. I take this to imply that for Aquinas, faith is warranted or justified belief, even in the absence of evidence. How this position of Aquinas' differs substantially from the theological foundationalist who holds that theological beliefs may be properly basic but are nonetheless still subject to mediate justification is not clear to me.[56] As such, theological foundationalism does not seem to necessitate a reformation of traditional natural theology, but, rather, to re-affirm it.

NOTES

1. This seems to be the position of Mark S. McLeod in his "Can Belief in God Be Confirmed?" *Religious Studies* 24, pp. 311–323. On p. 314, he states: "But given the lack of success with natural theology . . . it hardly seems likely that we should turn there for validation of the practice or, by extension, the confirmation of belief." And on p. 316, the exclusion of natural theology from theological foundationalism is endorsed even more rigidly: "The possibility of using confirmation which relies on natural theology seems an unlikely one. The use of discursive reasoning which relies on empirical facts to justify the linking belief about God is nothing more than an attempt at having independent confirmation for the belief in question. Since the

motivation for arguing that belief in God can be properly basic is that such justification is not available, it would be illegitimate (and quite likely unsuccessful) to use it here. Its use cannot be justified, thus it cannot be legitimately slipped in through the back door. It must be avoided." I think that McLeod is generally wrong about the motivation for arguing that belief in God can be properly basic. But even if he is generally right, the thesis I shall defend is that the theological foundationalist is in no way inextricably bound to believing in the failure of natural theology, and in fact it would be ultimately detrimental to his cause if natural theology does fail.

2. Plantinga's position is presented in most detail in "Reason and Belief in God," in *Faith and Rationality: Reason and Belief in God,* ed. by Alvin Plantinga and Nicholas Wolterstorff (Notre Dame: University of Notre Dame Press, 1983), pp. 16–93. See also Plantinga's "The Foundations of Theism: A Reply," *Faith and Philosophy* 3, no. 3 (July 1986), pp. 298–313; and his "Justification and Theism," *Faith and Philosophy* 4, no. 4 (October 1987), pp. 403–426.

3. William P. Alston's articles in epistemology have been collected in his *Epistemic Justification* (Ithaca: Cornell University Press, 1989). See also his "Christian Experience and Christian Belief," in *Faith and Rationality,* pp. 103–134; "Religious Diversity and Perceptual Knowledge of God," *Faith and Philosophy* 5, no. 4 (October 1988), pp. 433–448; "A 'Doxastic Practice' Approach to Epistemology," in *Knowledge and Skepticism,* ed. by Marjorie Clay and Keith Lehrer (Boulder: Westview Press, 1989), pp. 1–29; "Plantinga's Epistemology of Religious Belief," in *Alvin Plantinga,* ed. by J. Tomberline and P. Van Inwagen (Dordrecht: Reidel, 1985), pp. 289–311; *Perceiving God* (Ithaca: Cornell University Press, 1991).

4. Classical foundationalism is the favorite target of theological foundationalists. See the articles by Alston, Plantinga, and Wolterstorff in *Faith and Rationality,* and by Konyndyk, Plantinga, and Wolterstorff in *Rationality, Religious Belief, and Moral Commitment: New Essays in the Philosophy of Religion,* ed. by Robert Audi and William Wainwright (Ithaca: Cornell University Press, 1986).

5. Alston seems to recognize this danger in "A 'Doxastic Practice' Approach to Epistemology," on pp. 5–6, where he states that "what is natural to count as distinct doxastic practices are by no means wholly independent."

6. See, e.g., Plantinga's "Reason and Belief in God," p. 78 (hereafter "RBG").

7. Ibid., p. 81.

8. Ibid.

9. See Alston's *Epistemic Justification* (hereafter *EJ*), pp. 104–105, 37.

10. See, e.g., Alston, *EJ*, pp. 82, 111, 235–236, 334, 342.

11. See Plantinga, "RBG," p. 79; Alston, *EJ*, p. 108.

12. See Plantinga, "RBG," pp. 56–63.

13. Ibid., pp. 81–82.

14. Ibid., pp. 83–84; Alston, *EJ*, pp. 109–110, 238–239.

15. See Alston, *EJ*, p. 60.

16. I consider these issues in "A Critique of Plantinga's Theological Foundationalism," *International Journal for Philosophy of Religion* 28 (1990), pp. 173–189.

17. Richard Grigg, "Theism and Proper Basicality: A Response to Plantinga," *International Journal for Philosophy of Religion* 14 (1983), pp. 123–127; Philip L. Quinn, "In Search of the Foundations of Theism," *Faith and Philosophy* 2, no. 4 (October 1985), pp. 469–486; Robert Audi, "Direct Justification, Evidential Dependence, and Theistic Belief," in *Rationality, Religious Belief, and Moral Commitment*, pp. 139–166; Robert McKim, "Theism and Proper Basicality," *International Journal for Philosophy of Religion* 26 (1989), pp. 29–56.

18. I use the term "anti-theological foundationalism" to refer to the position that no theologically loaded beliefs can function as epistemically foundational.

19. Plantinga, "RBG," p. 76.

20. Alston, "A 'Doxastic Practice' Approach to Epistemology," p. 5.

21. Ibid.

22. In "A 'Doxastic Practice' Approach to Epistemology," Alston credits Wittgenstein and Reid for inspiration and correlates Wittgenstein's notion of "language-game" with his own notion of a "doxastic practice" (Alston, "A 'Doxastic Practice' Approach to Epistemology," pp. 3–5).

23. Ibid.

24. My interpretation of Wittgenstein's notion of criteria follows that of Newton Garver in his "Grammar and Criteria" (Ph.D. dissertation, Cornell University, 1965), chapter 3.

25. This is at least Garver's interpretation (see "Grammar and Criteria," p. 189).

26. See Wittgenstein, *The Blue Book* (New York: Harper and Row, 1965), pp. 24–25.

27. Alston, "Christian Experience and Christian Belief," p. 125.

28. Ibid., p. 128.

29. Ibid.

30. Ibid., pp. 128–129.

31. Alston, "Religious Diversity and Perceptual Knowledge of God," p. 439.

32. Plantinga, "RBG," p. 77.

33. Alston, *EJ*, p. 287.

34. Ibid., p. 106.

35. See, e.g., Alston's "Concepts of Epistemic Justification" and "An Internalist Externalism," both in *EJ*.

36. Alston, *EJ*, p. 314.

37. Ibid., p. 301.

38. Ibid., p. 99.

39. Ibid., p. 315.

40. St. Theresa describes one of her experiences in this way: "How is it that I can understand and maintain that he stands beside me, and be more certain of it than if I saw him? . . . He renders Himself present to the soul by a certain knowledge of Himself which is more clear than the sun" (quoted and translated in Evelyn Underhill's *Mysticism* (New York: World, 1955), pp. 284–285).

41. On *prima facie* versus unqualified justification, see Alston, *EJ*, pp. 109–110, 238–239.

42. In this way, my position contrasts with Plantinga's, who holds that "God has so created us that we have a tendency or disposition to see his hand in the world about us. More precisely, there is in us a disposition to believe propositions of the sort *this flower was created by God* or *this vast and intricate universe was created by God* when we contemplate the flower or behold the starry heavens or think about the vast reaches of the universe" ("RBG," p. 80).

43. Alston defines "infallibility" with respect to a type of proposition as: "For any proposition, S, of type R, it is logically impossible that P should believe S, without knowing that S" (*EJ*, p. 261). For the definitions of omniscience, indubitability, and incorrigibility *vis-à-vis* belief, see Alston, *EJ*, p. 254. Some may wish to argue that properly basic M-beliefs are indubitable, incorrigible, and omniscient in Alston's sense; I do not wish to argue that they are or that they are not, for my main thesis concerning truth-warrant for M-beliefs is neutral in respect to both positions.

44. Plantinga is responsible for dignifying consideration of belief in the Great Pumpkin in "RBG," pp. 74ff.

45. Alston, *EJ*, p. 64.

46. Ibid., p. 60.

47. Ibid., pp. 340–341.

48. Ibid., p. 342.

49. In "The Epistemology of the Perception of God," a handout for a lecture that he delivered at SUNY Buffalo in September 1990, Alston lists as one of the salient features of a mystical experience (i.e., what a subject takes to be a direct experience of God) "a *presentation* to experience of (what is taken to be God) *as* being or doing so-and-so."

50. St. Theresa told her confessor of her experience and was asked by him how she knew that it was Christ who appeared to her. She replied "that I did not know how I knew it; but I could not help knowing that He was close beside me . . . there are no words to explain—at least, none for us women, who know so little; learned men can explain it better" (quoted and translated in Underhill, *Mysticism*, pp. 284–285).

51. Religious claims, like any other sort of claim, are most typically warranted on the basis of reliable testimony. M-beliefs have an important but very small role in Christian doxastic practice. In fact, all warranted M-beliefs are themselves testimonial beliefs, the testimony coming from God, which also explains why properly basic M-beliefs would have greater certitude than other types of testimonial beliefs. A certain degree of skepticism about *all* fallible authorities, no matter how reliable, is justified. But if one is warranted in believing that the testimony is from an infallible source, unlimited trust is rational. And I would argue that believing on the basis of testimonial evidence for religious beliefs (excluding preambles here) is warranted only if there is a causal chain stretching back to one who is immediately justified.

52. See George Mavrodes, "Enthusiasm," *International Journal for Philosophy of Religion* 25 (1989), pp. 171–186.

53. Underhill, *Mysticism*, pp. 284–285.

54. See George Mavrodes, *Revelation in Religious Belief* (Philadelphia: Temple University Press, 1988), pp. 106–108.

55. Plantinga, "RBG," pp. 47–48.

56. In "RBG", Plantinga quotes from *SCG*, I, 6 as evidence of Aquinas' evidentialism (p. 45). Two pages later, he then quotes from *SCG*, III, 38, where Aquinas seems to endorse an immediate or intuitive knowledge of God. But I think it is also endorsed in *SCG*, I, 6 where he states: "there is the inspiration given to human minds, so that simple and untutored persons, filled with the gift of the Holy Spirit, come to possess instantaneously the highest wisdom and the readiest eloquence." And in *SCG*, I, 4 he states: "Beneficially, therefore, did the divine mercy provide that it should instruct us to hold by faith even those truths that human reason is able to investigate. In this way, all men would easily be able to have a share in the knowledge

of God, and this without uncertainty and error." See also the *Summa theologica*, I, 1, 1 and I, 12, 13 ad 3. Nicholas Wolterstorff, in his "Can Belief in God Be Rational," in *Faith and Philosophy*, states that: "Taking Anselm and Aquinas as typical, it becomes clear, then, that the medievals were doing something quite different in their project of natural theology from meeting the evidentialist challenge. They were engaged in the transmutation project of altering belief (faith) into knowledge." (p. 141) As I read Aquinas, there is no dichotomy between faith and knowledge. Faith is a sort of knowledge. The transmutation project is then to transmute faith which is already a knowledge (cognitio) into demonstrative knowledge (scientia). For an elaboration of Aquinas' position, see James F. Ross, "Aquinas on Belief and Knowledge," in *Essays Honoring Alan B. Wolter*, ed. by W. Frank and G. Etzkorn (St. Bonaventure: Franciscan Institute Press, 1984), pp. 245–269. An earlier draft of this paper was presented at a Canisius College Philosophy Department Colloquium. I would like to thank my colleagues in the department, and in particular Herbert J. Nelson and Janice Schultz, for their penetrating criticisms and supportive suggestions. I also wish to thank the editor of this collection, Linda Zagzebski, for her comments on an earlier draft. Research for this paper was supported by a grant from Dean Walter Sharrow and Canisius College.

3. Faith, Foundationalism, and Nicholas Wolterstorff

Hugo Meynell

Many contemporary philosophers claim that the traditional assumption, that knowledge rests on foundations which are themselves certain and indubitable, has now been shown to be untenable. The foundationalist account of knowledge has certainly had a long and impressive innings from Descartes and Locke in the seventeenth century to Husserl, Russell, and the logical positivists in the twentieth; and indeed roots may be found much earlier than Descartes, in ancient philosophy. Notoriously, the thrust of the last version of foundationalism that was fashionable, the radical form of empiricism known as logical positivism, was atheistic; God-talk appeared absurdly false on one interpretation (where God was envisaged as a being capable in principle of being observed), meaningless on another (where, in accordance with the beliefs of most theists of any sophistication, God was not supposed to be observable in any circumstances). More recently, philosophers have come to doubt not only the logical positivist form of foundationalism—which, as is well known, is subject to very damaging objections—but whether any form of foundationalism at all is defensible. It is perhaps no wonder that some religious believers who are philosophers have welcomed the coming into fashion of antifoundationalism. Atheists had argued that theism was to be rejected on the basis of certain alleged foundations of knowledge. But, clearly, if there are no foundations of knowledge, such a claim must in principle be baseless.

1. WOLTERSTORFF'S ANTI-FOUNDATIONALISM

Among recent writers who have argued in this way, Nicholas Wolterstorff is notable; I would like in what follows to consider the position set out in his book *Reason within the Bounds of Religion.*[1] Wolterstorff admits that religious persons have "control beliefs" arising from their faith which determine what they consider evidence on many matters and how they treat that evidence. A foundationalist is liable to argue that such "control beliefs" have no foundation, or perhaps that their contradictories have a better foundation; and therefore that they ought to be rejected. But if foundationalism is erroneous in all its forms, it looks as though the opponent of Christian faith and its theistic implications is just as much wedded to his own unfounded "control beliefs" as is the Christian theist. As Wolterstorff describes the action of "control beliefs," the original logical positivists set out to defend science on the basis of the "verification principle" which they claimed to be foundational. But when it turned out that science could not be defended on such a basis, they did not abandon it; they went on defending science, thus showing that the overall truth of science, or at least the appropriateness of scientific method for finding out the truth about the world, was for them a "control belief."[2]

My own view is that reason has no business to be confined within the limits of religion, or indeed of anything else. I am troubled by the fact that, as it seems to me, no belief is so cognitively bizarre or morally frightful that it could not be defended on the basis of the kind of account that Wolterstorff advances. He strenuously denies—though he admits that the claim is often made—that "anything goes" can validly be inferred from his anti-foundationalist position.[3] But I am not convinced by his assurances, for the following reason. Suppose one is confronted by any claim whatever, as plausible or preposterous as the reader pleases. In accordance with foundationalist assumptions, one may ask: "Is this proposition better founded, has it more reliable foundations, than its contradictory? Or: Is it or has it not?" If better founded or having more reliable foundations, then one is in the position rationally to accept it; if not, to reject it. When it comes to the "control beliefs" that in fact characterize the positions of the parties to any disagreement (whether on matters of science, morality, politics, or religion), one may ask how well each of these beliefs is founded. But on Wolterstorff's view, no set of "control beliefs" has foundations any more reliable than any other, and so conflicts between "control beliefs" are in principle undecidable, except in an arbitrary fashion. Since the position admits that reason can find no foundation on the basis of which it can even in principle resolve such conflicts, more or less inevitably, where the issues are regarded as of importance, resort will be had to indoctrination or coercion. In fact, I regard the consequences of Wolterstorff's position on this matter, and indeed those of anti-foundationalism in general, as lamentable a well as absurd.

Fortunately, I believe, there is a version of foundationalism which is proof against the objections alleged by Wolterstorff and others. After sketching this version, I shall attempt to show briefly how these foundations might be used for a vindication of theism and of Christianity.

Someone might object that for a belief to have foundations in the minimal sense implied by what I have said—for it to be better founded than its contradictory—is not for it to have foundations in the sense objected to by Wolterstorff and other philosophers. Let us try to get a more detailed picture of what it is for one proposition to be better founded than another. Suppose Smith says, "There is a yellow book by Z. Y. Jones on the desk in Robinson's office," where Smith and Robinson are academic colleagues well known to one another. What would it be for such a statement to be well founded, founded to some extent, or not founded at all? It would presumably be very well founded if Smith could truly explain her reasons for making it somewhat as follows: "I was in Robinson's office a minute ago, no one to my knowledge has been there since, and I had a vivid impression of seeing the book on his desk just before I left." It would be rather less well founded if Smith could claim only to have recently heard Robinson talking in an animated fashion about Jones's work and saying that he was writing a paper on the subject; and if she knew that Jones's most influential and seminal book had a yellow cover. In this case, the proposition would amount to a sensible guess; even if it turned out to be accurate, there might be some reason for denying that Smith *knew* when she made the statement that it was so. (It has been very widely held, since Plato first made the suggestion in the *Theaetetus*,[4] that for it to be the case that someone knows the *p*, she must believe truly that *p*, and the belief must have some justification). The proposition would not be well founded at all if no relevant experience could be cited by Smith; and if Jones were the author only of texts on thermodynamics, a subject about which Robinson had never been heard either to evidence knowledge or to express interest. In this case, the contradictory of the proposition would be better founded than the proposition itself.

What is at issue in this "founding"? Evidently the experience of one's senses does come into it. In the first case, Smith retains the memory of an experience as of a yellow book,[5] with Z. Y. Jones's name on the cover; and memory does not usually deceive normal people over such a short lapse of time, at least when there is no motive for self-deception. In the second, she might remember the sound of Robinson's voice and her own initial remarking of his apparent interest in Jones; and experiences as of seeing or hearing about the yellow cover on Jones's book. In the third, there is no such course of experience to be appealed to *for*, and a good deal *against*, the truth of the proposition. Whether the proposition is well founded and the degree to which it is well founded seems to depend at least to some extent on evidence in experience. This tendency of well-founded knowledge-claims to depend on experience, of course, has always been emphasized *ex officio* by empiricists.

But there are other aspects to the matter as well. The presence of the book at that place at that time is one possibility among others. Even in the first case, error is possible; someone might have slipped surreptitiously into the office and removed the book, or even to have torn it in half and flung one bit on the floor (so that it would be misleading to say *tout court* either that there was, or that there was not, such a book on the desk). In the second case, the contradictory possibility, that there is not such a book on Robinson's desk, may be just about as probable—Robinson may not have been attending to that particular book at all for the purposes of his research, or may have been lying (perhaps to impress his colleagues) when he claimed to be making a special study of Jones's work; or he might for some reason have taken the book from the desk when leaving his office and put it on a bookshelf. To draw the moral, in assessing the foundations for a statement like this, one has not only to attend to a course of experience, but to envisage a range of possibilities; the best-founded statement, the one most liable to be true, will be that of the possibility which is best corroborated by the whole relevant range of experience. A proposition *fails* to be well founded and so is the less likely to be true so far as the person who entertains it (or her informant) has not attended to the relevant experience, has not envisaged the possible ways of accounting for it, and does not judge to be the case the possibility best supported by the evidence.[6]

Can what we have abstracted from our example be applied to other instances of well- or ill-founded belief? It seems to me that it can. Let us take three types of case: in science, in reference to the past, and in reference to the thoughts or feelings of another person. Why, and in what sense, is the belief well founded that the addition of hydrochloric acid to caustic soda will yield common salt and water? Plainly, very many persons over very many years have identified the two sorts of corrosive liquid by observing the sensory and causal properties of each, and have gone on to observe the results of their mixture. This series of observations fits the hypothesis mentioned far better than it does any alternative—for example, the one that might be maintained by someone wholly ignorant of chemistry, that the mixing of these highly corrosive substances would yield a substance still more corrosive than either. The explanatory schema that accounts for the accepted result, furthermore, accounts also for the observable properties of a vast range of other substances, and appears falsified hardly ever, if at all.[7] In rather a similar way, that a battle was fought at a particular place and time, or that my friend is feeling annoyed at what I have been saying to her, may be the possibility that is supported more adequately than any other by the relevant observations, and so is the most likely to be the case. Let us say that an investigator into any state of affairs is *attentive* so far as she takes into account the relevant evidence in experience, *intelligent* so far as she envisages the range of possible ways in which the situation might be explained, and *reasonable* so far as she judges to be so that possibility which does best explain the evidence.[8] I propose that in general a belief is well founded, has adequate foundations, so far as it has been attentively, intelligently, and reasonably arrived at. This view, I fear, is certainly a version of foundationalism. Worth mentioning is that discourse of each of the three types that I have just considered has proved something of a thorn in the side of empiricism, since one cannot strictly *have experience of* another person's thoughts and feelings, a beta particle, or the Battle of Carchemish. But I can perfectly well make well-founded *judgments* on all these matters on the basis of evidence which *is* available to me in experience.

It may be objected that for a belief to be well founded is not necessarily for it to be true. However conscientious the deliberations of a court that has gone over all the available evidence on a case in a meticulous fashion and has carefully considered every possibility that presents itself, the court may still identify the wrong person as the criminal. On the other hand, a fortune-teller who looks into his crystal ball may just happen to come up with the right answer. While these things must be admitted, it is to be maintained all the same that attentive, intelligent, and reasonable investigation is the means *par excellence* of arriving at the truth and, furthermore, is the only way in which, when the truth is arrived at by other means, it is to be recognized and confirmed as being the truth. What after all would it amount to, to discover that the crystal gazer had been right and the court wrong? It would depend on the finding of further evidence or the envisagement of more hypotheses than had been at the disposal of the court in making its judgment. In other words, it would be a matter of applying even more extensively and thoroughly the method that had been used by the court.

Traditionally, empiricists and rationalists have wrangled over the nature and the foundations of knowledge, and it must be admitted that the views of both parties have much to recommend them. It is difficult to deny that experience does play a role in the acquisition and confirmation of knowledge. On the other hand, if any belief is to count as knowledge, the belief must fit into a coherent whole with the set of other such beliefs, and be such that it can be inferred from some members of the set, and that others can be inferred from it. In the terminology that I have suggested, empiricists stress the role of attentiveness in acquiring knowledge; rationalists, intelligence and reasonableness. The view of the foundations of knowledge that I have sketched allows a certain merit both to empiricism and to rationalism while implying that each stands to gain from the corrective supplied by the other.

The requirement of attentiveness to experience is somewhat reminiscent of the "verification principle" of logical positivism; and, as Wolterstorff brings out,[9] one of the more immediate reasons for the present vogue of anti-foundationalism is that the foundations of knowledge proposed by the logical positivists have turned out to be self-destructive. It is by now notorious that there is no course of experience by which one can verify or falsify the putatively meaningful non-analytic proposition that every meaningful non-analytic proposition must be verifiable or falsifiable by some course of experience. The question may be asked whether the foundational principles that I have sketched are similarly self-destructive. The answer is that, so far from this being the case, it is their *contradictories* which are self-destructive. Suppose someone denies that beliefs are well founded and so tend to represent the truth about things, so far as they are attentively, intelligently, and reasonable arrived at. Has she attended to the relevant evidence? Has she envisaged a range of possible ways in which that evidence might be explained? Does she offer her opinion as the possibility that does best account for the evidence? If she has done all of these things, she is employing in support of her truth-claim the very mental operations the relevance of which to the support of truth-claims she is denying. But if she has failed to do one or more of these things, what is the point of paying any attention to her, as her denial is not even advanced as being any more worthy of acceptance than its contradictory?[10]

It might be protested that, if someone proposes an alternative account of well foundedness, and uses *that* to defend her judgments, she is doing just the same as the proponent of the view that I have just sketched. I do not think that this objection can be sustained. Let us call the hypothetical alternative account A. If A is defended on the ground that it is the best hypothesis to account for the relevant evidence, A is *ipso facto* not strictly foundational but depends on a foundation which is other than itself. If it *cannot* thus be defended, it is to be objected to as arbitrary (if it is not self-destructive, as alleged foundations have often notoriously turned out to be). If A differs not materially but only verbally from the account that I have outlined, A does not count as a genuine alternative to my account. The main difficulty about supposed foundations of knowledge, which has in fact been the prime reason for the widespread conviction that the very attempt to find and establish such foundations must be abandoned, can be expressed briefly as follows. If one is to set out a view of how judgments may be well founded, presumably that view has itself to consist in a series of judgments. But how can these judgments themselves be anything but arbitrary? The alternative is that they must be, as one might express it, successfully self-referential; that is to say, they must establish their own well-foundedness, as well as that of all other well-founded judgments. And the judgment, that every judgment is well founded so far as it is more reasonable to hold it than its contradictory on the basis of the evidence, certainly appears to be well founded, as may be shown by the self-destructiveness of its negation. It would be strange to purport to adduce evidence in favor of the truth of the hypothesis that one does not tend to get at the truth by adducing evidence in favor of one's hypotheses. I do not know of any other account of the foundations of knowledge which is self-vindicating in this way, though I have no doubt that what is at bottom the same point can be expressed in a variety of ways.

Someone who doubts the point I have just been trying to establish should ask herself, just what is minimally involved in soundly arguing for the truth of any position, including the position that one does not tend to *establish the truth of any position by arguing soundly for it? One has to consider as much as possible of the relevant evidence; one has to envisage the range of possibilities which might account for it; and one has to judge that the position is actually the one among the many possibilities that does best account for the evidence. How could establishing a position consist in any *less* than engagement in these three types of mental activity? Yet to engage in them all is nothing else than to be attentive, intelligent, and reasonable in the senses that I have discussed.

2. DIFFICULTIES IN FOUNDATIONALISM

It is often objected to foundationalism, and Wolterstorff reiterates the objection,[11] that foundationalism is committed to the view that knowledge must be erected on a basis which is certain by procedures which themselves are certain, but that no such certainties in basis or procedures can be found. The foundation for knowledge that I have suggested is not a "certainty," however of a kind that immediately presents itself to naive consciousness; rather, it has to be established by philosophical reflection. The philosophical reflection involved is very close to Descartes's systematic doubt; and its conclusion, to Descartes's thesis that one cannot coherently doubt that one is a doubter.[12] It is unreasonable to judge, on the basis of possibilities thought up to explain the relevant evidence, that one is not a being capable of judging reasonably on the basis on possibilities thought up to explain relevant evidence. And the contradictory judgment, that one *is* such a reasonable being, is consequently well founded.

Another possible objection: the mental transactions thus described all take place, so to say, *within* the conscious subject and can thus have no bearing on the real world of objects supposed to exist *prior to and independently of* the conscious subject and her mental transactions.[13] Is not the upholder of this view forced, like Descartes, to appeal to something like the special providence of God, in order to ensure that our thoughts can attain the truth about what exists independently of our thoughts?[14] But the belief that the subject as so conceived must be cut off from the world seems to be a mistake. What can "the world" or "reality" be after all, in the last analysis, *apart from* what one tends to get to know so far as one is attentive, intelligent, and reasonable in the senses that I have outlined? Except against the background of these basic mental processes employed only so far, as opposed to further or indefinitely, the distinctions between truth and falsity, and between reality and mere appearance, can get no purchase on our thought or language. A "real world," like that consisting of Kant's "things in themselves," which cannot conceivably be known by the utmost efforts of attentiveness, intelligence, and reasonableness, turns out in the last analysis to be a mere chimera.[15] (I might note that, even though Descartes was wrong to maintain that we had to believe in the existence of God to have grounds for belief that our thought was capable of attaining to a reality independent of itself, he may still have been correct in supposing that there is some important connection between the one belief and the other. I shall return to this point later.)

Wolterstorff[16] and others are surely on secure ground in arguing that, even if there are immediately self-evident certainties (such as I may have that I am at present undergoing sensations or feelings of a certain type), these are quite insufficient, at any rate when taken by themselves, as foundations for knowledge. However, I think it may properly be said that sensations of which one may be claimed to be certain at the moment of enjoying them are *among* the foundations of knowledge. Such are, in typical cases of coming to know about things, the basic data to which one has to be attentive in the sense that I have described. Wolterstorff rightly points out difficulties in the claim that knowledge of an inter-subjective reality can be obtained either by deduction or by induction from such sensations.[17] What, after all, about the existence of a state of affairs within the public world, can possibly be deduced validly from the fact that I enjoy a series of private sensations? And the justification of induction in general has notoriously been a thorn in the side of philosophy ever since the time of Hume.

However, that reality is to be known as the most reasonable explanation of the fact that I have the experiences that I do, and of the experiences reported (as it seems on the basis of my own experiences) by others, is a thesis which does not seem to fall foul of these objections. Deduction is one aspect of the operation of what I have called reasonableness; in matters of common sense as well as in the sciences, having conceived a range of possibilities, I may make deductions from them which may be either falsified or corroborated by my experience. It seems to me that what is generally known as "induction" consists of an untidy bundle of all those mental operations involved in coming to know which are not reducible either to the undergoing of and attending to sensations, or to the performance of deductions. The move from a number of observed instances to the hazarding of a generalization, for example from a number of perceptions of black ravens to a grasp of the possibility that all ravens are black, is a matter of what I have called intelligence. However, the categorical judgment that all ravens are black, without further attention to and marshaling of the evidence, immediately the possibility had occurred to one, would seem to be hasty rather than reasonable. (For some time, after all, it was generally believed by Europeans that all swans were white, until they unexpectedly encountered black swans.) Sophisticated instances of scientific theory are not essentially different from these simple examples according to the schema that I have been commending. When Einstein proposed his general theory of relativity, observational consequences were deduced (relating to the motion of the planet Mercury and the apparent positions of stars visible in the neighborhood of the sun when the sun was eclipsed); and it seemed more reasonable that the theory should be accepted when deductions from it turned out to be in conformity with the relevant observations, when these were not compatible with theories which had prevailed previously.

Wolterstorff mentions the empiricist and falsificationist versions of foundationalism, and finds them both wanting.[18] I agree that both of them are wanting as they are usually presented; but I would urge that they appear in a better light when seen as approximations to the kind of foundationalism for which I have been arguing. The empiricist is quite correct that experience is *one* crucial factor in knowledge, and that, at least in cases of commonsense beliefs or those of natural science, it affords the decisive evidence for preferring any judgment as more liable to be true than its contradictory. But she is apt either to overlook or to misrepresent the other components of the mental process required for arrival at true judgments. The falsificationist has a grasp of the role of creative understanding and hypothesizing in the acquisition of knowledge; she realizes that one has to have thought up a range of possible explanations for an observed phenomenon before one is in a position to make deductions from these explanations, and that one ought to retain (with more or less confidence) the explanations deductions from which are corroborated[19] rather than falsified by experience. But the trouble with falsification as a criterion is that it seems to be capable of being made precise only at the cost of becoming incredible; if it had been applied rigorously to almost any scientific discovery, that discovery would have been rejected very soon after it had been proposed.[20] Sometimes, when a judgment is in other respects well corroborated, it is wise not to abandon it too quickly when it is subject to *prima facie* falsification; occasionally further inquiry will turn out to vindicate the judgment after all. For example, when the oxygen theory of combustion was first proposed by Lavoisier, its opponents, such as Joseph Priestley, could point to phenomena which at first sight were incompatible with it; these were later explained all the same by refinements of the oxygen theory. Again, Prout's Law, to the effect that the atomic weight of all the elements was an integral multiple of that of hydrogen, seemed confirmed in the case of the vast majority of other elements, but falsified in the case of chlorine; ultimately there turned out to be two isotopes of chlorine, mixed together in natural samples but each separately conforming with Prout's Law.[21] The principle of falsification is good enough as a rule of thumb; but when applied strictly, the principle conflicts with some instances of reasonable judgment. However, falsification cannot apparently be relaxed in a convincing manner in such a way as to be consistent with such cases.[22] Yet it remains that reasonable judgment on the evidence provided by experience is possible.

A difficulty in relating reasonable judgment to experience has been put forward by W. V. O. Quine and reaffirmed by Wolterstorff.[23] Quine points out that when a judgment seems to conflict with experience, especially in science, it is always possible to save the judgment in question by changing our system of judgments elsewhere. He retains a kind of empiricism by concluding that our ensemble of judgments is supported by experience as a whole, rather than each judgment being supported by its own fragment of experience; but others have drawn the anti-foundationalist inference that our judgments are not really founded on experience at all.[24] My own view is that Quine has put his finger on a real difficulty but that it should be resolved in a way different from what he himself has proposed. I believe that characteristically our judgments are supported each by a range of experience, but not in such a way that the judgment depends *unconditionally* for its support on any *one* item within this range. For any judgment of common sense or of science one can say something like, "If *this* judgment were not true, you would not expect people to make *those* kinds of observations or come up with *those* sorts of experimental result." But, at more or less of a pinch, the judgment can be salvaged if *any particular part* of this observational support turns out to be lacking, given that there is compensatory support elsewhere.

An analogy may serve to make clearer the point that I am trying to make. Plainly the reader is in general dependent on her perception of the letters of that last sentence in apprehending the statement that I was making. But the change of no single one token (or probably even type) letter will render such apprehension impossible. If, say, any four sufficiently widely distributed letters in the sentence had been omitted, substituted for, or misplaced, my unfortunate reader would probably soon have realized what I intended to write. The fact that the reader's apprehension of what I originally intended to write does not depend on her perception of any particular (token or type) letter in that sentence does not imply that it does not depend on her perception of the ordered collocation of letters constitutive of that sentence as a whole. And there is a similar relationship, I believe, between particular human judgments and particular items of human experience.

Given the qualifications that I have just made, one may say that the marks on the paper which the reader appeared to see, together with her powers as an intelligent and reasonable being, are the foundations for her judgment that I originally wrote or at least intended to write the sentence in question. A number of philosophers, since the heyday of "sense-data" in philosophy more than a generation ago, have been inclined to make fun of the view that we arrive at statements of fact by inference from the immediate contents of our experience.[25] But

I think it is important in this context to attend to the distinction between use of our mental powers, on the one hand, and advertence to our use of them, on the other. Many contemporary psychologists take for granted that "this 'construction' of the world out of our raw sensory input normally proceeds automatically and without awareness."[26] Rather similarly, it may be pointed out that people argued and inferred more or less logically before Aristotle first set down rules for doing so. And Noam Chomsky has accustomed us to the idea that we are all in possession of certain constructive capacities to generate well-formed sentences, of whose precise nature even the most expert authorities in linguistics are in doubt.[27] It may be urged: a mental capacity of a similar kind, which requires effort to become fully conscious, is involved in our making of judgments about a real "objective" world on the basis of our "subjective" experiences. Thus it is one thing to say that, on the basis of a range of experience, I spontaneously judge that something is so; quite another to maintain that I am first aware of my experiences as such, and then consciously and laboriously infer from them that something is the case as the best explanation of the fact that I have the experiences. When I am liable to make a mistake in such a judgment of fact, owing to my own inattention or haste perhaps, or due to the artfulness of others, I am apt to become conscious of the assumptions that I bring to my experience. Suppose I "see" a music stand in the middle of a pool of light inside a darkened room that is part of a psychology laboratory. I may well wonder whether the actual presence of a music stand where it appears to be is the best explanation, all things considered, of the fact that I have the experience that I do, or whether the best explanation is rather that one of the staff has arranged things in such a way that I will have experiences as though this were the case, when in fact it is not so.

3. ALLEGED ALTERNATIVES
TO FOUNDATIONALISM

I have claimed that the only alternative to foundationalism of some kind, contrary to what Wolterstorff asserts, is the view that "anything goes." I believe that this issue is blurred by the tendency of philosophers to fall back on positions alleged to be *alternatives* to foundationalism but which in my view are themselves in part able to be shown to be unsatisfactory, in part reducible to foundationalism. The alternatives all offer accounts of what it is for one statement to be better *founded* than another, for all that they differ from "foundationalism" in what may be regarded as its classical form. In maintaining that there is a self-consistent stopping place between foundationalism and the view that "anything goes," Wolterstorff might well appeal to any of them. (In fact he does not do so in the book that we are discussing, but rather, he states more or less baldly that foundationalism and the view that anything goes do not exhaust the available options.) The three most obvious such positions are conventionalism, coherentism, and pragmatism. I will say something very brief about each; to cover any one of them adequately surely could be done only at much greater length.[28] None of these supposed alternatives to foundationalism are, so far as I know, defended as a matter of fact by contemporary Reformed philosophers; but the alternatives constitute such a natural first position of retreat for anti-foundationalists, when the *prima facie* absurd consequences of their position are pointed out, that it seemed essential to deal with the other options briefly here.

According to the conventionalist view, a statement is true so far as it is accepted as such by one's society or group within society.[29] Now suppose it is the case, as I think most people would agree, that Alfred Tarski's view[30] is correct, that a proposition "*p*" is true if and only if *p*—to take the well-worn example, "snow is white" is true if and only if snow is white. Then it appears to follow that in all cases, if the truth of a proposition "*p*" is due solely to social convention, the existence of the corresponding state of affairs *p* is also brought about solely by social convention. I submit that this is a little hard to swallow. Does society really bring it about that the planet Neptune is larger than the planet Mars, that the fulmar is abundant in the north Atlantic, or that Sebastian del Cano was among the first human beings to circumnavigate the earth? Short of extreme subjective idealism, such things are so prior to, and independent of, the assertion of any individual or group that they are so. Their being so is not brought about by any human convention; and thus, short of a very implausible view of the nature of truth, the truth of the propositions that they are so is not brought about by convention either. It must certainly be acknowledged that the human ability to say what is true depends on certain conventions, about which words have which meanings assigned to them; but that is a different matter.

A strong version of conventionalism might imply that all that was *meant* by the "truth" of a statement was acceptance by one's society or group; a weaker version only that it was always the case *as a matter of fact* that statements so accepted were true. But the conventional beliefs of different societies, or of different groups within the same society, frequently contradict one another; and how could a fact, and the contradictory of that fact, both be the case? And it may further be wondered *by virtue of what*, on this view, the conventional beliefs of a society, or of some group (say, of prestigious academics) within a society, are true of a world which exists largely prior to, and independently of, that society or group. The foundationalist will maintain, of course, that the conventional beliefs of a society or group are liable to be true just so far as they are well founded; that is to say, in terms of the version of foundationalism that I have outlined, so far as they have been arrived at attentively, intelligently, and reasonably.

Similar points have to be made about coherentism. It is true that a necessary condition of the truth of any proposition is that it should turn out to be consistent with other true propositions. But why should there not be many comprehensive systems of propositions such that each system is internally consistent within itself but contradicts the others? And in that case, how could more than one such system represent the truth? Other points that may be made against coherentism are that it seems tailor-made for the defense of any deeply entrenched belief whatever and that it misrepresents the way we normally go about testing beliefs, whether in science or in ordinary life. Subtle forms of coherentism, which purport to take into account the place of observation in knowledge (the obvious *prima facie* Achilles' heel of coherentism), have been developed by some recent authors, notably Laurence Bonjour and

Jonathan Dancy.[31] I have no space here to attend to their arguments in detail; but one point can be made that I take to be fundamental. Either the "cognitively spontaneous beliefs," which Bonjour concedes must be integrated into any set of coherent beliefs with pretensions to truth, are arbitrary; or they are in effect identical with the direct records of sensation alluded to by empiricists. In the former case, the way is open to an indefinite number of mutually incompatible sets of coherent beliefs; in the latter, one is back with foundationalism. What applies to Bonjour's coherentism appears to me to apply *mutatis mutandis* to Dancy's.

Coherentism may be eked out by pragmatism; one may urge that of the many possible coherent systems of propositions, the one that is most likely to be true supports the most successful practice. For example, if a dog is dangerous, belief that it is dangerous will provide a more successful basis for coping with the animal than the absence of belief that it is so. But is it not notorious that many societies have flourished partly by dint of believing damaging falsehoods about minorities or about members of other societies? And even if one were to argue, against a substantial amount of *prima facie* evidence, that such a state of affairs never in fact obtains one would have difficulty holding that it could never *conceivably* obtain, as would follow from the premise that the truth of beliefs was *definable* in terms of their practical effectiveness. It is true, and important, that a significant index of truth, or at least of approximation to truth, in the case of many of our beliefs, is that we can carry out rather elaborate and successful programs of action in accordance with them, in a way that we cannot in accordance with such alternatives to them as we can conceive. For example, it is strong evidence for at least the approximate truth of contemporary theories of dynamics and gravitation that we can send human beings to the moon on the basis of the assumption that they are true. But the implications of this kind of pragmatism seem in an obvious sense foundationalist; what it amounts to is that a range of occurrences which are what we would expect if a theory were true, and which are of practical importance for us, constitute proper *foundations* for acceptance of that theory. The foundationalist need not, and in my opinion should not,

maintain that coherentism and pragmatism are simply erroneous. The kind of foundationalist whose position I have outlined
would maintain that coherence with other reasonable judgments is at least *among* the most important criteria of the reasonableness of any judgment, as are the successful practices
facilitated by belief that it is true.

I conclude a (necessarily brief) discussion of supposed alternatives to foundationalism, as devices for ruling out the conclusion that "anything goes," with the suggestion that they all
either collapse under examination or turn out themselves to be
versions of foundationalism, or at least to point to aspects of
the actual foundations of knowledge. Nevertheless, it appears
that consideration of conventionalism, coherentism, and pragmatism, as *alternatives* to foundationalism by means of which
one might avoid the conclusion that "anything goes," is superfluous in the immediate context of a consideration of Wolterstorff's views as set out in his book. Each of the alternatives
amounts to a general set of criteria by means of which "control
beliefs" might at least in the long run be evaluated, and so presumably is a *version of* rather than an *alternative to* the sort of
foundationalism that Wolterstorff wishes to reject.

How closely is the view of foundations that I have com-
mended related to the "classical foundationalism," as it may be
called, the actual or alleged breakdown of which has led to the
present vogue of anti-foundationalism? The nature of this
"classical" view has been conveniently summarized in a recent
paper by Kai Nielsen. "Foundationalism," he writes, "is a philosophical attempt which seeks to isolate, by some kind of philosophical method, a set of basic beliefs which are foundational
for all the rest of the things that we may reasonably claim to
know or reasonably believe. Classical foundationalism holds
that the only properly basic beliefs are those that are self-
evident, incorrigible reports of experiences or are evident to
the senses. On such an account, other beliefs can be rationally
held only if they are supported either deductively or inductively by such properly basic beliefs."[32] Now on the account
which I have given it is a series of *assumptions,* which, though
virtually universal among humankind, seldom reach the level
of formulation into explicit *beliefs* that are properly basic. It is

one thing to *be* attentive, intelligent, and reasonable in the senses sketched earlier in this paper; it is another to set out clearly and distinctly just *what* it is to be so. These three mental operations are the foundations of knowledge, or of properly grounded true belief. In spite of what has been claimed by so many contemporary philosophers, representatives of the epistemological tradition in philosophy from Descartes up to Husserl and Russell, were quite correct in trying to state clearly the nature of these foundations and to justify them as such.[33]

Someone may suggest that what I am advancing here is a non-propositional account of foundations, and it is not clear that such an account is incompatible with Wolterstorff's position. It is true that certain mental activities, rather than propositions as such, are on my account the foundations of knowledge. However, the fact that they are so may be expressed in the form of propositions—e.g., "Knowledge, or justified true belief, is to be approximated to so far as one's beliefs are attentively, intelligently, and reasonably arrived at." But even if it is granted that my account is not in essential contradiction with the account that is characteristic of contemporary Reformed philosophers, I would still urge that their position *needs supplementing* in the manner that I have proposed, if the intolerable conclusion that "anything goes" is to be avoided.

Inference to the best explanation from the evidence available to the senses involves what is usually called "induction" as well as deduction; so I suppose that the reasoning by which one builds on the foundation may not improperly be said to be both inductive and deductive. At all events, one has both to hazard explanations and to work out their consequences.[34] The philosophical method by which one may isolate the basic beliefs, or rather by which one may turn the basic assumptions into articulate convictions, is such as I have already described.

The Achilles' heel of classical foundationalism, as Nielsen well brings out, is that it is self-refuting. "The very proposition asserting what classical foundationalism is is, on the one hand, neither self-evident to the senses or an incorrigible report of experience, nor, on the other, deducible from such propositions or inductively justified by them. In fine, classical foundationalism hoists itself by its own petard."[35] Does this objection apply to the alternative form of foundationalism that I have put forward?[36] It does not. On the contrary, its *contradictory* is self-destroying, for the reasons that I have already given. One could not intelligently and reasonably, in the light of the relevant evidence, judge that one does *not* tend to get at the truth about things by judging intelligently and reasonably in the light of relevant evidence.

As grounds for rejection of the view that the confidence with which we maintain our judgments should be in proportion to the evidence which we have for them, Anthony Kenny points out that there are some judgments, such as "There is such a place as Australia," which are much more certain than any evidence which we might adduce in support of them.[37] I believe that this is true, at least in one sense; but it is worth giving some attention to *why* it is true and *in what sense*, and what its truth implies. It is important to remember that some people have enjoyed *feelings* of certainty about propositions that others have felt equally strongly to be false (such as that God as conceived by Christians or Muslims exists, that the earth is spinning round on an axis, or that one ought not to own slaves). How can we discriminate at least in principle between what we may call actual certainties, or propositions which some people feel certain of and are in fact true, and what we may label pseudo-certainties, of which some people feel certain but which are in fact false? The question is no trivial one; people have *felt* certain of the truth of many propositions which we regard as intellectually absurd or morally frightful.

As a step towards achieving such a discrimination, I suggest that we may make a pair of distinctions, between spontaneous actual certainties or pseudo-certainties on the one hand, and fully critical actual certainties on the other; and within the class of fully critical actual certainties, between those which are basic and those which are derived. Spontaneous actual certainties can be turned into fully critical certainties, and so be discriminated from spontaneous pseudo-certainties, by being derived from fully critical certainties. Basic fully critical actual certainties, such as that I am capable of speaking the truth, and that I tend to speak the truth so far as I judge in accordance with the relevant evidence, are vindicated by the self-destructiveness of their contradictories, in the manner that I have already briefly shown. That there is such a place as Australia is a spontaneous actual certainty that may easily be turned into a derived fully critical actual certainty. My memory contains a vast fund of evidence that tends to establish it, and none that goes against it; I can confirm it at any time by asking a well-disposed friend, or looking at an atlas. It should be noted that, while no individual scrap of evidence for the fact that Australia is an island is anything like as certain as the fact itself, this does not imply that the evidence cannot properly form the foundation of such a certainty when taken together.

Now basic fully critical certainties, so far from being matters of spontaneous actual certainty, are never adverted to by most people and are a matter of obscurity even to some philosophers; thus there is unquestionably a sense in which the fact that Australia is an island is more certain than any of the evidence on which we may base it. But this does not strictly imply that it is not able to be supported by principles that are, in a rather different sense, more certain than itself. In one respect, many spontaneous actual certainties are more certain than basic fully critical actual certainties; in another sense, they are not. Thus Kenny's argument does not after all impugn the thesis that the confidence with which we hold our beliefs should be proportionate to the evidence that we have for them.

4. THE RATIONALITY OF THEISM

Alvin Plantinga has suggested that if any beliefs are to be taken as properly basic, then the theist may take belief in God to be so.[38] For all the brilliance with which Plantinga defends this position, I find it both implausible and profoundly disquieting in its implications. If belief in God is properly basic *for* the theist, why should not belief in the Great Pumpkin be equally basic *for* the devotees of that putative entity? No doubt belief in the Great Pumpkin is absurd *for* Christian theists and atheistic rationalists alike; but why should not belief in God or in the Oscillating Universe (or whatever it is that an atheistic rationalist may believe in) be just as absurd *for* the Great Pumpkin's votaries? Either there are overall criteria, which are not relative to cultural or religious groups, for assigning beliefs to the category of properly basic beliefs; or there are not. If there are, we are back with a form of foundationalism. If there are not, we seem to be committed once again to the view that "anything goes," so far as it is maintained with enough confidence and affirmed with sufficient existential *panache* by the religious or cultural group with which one happens to identify. Plantinga will have it that if the Christian or the Jew finds that belief in God is not derivative from any of her other beliefs, she is within her intellectual rights to maintain that this belief is properly basic *for her*.[39] But what belief, however absurd or frightful, cannot be rescued by such a maneuver from attack as unreasonable? An individual or a community may be committed to the belief that the interior of the earth consists of jam; or that the whole human race will perish in agony if elderly spinsters who own black cats are not burned alive. If such beliefs prove indefensible by reference to the other beliefs of those who hold them, why should they not, on Plantinga's account, be advanced as properly basic by those so disposed?

A similar objection has been made to Plantinga's position on the matter by Kenny:[40] "Plantinga has not shown us why what goes for belief in the proposition 'there is a God' does not go for belief in any proposition whatever." Plantinga has insisted that one can properly maintain that some beliefs (for example, that the Great Pumpkin returns every Hallowe'en) are not properly basic, without being able either to point to classical foundationalist criteria of what is properly basic, or even to articulate alternative criteria.[41] I concede that a person might in a sense non-arbitrarily refuse to assign belief to the category of the properly basic, even if she was *herself* unable to specify the criteria, given that all the same *some* such criteria existed and could *in principle* be specified. But "that the Reformed Epistemologist not only rejects those criteria for proper basicality" supplied by classical foundationalism, "but seems in no hurry to produce what he takes to be a better substitute,"[42] appears to her opponents to be *prima facie* evidence for the view that there is no substitute to be produced. It seems merely sophistical to assert that belief in God has warrant, whereas belief in the Great Pumpkin does not, if one is not prepared to go on to show in what such warrant consists, other than a tendency to support one's own beliefs and undermine those of one's opponents. And what goes for "warrant" obviously goes as well for that "proper use of one's cognitive faculties" which is supposed to keep God in the bath and let the Great Pumpkin out with the bathwater. In this connection, Reformed philosophers display what seems to me an unfortunate tendency to multiply epistemological distinctions, for instance between beliefs which have "warrant" (that is to say, one's own, whether defensible against their contradictories according to some articulate set of principles or not), and those for which there is "evidence" (that is, which can be thus defended). In my view, in opposition to that typical of Reformed philosophers, either reasons cannot even in principle be given for a belief, in which case there is no *warrant* for it; or they can, in which case there is *evidence* for it. It is important to note that this point in no way impugns the acceptance of belief on authority, which is very often reasonable. I am no expert on chemistry; so it is more reasonable for me to accept than to reject the claims of those who are expert on the nature of rare earth elements.

Many people are certain of God's existence, many of God's non-existence; the problem, to use the terminology we introduced above, is whether the proposition that God exists is a spontaneous actual certainty, or a spontaneous pseudo-certainty. If it is a basic belief in Plantinga's sense, the question cannot be resolved one way or the other by appeal to rational principles that do not presuppose what they are to establish.

A parallel has often been alleged between the rationality of belief in God on the basis of events supposed to be revelatory of God, and the rationality of belief in material objects on the basis of sense-experience.[44] Few, apart from some philosophers, would deny that it is rational for us to believe that material objects exist, for all that the kind of reasoning which justifies our belief in them on the basis of our sense-experiences has proved notoriously elusive. But in that case, it is asked, why should it not be rational for the theist to believe that there is a God on the basis of supposed revelatory events, for all that the exact nature of the rationality involved cannot be spelled out in this case either?

I believe that this "parity" argument is very telling against those philosophers who have dismissed the rationality of belief in God on the basis of assumptions about rationality that would equally impugn a large number of our commonsense beliefs. (It may be noted that the account of rationality that I sketched at the beginning of this paper makes it thoroughly rational to believe in material objects; it is far more intelligent and reasonable to judge that there is a world of things which exist prior to, and independently of, any sensations of them, than that there is not.) However, it is to be presumed that, on almost any account of rationality, for a belief to be rational is at least conducive to its being true. But to what extent could this principle apply to beliefs which are reasonable *for me*, but which I admit to be unreasonable *for someone else?* It appears to me that the link between "it is reasonable for me to believe that *p*," and "it is liable to be true that *p*," is broken so far as I concede that it is no less reasonable for someone else to believe that not-*p*, at least when the state of affairs *p* is supposed to be something which is not *made* to be true, like the survival of Tinkerbell in *Peter Pan*, by a belief to the effect that *p*. I do not think that Plantinga or Wolterstorff would be content with the kind of view which is often associated with D. Z. Phillips, that God exists in the world of the theist but does not exist in the world of the atheist. Yet it seems to me that they are liable to be driven to this account, unless they allow that what is *reasonable* is not reducible to what *happens to be reasonable for*, or rather *to be deemed reasonable by*, particular human ideological groups. But if they think that belief in God is more reasonable than unbelief in some absolute sense, which is not merely a matter of conformity with the "basic beliefs" or "control beliefs" of any particular set of human beings, then there is owing an account of such rationality, and of the basis of the beliefs which are to be deemed rational in accordance with it. However, to postulate such a basis is *ipso facto* to be committed to foundationalism in the very sense in which it is repudiated by Wolterstorff.

If one does not take belief in God as itself foundational, with Plantinga, or as a "control belief," with Wolterstorff, is there any hope for theism on a foundationalist basis? The most recently prevalent form of foundationalism, radical empiricism, would seem to suggest very strongly that there is not. But radical empiricist foundationalism is demonstrably and fatally defective, as would now almost universally be acknowledged. What of the prospects for rational theism on the basis of the type of foundationalism that I have sketched, where the foundations of knowledge are a matter of the application of intelligence and reasonableness, not merely of principles of logic in a strict sense, to experience? I have tried to show at some length elsewhere[45] that this may indeed provide the basis for a sound argument that a being exists very like that which has always been called "God"; perhaps a brief sketch of this argument will be in place here. Its essence may be set out in two theses: on the account of knowledge and its foundations that I have already given, the world is essentially knowable, and therefore intelligible; and the best explanation of the existence of an intelligible world is that it is due to the will of an intelligent being.

It is self-destructive, as we have already suggested, to deny that we can think or speak the truth about anything, or that we tend to get at the truth so far as we ensure that there is the best possible foundation for our statements—where a statement is well founded so far as it is attentively, intelligently, and reasonable asserted. Now the world or reality can be nothing other in the last analysis than what tends to be known so far as our beliefs are thus well founded. What could "reality" be other than what we tend to get to know so far as we avoid error, and what could the systematic avoidance of error be other than the subjection of our beliefs to the kind of procedure described? Now intelligence is a matter of framing hypotheses; reasonableness, a matter of asserting that some of these are probably or certainly the case according to the evidence of experience. We do not and cannot know here and now what the nature of the world is in detail, since we have not attended to all the relevant evidence, or envisaged all the relevant hypotheses, or reasonably marshaled the evidence to determine which of all these hypotheses is liable to be true. But we can know here and now that the world must ultimately turn out to be a realization of some set of intelligible possibilities. In other words, it is an intelligible world.

What explains the intelligibility of the world? One might say, in Kantian fashion, that the world is not intelligible in itself, but that we impose intelligibility on it by our acts of understanding. But, as Fichte and Hegel pointed out, "things in themselves" which are other than the potential objects of sense or intelligence are in the last analysis inconceivable. We may protest that the intelligibility of the universe is a mere matter of fact without explanation; but it has been rightly remarked that the refusal to ask the question "Why?" about any matter of fact only provokes a healthy mind to go on asking the question more insistently. That the world combines intelligibility with matter-of-factness, as it does, is perfectly explained if it is conceived and willed by a being whose intelligence accounts for its through-and-through intelligibility and whose will explains that it has the particular kind of intelligibility that it has—in terms of phosphorus rather than phlogiston, of protons and electrons rather than Democritean atoms, and so on. And, of course, the intelligent will on which the rest of what exists depends is what, as Aquinas would say, "all call God."[46] If God is the intelligent will on which *all* else depends, the same kind of question cannot on principle arise about why God exists, as can arise about the rest of what exists. In at least one passage in his writings, Plantinga suggests that an adequate account of knowledge must recognize a difference between the proper and the improper use of our cognitive faculties; and that this difference makes much more sense if one believes in God than if one does not.[47] Naturally I find this line of argument promising, approximating as it does to my own views as summarized here. But its whole force depends on the assumption that belief that there is a God is *not* a properly basic belief but is to be justified by appeal to more basic beliefs about the nature and conditions of justified belief as such.

Given the existence of God, I believe that an argument could also be advanced for the truth of Christianity; its special doctrines might be at once corroborated by historical investigation and vindicated as claiming in effect that God had done the sort of thing that would effectively remedy the human moral plight.[48] But there is no space to go further into these points here.

Adherents of Reformed Christianity frequently claim that what is called "natural theology" is unnecessary, even if its arguments are successful. The claim is usually made from the point of view of belief in divine revelation; if God is self-revealed, it may be asked, is not any attempt to test whether God is really so at best superfluous, at worst downright blasphemous? I think the right response to this claim can readily be inferred from the whole tenor of this paper so far. Some feel certain that there is no God; some feel certain that God is revealed exclusively or climactically in one way, some in another. To revert to the terminology that I introduced earlier, there thus inevitably arises the question of which of these certainties are actual and which are pseudo-certainties; since the claims contradict one another, they cannot all be actual certainties. Short of "natural theology," or the attempt to use reason to establish that there is a God rather than that there is not, or that God is displayed to human beings through a particular form of revelation rather than that God is not, I do not see how the question of which are actual certainties can be settled in any other manner than sheer assertion one way or the other. And, as the Scholastics used to say, whatever is affirmed gratuitously is denied gratuitously. Those who abandon resort to reasoning on the basis of evidence but all the same wish to convince others of what they believe—as of course all Christians are bound to do—will almost inevitably be led to indulge in more sinister means of persuasion, such as indoctrination or less subtle forms of coercion. (By "indoctrination" I mean the causing of someone to accept a belief by some means other than convincing her that this is the most intelligent and reasonable thing to do on the basis of the relevant evidence.) In conclusion, I have to admit that my own view on this matter amounts to a very crass form of what Reformed philosophers are wont to denounce as "evidentialism."[49]

NOTES

1. N. Wolterstorff, *Reason within the Bounds of Religion* (Grand Rapids: Eerdmans, 1976); 2nd edition (1984). References will be to the 2nd ed.

2. Wolterstorff, op. cit., 20; cf. 11–12, 17–18.

3. Ibid., 56.

4. Plato *Theaetetus* 202C.

5. " . . . experience *as* of a yellow book," since "experience *of* a yellow book" might seem to entail that a yellow book was actually present in Smith's vicinity, as well as that Smith had had the appropriate experience.

6. This account of the threefold mental process involved in coming to know has been most exhaustively set out in B. J. F. Lonergan's *Insight: A Study of Human Understanding* (London: Longmans, Green, 1957).

7. The qualification "hardly ever, if at all," allows for unexpected results which are not repeated, isolated experiments which come out "wrong," and so on.

8. This terminology is used by Lonergan in *Method in Theology* (London: Darton, Longman, Todd, 1972), chapter 1.

9. Wolterstorff, op, cit., 20.

10. Lonergan, *Method*, 16–17.

11. Wolterstorff, op, cit., 46. Essential to foundationalism is the view that some propositions "are not only true but can be known non-inferentially and with certitude."

12. R. Descartes, *Meditations on First Philosophy* (Indianapolis: Bobbs-Merrill, 1960), 24–28 (First Mediation).

13. Wolterstorff, op, cit., 53–54. For an ingenious defense of this thesis, see J. Kekes, "Link-Concepts and Epistemology," *Ratio* (December 1985).

14. Descartes, op. cit., 51 (Fourth Meditation).

15. P. F. Strawson, *The Bounds of Sense* (London: Methuen, 1966), 250.

16. Wolterstorff, op. cit., 53–54.

17. Ibid., 37–40.

18. Ibid., 19:40–43.

19. I.e., which survive attempts to falsify them, when they could very well conceivably have been falsified. Cf. K. Popper, *Objective Knowledge* (Oxford: Clarendon Press, 1972), especially 17–20, 82–84, 98, 103.

20. On difficulties with falsificationism, see T. S. Kuhn, *The Structure of Scientific Revolutions* (Chicago: University of Chicago Press, 1962), 5–6, 24, 39, 77, 82, 145; P. K. Feyerabend, *Against Method* (London: New Left Books, 1975), 65–66, 143, 182ff.; Feyerabend, "Consolations for the Specialist," in *Criticism and the Growth of Knowledge*,

ed. I. Lakatos and A. Musgrave (Cambridge: Cambridge University Press, 1970), 215.

21. Cf. I. Lakatos, "Criticism and the Methodology of Scientific Research Programmes," *Proceedings of the Aristotelian Society,* 1968–1969, 149–186.

22. Feyerabend, "Consolations for the Specialist," 216.

23. Wolterstorff, op. cit., 43–44, Cf. Quine, *From a Logical Point of View* (Cambridge, Mass.: Harvard University Press, 1953), 41.

24. Cf. R. Rorty, *Philosophy and the Mirror of Nature* (Princeton, N.J.: Princeton University Press, 1979), chapters 4 and 5.

25. See J. L. Austin, *Sense and Sensibilia* (Oxford: Clarendon Press, 1962); J. Beversluis, *C. S. Lewis and the Search for Rational Religion* (Grand Rapids: Eerdmans, 1985), 60–61.

26. F. Watts and M. Williams, *The Psychology of Religious Knowing* (Cambridge: Cambridge University Press, 1988), 65.

27. N. Chomsky, *Syntactic Structures* (The Hague and Paris: Mouton, 1957).

28. I believe that the failure of particular accounts of what it is for our knowledge-claims to have foundations, together with the fact that everyone goes on making knowledge-claims just the same, have made some philosophers assume too readily that knowledge-claims may properly be made without foundations and to repress the concerns that made earlier generations of their colleagues search for such foundations in the first place.

29. Cf. D. Bloor: "To appraise an argument for validity is to apply the standards of a social group. It cannot be other, or more, than this because we have no access to other standards. . . . The authority of truth is the authority of society" ("Popper's Mystification of Objective Knowledge," *Science Studies* [1974], 75–76).

30. A. Tarski, *Logic, Semantics, Metamathematics* (Oxford: Clarendon Press, 1956), 152–278.

31. L. Bonjour, *The Structure of Empirical Knowledge* (Cambridge, Mass.: Harvard University Press, 1985); J. Dancy, *Contemporary Epistemology* (Oxford: Blackwell, 1985).

32. K. Nielsen, "Philosophy as Critical Theory," paper delivered at The Future of Philosophy: Sixty-first Annual Pacific Division Meeting, San Francisco, California, 27 March 1987, 92. On the relevance of classical foundationalism to belief in God, and the collapse of this kind of foundationalism, cf. also A. Plantinga, "Reason and Belief in God," in *Faith and Rationality,* ed. A. Plantinga and N. Wolterstorff (Notre Dame, Ind.: University of Notre Dame Press, 1983), 59–63.

33. This is the thesis which is primarily under attack in Rorty's *Philosophy and the Mirror of Nature.* Cf. H. Meynell, "Reversing Rorty," *Method* (April 1985).

34. On the problematic nature of the notion of "induction," cf. K. Popper, *Objective Knowledge* (Oxford: Clarendon Press, 1972), chapter 1.

35. Nielsen, loc. cit. Plantinga has made what is effectively the same point in many places in his work.

36. It might be called pre-classical, as it was at least adumbrated by Aristotle and Aquinas. See Lonergan, *A Second Collection* (London: Darton, Longman, Todd, 1974), 53; Aristotle *Metaphysics* 4.4.1005b–1006a 28; Aquinas *In III De Anima* lect. 7 690.

37. A. Kenny, *Faith and Reason* (New York: Columbia University Press, 1983), 18–24.

38. A. Plantinga, "Rationality and Religious Belief," in *Contemporary Philosophy of Religion,* ed. S. M. Cahn and D. Shatz (New York: Oxford University Press, 1982).

39. Ibid., 276: "The Christian or Jew will of course suppose that belief in God is entirely proper and rational; if he doesn't accept this belief on the basis of other propositions, he will conclude that it is basic and quite properly so." Wolterstorff applies the same moral to the Buddhist (Wolterstorff, op. cit., 11–12) but not to the astrologer or the flat-earther.

40. Kenny, op. cit., 16.

41. Plantinga, "Reason and Belief in God." 74–75.

42. Ibid., 75.

43. I do not find that Plantinga's "Justification and Theism" *(Faith and Philosophy* [October 1987]), interesting and valuable as it is in many respects, as a whole (but cf. below, note 47) adds anything that is relevant to the treatment of this question.

44. For the presentation of this "parity" argument, I am much indebted to an unpublished paper by T. Penelhum, "Revelation and Philosophy." Cf. also T. Penelhum's *God and Skepticism* (Dordrecht: Reidel, 1983), 147–158.

45. See H. Meynell, *The Intelligible Universe* (New York: Barnes and Noble, 1982). For a magisterial presentation, see Lonergan, *Insight,* chapter 14.

46. Thomas Aquinas *Summa Theologica* 1.ii.3.

47. Plantinga, "Justification and Theism," 411.

48. I have outlined such an argument in "Faith, Objectivity, and Historical Falsifiability," in *Language, Meaning, and God,* ed. B. Davies (London: Geoffrey Chapman, 1987).

49. I find astonishing Wolterstorff's claim that Thomas Aquinas, who is shown in every article in the *Summa* to be among the most obsessive of "evidentialists," is not an "evidentialist" at all (see Wolterstorff, "The Migration of Theistic Arguments: From Natural Theology to Evidentialist Apologetics," in *Rationality, Religious Belief, and Moral Commitment: New Essays in the Philosophy of Religion*, ed. R. Audi and W. J. Wainwright [Ithaca: Cornell University Press, 1986]); but there is no space here to pursue that matter.

I am grateful to Linda Zagzebski, from whose comments on an earlier draft of this paper I have greatly profitted.

4. Resolute Belief
and the Problem of Objectivity

Thomas D. Sullivan

1. THE PROBLEM

In an extraordinary statement that deserves to be far better known, the nineteenth-century philosopher of religion W. G. Ward expressed what he took to be—rightly, I think—"the chief stronghold of philosophical objectors against the Church." The objection that Ward voices for the rationalist assails Catholicism directly but bears on any religion requiring firm faith in its creeds.

> Catholics are taught to regard it as a sacred duty that they shall hold, most firmly and without a shadow of doubt, the truth of certain marvels which are alleged to have taken place nineteen centuries ago. As to examining the *evidence* for those truths, the great mass of Catholics are of course philosophically uncultured and simply incompetent to such a task.

Moreover, even those capable of examining the question are sunk in irrationality.

> I place before him some serious difficulty, which tells against the most central facts of his religion; he has never heard of the difficulty before, and he is not now at all sure that he will be able to answer it. I should have expected, were it not for my knowledge of Catholics, that the confidence of his conviction

would be *diminished* by this circumstance; for plainly, an unanswered difficulty is no slight abatement from the body of proof on which his creed reposes. But he says unblushingly that if he were to study for ten years without seeing how to meet the point I have suggested, his belief in his Church, whose claim of authority he recognizes as divinely authorized, would be in no respect or degree affected by the circumstance.

Nor is it for themselves alone, but for all mankind, that Catholics prescribe this rebellion against reason. They maintain that every human being, to whom their Gospel is preached, is under an obligation of accepting with firmest faith the whole mass of Catholic facts—the miraculous Conception, Resurrection, Ascension, etc.; while it is simply undeniable that 999 out of every 1000 are absolutely incapable of appreciating ever so distantly the evidence on which these facts are alleged to repose.

Nor, to do them justice, do they show the slightest disposition to conceal or veil their maxims. The Vatican Council itself has openly anathematized all those who shall allege that Catholics may lawfully suspend their judgment on the truth of Catholicity, until they have obtained for themselves scientific proof of its truth.

I have no general prejudice against Catholics; on the contrary, I think many of them possess some first-rate qualities. But while their avowed intellectual maxims are those above recited, I must regard them as external to the pale of intellectual civilization. I have no more ground on which I can argue with a Catholic then I have ground on which I can argue with a savage.[1]

All this from a Catholic.

Ward's vigorous statement on behalf of rationalism includes three points easily lost sight of in arguments about religious belief.

First, Ward's rationalist makes two distinct complaints against religious faith as such. That believers often have little or no evidence for their firmly held beliefs is only the beginning of the problem. The more serious criticism is that even while conscious of rationally based objections they persist in believing highly contested propositions with all the confidence due known truths. As we shall see in a moment, standard replies to the rationalist challenge often address only the first charge.

Second, the point of the challenge is not merely that religious persons are somehow irrational or irresponsible, but that the very requirement of undoubting faith constitutes proof that the church is not, in Newman's terms, "the oracle of God." Obviously, the same applies to Scripture or any other putative source of an obligation to believe without proof.

Third, the genius of the objection is that it attacks revealed truth without ever having to examine in any detail the particular grounds for the claims. Locke charged that a Catholic "swallows" the doctrine of transubstantiation "not only against all probability, but even the clear evidence of his senses."[2] Others have gone further, maintaining that the doctrine of transubstantiation involves flat contradiction. But whether such teachings are improbable or outright contradictory, they are at least *difficult* to accept, i.e., they involve intellectual difficulties. The solitary fact that the church teaches its members to expel doubt in the face of difficulties is enough to show that whatever credentials the church offers, it cannot be an unerring transmitter of the divine message.

Although I will follow Ward in considering the problem with special reference to Catholic belief, my general aim is to provide at least the beginnings of a satisfactory reply to the challenge to religious belief as such. My focus is on the first point, which is the foundation of the second and third. Section II successively refines the objection—hereafter "the Chief Stronghold" (CS)—in light of some standard replies to rationalists' complaints against committed religious belief. Section III examines the claim that Christian belief is a form of knowledge and is therefore not to be condemned along with prejudice or credulity. This claim that faith is a form of knowledge is rejected. Section IV argues against the central claim of CS. Section V then offers a positive argument for firm religious belief. The remaining section, VI, considers some possible objections and replies, focusing on the problem of objectivity.

2. SOME POSSIBLE REPLIES AND REFINEMENTS

One way to structure CS is this:

Version A:

A-1   It is always wrong not to proportion belief to evidence.

A-2   Christians do not proportion belief to evidence.

Therefore:

A-3   By not proportioning belief to evidence Christians do something wrong.

The first premise of this version of the argument is a form of the proportionality precept made famous by Locke, Hume, Clifford, and their followers. Despite its fame, however, this precept carries with it obviously unacceptable consequences. As Ward observes, children who love their parents would be especially obliged, because of their affection and partiality, to scrutinize their parents' behavior in order to detect all their faults. Moreover, the children would be obliged to delay accepting even the most fundamental instructions of their parents until they had tested them in the light of their own experience.[3] It seems quite evident from such examples that most of our dispositional beliefs are properly left undisturbed unless some fact, incongruent with those beliefs, provokes us to reconsider matters. In any event, we cannot possibly at once raise to consciousness every dispositionally held belief for simultaneous scrutiny. So the proportionality precept condemns all of us no matter how scrupulously we would proportion belief to evidence. Moreover, the duty to proportion belief is not our only duty. I should be able to go about my daily business without checking on my dispositionally held belief that I ate Wheaties as a child. As Newman observed in his time, and Alvin Plantinga, Nicholas Wolterstorff, and others in the Reformed tradition have effectively shown in ours,[4] we properly begin by believing many things without any evidence or argument. The proportionality precept simply stated is too obviously flawed to serve as a solid foundation for a successful attack on faith ungirded by evidence.

We thus have a partial answer to the problem Ward puts in the mouth of the philosophical objector. But the answer is incomplete. For it is one thing to say that we properly begin by believing many things without evidence or argument; it is quite another thing to say we properly continue with unwavering belief in the face of genuine difficulties. At one stage in life we were within our epistemic rights to follow our credulity dispositions and believe firmly in Santa Claus, but not now. If it is not true that we are always and everywhere obliged to proportion belief to evidence, we nonetheless seemingly are obliged to reduce confidence in the face of objections. This yields a second version of CS.

Version B:

B-1   It is always wrong not to proportion belief when aware of unanswered objections.

B-2   Christians do not proportion belief when aware of unanswered objections.

Recognizing that counterevidence cannot simply be dismissed, a Christian might claim that evidence properly determines whether something ought to be believed at all, but that once a certain threshold of probability is reached one is free to believe with any pleasing degree of firmness. "It seems hard," writes George Mavrodes, "to think of what that wrong [of believing disproportionately] might be, or of how the *strength* of belief, as distinct from the *fact* of belief, could be a defect in my cognitive life."[5] But I am afraid we do know what that wrong may be: Overbelief may bias the search for truth. As Mavrodes suggests, perhaps strong belief in the face of seeming counterevidence is not a *cognitive* defect. But that does not rule out its being a *moral* defect, a defect of the *will,* consisting in an insufficient openness to the truth.

Nonetheless, there seems to be a rather easy way to respond to the argument as stated. I believe that some things move, but I am uncertain about how to resolve all of Zeno's paradoxes. You believe that the world exists independently of your mind, and yet you perhaps are puzzled by certain skeptical arguments. On *B-1* we should not believe wholeheartedly that some things move in a world external to our minds. A rationalist could insist that unresolved perplexities do demand a reduction of confidence. But such a strong claim would weaken the argument against willful religious belief; for then the argument would depend on assuming the truth of a species of skepticism that faults firm belief in just about everything of importance. CS is more telling if we construe it as condemning willful belief in what is *unknown*. We need to replace *Version B* with a more sharply formulated statement of the objection.

For this purpose it will prove helpful to fix definitions for three concepts. First, we will say "S is troubled about p" if and only if (i) S accepts p, (ii) S does not know p to be true, and (iii) S is conscious of intellectual difficulties about p. Second, we will say "S is (merely) perplexed about p" if (i) and (iii) hold, but not (ii). What distinguishes being "troubled" from being "perplexed" is knowledge. Magicians' tricks are perplexing, not troubling. We cannot explain how a bird suddenly emerges "from nowhere," and so we are "perplexed." Since, however, we know the magician does not produce the bird *ex nihilo*, we are not "troubled." With this distinction in mind, we now say "S resolutely believes p" if (a) S is troubled about p, and (yet) (b) S gives unqualified assent to p.

We can now restate the proportionality precept and the argument.

Version C:

C-1   If you are troubled about a proposition p, then you should proportion belief in the proposition to the evidence.

Therefore,

C-2   It is always wrong to believe resolutely.

But,

C-3   Christians believe resolutely.

Therefore,

C-4   In believing resolutely Christians do something wrong.

At this point, it is quite tempting to invoke the time-honored solution touched on earlier. The trouble with *C-1* is that it fails to consider the multitude of competing duties. Duty to truth is just one of many duties. Resolute belief may therefore legitimately serve other ends, among them preserving the bonds of affection. We believe completely in our parents, spouses, and loved ones, even when there are difficulties. No one is our friend who believes in our good intentions only to the degree they are proved. We expect our friends to be slow to accept evidence against our intentions. Such confidence between friends, C. S. Lewis notes, "is universally praised as a moral beauty."[6]

This is true, but not entirely convincing. For while personal trust is a thing of beauty, it is not blind partiality that makes it beautiful but a love that sees what others do not see. Truth is the foundation of genuine friendship.

After all, for Christians, truth is the foundation of everything.[7] For God is truth. "God is light, and there is no darkness in him at all" (1 John 1:5). Since life with God is the goal of our existence, truth is the goal of our existence. "I am the Way, the Truth, and the Life" (John 14:6). Christ came into the world to bear witness to the truth (John 18:37). All genuine human friendship, rooted in friendship with God, is thus rooted in truth. Since truth is the master goal, then it should never be sacrificed for lesser ends. We should never indispose ourselves to the truth.

A qualification, however, is in order. There is a hierarchy among truths. Some truths are more worth knowing than others. The obligation to dispose ourselves for the reception of truth cannot plausibly mean anything as simple and mechanical as disposing ourselves to believing the most truths. We are not obliged to forgo working or visiting the ill in order to learn all about the lives of the rich and famous. Quite the reverse. Curiosity is a vice, a disordered desire for the truth.[8]

To see clearly where we are, it will be helpful to insert into the objection tacit premises for the key proposition *C-1*.

Version C (amplified):

> C-1   If you are troubled about a proposition *p*, then you should proportion belief in the proposition to the evidence.
>
> Since   C-1a   It is always wrong for you to indispose yourself to the (ordered) reception of truth.

And   *C-1b*   Necessarily, if you do not proportion belief in a proposition when troubled about it, then you indispose yourself to the ordered reception of truth.

Therefore,

C-2   It is always wrong to believe resolutely.

And since,

C-3   Christians believe resolutely,

Therefore,

C-4   In believing resolutely Christians do something wrong.

Accepting *C-1a*, as I have argued we should, leaves us with two alternatives: deny *C-1b* or deny *C-3*. Let us defer consideration of *C-1b* in order to take up what surely will seem to some the better way out.

3. FAITH AS A FORM OF KNOWLEDGE

Faith and Super-Superabundant Evidence

The better way, as some see it, it to claim that faith is a form of knowledge. If it is, Christians are not resolute believers in the defined sense of that expression. For though Christians are conscious of difficulties, they are like those who know that things move but cannot answer Zeno. Since Christians know the content of faith is true, they can only be "perplexed," not "troubled." Consequently, their belief is not "resolute" in the defined sense.

How, though, can it plausibly be maintained that Christians *know* the objects of belief? Christians do not seem to know that Christ is the Second Person of the Blessed Trinity, that were will be a resurrection of the dead, or that God will reward the just with everlasting bliss. Christians accept these tenets on the authority of others. Their truth is not apparent to Christians.

But that is only one side of the story. Scripture does call faith "knowledge," and many Christians, including Calvin and

Aquinas, adopt the same language. Christians have recently developed this contention in at least two ways.

Some Catholics treat faith as grounded in overwhelming evidence. Pressed to respond to rationalist objections, they begin by arguing that Aquinas and other philosophers offer various demonstrations of God's existence. That established, extending the chain of reasoning to divine attributes such as omnipotence, omniscience, and perfect goodness is possible. Included among these attributes is unfailing truthfulness. Given God's unfailing truthfulness, we may have perfect confidence in any revelation God makes. Miracles and other evidence compellingly testify to the fact of revelation. At every stage of the way, then, reason supplies the grounds for belief, first establishing God's existence, then God's truthfulness, and then finally the fact of revelation. The result is a virtual transmutation of faith into knowledge, expressible as a syllogism. We know that (a) all that God reveals is true; we know that (b) God has indeed revealed X. So we know that (c) X is true. Ward declares that Catholics "have cognisance of various premises which (according to the accumulative method of reasoning) are super-superabundantly sufficient to establish the truth of that religion." Moreover, "God, in imparting and upholding the gift of faith, specially illuminates the Catholic's mind, so that he shall give those premises their due weight, and thus reasonably possess certitude."[9]

But this account will hardly do. For one thing, it is established Catholic teaching that faith is meritorious, and this because faith requires an act of will. The Second Vatican Council's Declaration on Religious Freedom gives a particularly succinct statement of the matter: "The act of faith is of its very nature a free act."[10] If the evidence were compelling, we would no more need to make an act of the will to believe in the real presence of Christ in the Eucharist than to believe in the real presence of the sun in the sky.[11] Such is the meritless "faith" of the fallen angels who cannot help but be convinced by the evidence they see more clearly than we do.[12]

Secondly, many Catholics and other believers simply do not claim to see the evidence as "super-superabundant," rendering all arguments on the other side obviously irrational. Even with the light of grace, for them the evidence backing the claims of the church is not on a par with the evidence for the truth, say, that there is a place called England. Reason plays its role, but just as Aquinas says, the certitude of the faith is rooted in the will.[13]

Faith, Knowledge, and the Proper Functioning of the Mind

So much, then, for Catholic versions of the thesis that faith is knowledge. We turn now in another direction. Like Aquinas, Calvin seems to hold that faith is knowledge only in a popular sense.[14] Nonetheless, working from within the tradition he occasionally refers to as "Reformed Epistemology," Alvin Plantinga has articulated a notion of knowledge that might well be adopted in order to defend the claim that revealed truth can be known in a strict sense of "known."

The basic idea is this: "Positive epistemic status," an expression Plantinga prefers to "epistemic justification," names the (possibly complex) normative property which, possessed to the proper degree, distinguishes knowledge from true belief.[15] Approaching this concept from a theistic standpoint, Plantinga suggests that we reflect on the fact that human beings, like ropes and linear accelerators, have been designed. God, of course, is the designer. Having made us in God's own image, God endows us with cognitive faculties devised in such a way as to achieve true beliefs. It is natural, then, to think of positive epistemic status as the property a belief has when the believer's cognitive capacities are working the way they were designed to work in the sort of environment for which they were designed.[16]

This account of knowledge opens the way to claiming that faith is a form of knowledge. I am not saying that this is in fact what Plantinga does or intends, but only that his definition suggests one way to reply to the rationalist objection. Plantinga's definition of knowledge—more precisely his definition of the key ingredient of positive epistemic status—does not restrict the scope of knowledge to propositions for which there is compelling evidence. Since Christianity is in fact true, we can know it is true simply by exercising our cognitive capacities in the way that they were meant to be exercised. As you look at the starry skies, your mind, operating precisely as God designed it to operate, in the setting for which God designed it, forms the true judgment that God exists. That is all there is to it. You rightly take it that God exists, as you might take it that you had breakfast this morning, and in so doing, you know it. Similarly, you hear the Word preached—"faith comes through hearing"—and your epistemic faculties, working properly in an appropriate environment, seize on the truth of the Word. There is no end to knowing Christian doctrine in this way. You need only to hear the Word, accept it, and hold it to the right degree—firmly.

Appropriating Plantinga's definition of knowledge has several advantages, particularly from the standpoint of those inclined to read Scripture and Calvin as holding that faith is knowledge, literally and nonanalogically. For though Plantinga's definition of knowledge is perhaps narrower than some contemporary rivals, the definition is broader than the stringent ones suggested by the classical foundationalism of Aristotle or Aquinas, which require that the known truth be immediately or derivatively evident. It is thus possible to hold that Christian belief is knowledge without claiming with the Catholics cited above that Christian belief is made certain by super-superabundant evidence displayed as such by the light of grace. Consequently there is no danger of restricting those who know the truth of Christianity to a small number of souls endowed with superior natural powers of reasoning or higher gifts of God. Anyone using ordinary epistemic powers in the way God had in mind can know Christianity is true.

But does this give us an adequate answer to CS? I do not think so. The trouble is not just that Plantinga's definition of knowledge is controversial,[17] but also that even if we accept the definition, many sincere Christians still will have no right to cling to their faith.

To begin with, Christians obviously disagree on some substantive points. Since there are points of conflict, some of us must be in error. Virginia believes the Roman Catholic doctrine of the real presence: the Eucharist *is* Jesus Christ. ("I am the bread of life. . . . I am the living bread which came down from heaven; if anyone eats of this bread, he will live forever, and the bread which I shall give for the life of the world is my flesh" [John 6:48, 51].) George, on the other hand, believes the Eucharist is only a symbol of Christ's love. He understands the scriptural words differently from Virginia. One of them must therefore be wrong. Suppose for the sake of argument that it is Virginia who is wrong. What, then, do we think she should do? Give up her belief in the real presence? Believe in it only tentatively? Do Christians who reject the doctrine of the real presence want to say Virginia has no right to believe it? I take it as evident that we do not want to start labeling one another's erroneous religious beliefs "immoral." So even if some beliefs qualify as knowledge in Plantinga's sense of the term, since many do not, we are left with no effective way to counter CS. Very large numbers of sincere Christians and others devoted to God will be unjustified in their beliefs.

Some Christians might disagree that this is an unacceptable consequence. George says, "All the argument shows is that poor Virginia and others like her wrongfully accept various teachings labeled 'Christian.' It proves nothing about proper religious belief. *My* religious belief is fully protected just by denying (1)."

But there are serious consequences of refusing to provide an umbrella for Virginia's erroneous beliefs, consequences that ultimately reach George. Virginia believes in the real presence for the same reason that she believes many elements of Christianity that George also believes. With George, Virginia believes God loves us. But Virginia's beliefs about divine love and the real presence radiate from the same source—the teaching of the church. She accepts both doctrines because she believes the church transmits the revelation of God. (One may think that Virginia should accept the doctrine of divine love for different reasons, but that is irrelevant. That the church preaches both doctrines may in fact be the decisive reason she holds the doctrines—this is in fact the decisive reason I hold them—and that is all that counts.) If, then, because the source is tainted, we think Virginia should not believe in the real presence, then for the same reason we ought to agree she behaves badly even by believing religious doctrines that are true.

Worse follows. Virginia has no right to believe even what she knows. The reason for this is a bit more complicated. To develop the point, fixing terminology for two concepts will be useful. An "evidential case" (or briefly, "case") for a proposition is all that may be said for it. This includes all relevant evidence, grounds, implicit and explicit reasoning, memories, perceptions—all the deliverances of epistemic faculties. An "appraisal" of a case for a proposition is an individual's judgment of what the case is worth epistemically. We will say an individual appraises a case if the individual judges the case to be strong or weak, etc., or, in comparative terms, stronger or weaker than another case.

Now as we can be faulted for believing too much or too little, given a case for a belief, so too we can be faulted for believing too much or too little, given our *appraisal* of that case. ("You *thought* it was a bad case, so why did you believe the contention?") This prompts the following:

(V-1)   If V appraises her cases for two propositions p and q as equal, then if V is unjustified in believing p (or believing it with a certain degree of firmness) *in virtue of her appraisal of p*, then V is unjustified in believing q *in virtue of her appraisal of q*.[18]

We are now in a position to apply the definitions and the principle. Until now we have been assuming that Virginia's belief in the real presence (hereafter R) radiates from the same source as her belief that God loves us (L). Let us, though, now suppose her belief in L instead has the same ultimate source as George's. She believes L because her cognitive powers are working just the way George's are working in circumstances similar in all relevant particulars, and she inclines towards believing L in just the same proper degree as George. Moreover, let us suppose, she appraises the cases for R and L as equally good. (It is surely possible for her to think the case for R is equal to the case for L; she may even think it better.) From (V-1) it follows that she has no more right to believe L than she has to believe R. So Virginia has no right to believe even what she knows.

Peculiar as this is, the result may be acceptable to someone who adopts Plantinga's definition of knowledge. But we have not reached the end of it. With a slight twist on (V-1), we get:

(V-2)   If *V's* appraisal of the case for *p* is the same as *G's*,
         then if *V* is not justified in believing *p* (or believ-
         ing it firmly) in virtue of her appraisal of the
         case for *p*, then neither is *G*.

On the present supposition that Virginia's appraisal of her case
for *L* is the same as George's appraisal of his case for *L*, George
now has no right to believe *L*. For Virginia, as we have seen, has
no right to believe *L*, even though she knows *L*. So, by (V-2),
neither does George. After all, what's so special about George?
Why should he be justified in believing *L* firmly on his appraisal of the case, if Virginia is not justified in believing it on
her appraisal of her case?

    We have been considering a concept of knowledge that
would permit belief in the truth of Christianity to count as
knowledge. Allowing that such belief is (or can be) knowledge
in Plantinga's sense of the term, there remain many problems.
The approach fails to protect against the charge of moral im-
propriety for first, sincere false belief; next, sincere true belief;
and finally, even what is known to be true. The upshot is that
this kind of response to the Chief Stronghold argument justifies the belief of very few people.

    In sum, whether we adopt a fairly classical view of knowl-
edge (identifying it with true belief backed by compelling evidence) or Plantinga's idea (linking knowledge to the proper
functioning of a designed instrument), the Christian should
not accept the claim that undoubting belief in the face of difficulties is justified only if what is believed is also known.

4. THE RECEPTION OF TRUTH

    If, as we have argued, Christians typically are resolute be-
lievers, then to reply to CS it must be shown that there is nothing wrong with resolute belief. Now recall that the ground for
thinking that there is something wrong with resolute belief is
C-1: If you are troubled about a proposition, you should proportion belief in the proposition to the evidence. This claim is
in turn backed by *C-1a* and *C-1b*. Proposition *C-1a* we accept. It
is always wrong to indispose yourself to the reception of truth.

This leaves *C-1b:* Necessarily, if you do not proportion belief in a proposition when troubled about it, then you indispose yourself to the reception of truth.

What, then are we to make of *C-1b* and, consequently, *C-1?* To answer this question we now need to take account of a significant omission in the statement of these propositions. As long as we speak broadly about proportioning belief to evidence, they have considerable appeal. As soon as we get more specific about *times,* however, the precept and its backing begin to look quite strange. Are we *at every moment* to proportion belief to the available evidence? As a juror in a civil trial between Smith and Jones, you first hear Smith tell the tale. Of course he tells it his way, and so as Smith concludes his testimony, the evidence favors Smith. Should you then immediately side with Smith before Jones gets to tell her side of the story? Clearly not. It might be observed that in such cases we know more evidence is in prospect, and besides, we have an obligation to wait until the evidence is in before coming to judgment. That is true, but it leaves the counter-example untouched. In fact it concedes the point at issue. Since on some occasions we are obliged to defer judgment, it cannot be true that immediately proportioning belief is obligatory. Punctilious adherence to the proportionality precept in some cases would operate contrary to the ends of human existence, including the very adjudication of the truth.

This is particularly so with respect to religious matters. Catherine Ward writes to Newman:

> Strong convictions I have at times that the church of Rome is the One true church—strong yearnings after her blessed teachings of the Holy sacrament—and then comes the fear, the shrinking from certain doctrines as the teaching of the evil one, and I am cast back, I cannot say into the English church, but alas no where—homeless as it were and houseless.... [19]

On the temporally quantified version of the proportionality precept, Catherine Ward should be a Catholic one moment and anti-Catholic the next. Whatever one thinks about Catholicism, this cannot be right.

It may be objected that all these cases show is that the proportionality precept requires some modification such as that of allowing reasonable time for assessment of all the essential evidence. But then when is all the relevant evidence in? A few days, a few weeks, a few months suffice for a trial. But for religious belief nothing less than a lifetime seems adequate for gathering all the relevant evidence. For if Christian doctrine is credible in part because its excellence testifies to a divine source, and if appreciation of that fact grows as one enters into the life, living the Creed and participating in the sacraments, then fresh evidence is always opening up to the believer. The believer and the nonbeliever are not looking at the same body of evidence. Since strong belief is a condition for acquiring essential evidence, the believer is not morally obliged to proportion belief to evidence.

This, then, is how I think we must reply to the argument Ward dubbed "the chief stronghold" of philosophical objectors. But we have so far hardly touched on positive reasons for resolute belief. What reason can be given for resolute belief in Christianity?

5. WHY RESOLUTE BELIEF?

The best short answer to the question I know of is Newman's. We have evidence enough to warrant the judgment that One to whom we owe absolute obedience commands us to believe certain truths without deliberate doubt.[20] "Reason does not prove that Catholicism is *true,* as it proves that mathematical conclusions are true . . . but it proves that there is a *case* for it so strong that we see we ought to accept it."[21]

For now we need not concern ourselves with what the case Newman refers to may be or whether it in fact is a strong case. For given two principles more or less explicit in this text of Newman's, all that counts is that some *appraise* the case as strong. The first principle is deontic.

(O)   Acts indispensable to an obligatory end are themselves obligatory.

The second adds a doxastic component.

(DO)   If S believes there is a better case for than against (1) an end E being obligatory and (2) an act A being indispensable for achieving E, then A is obligatory for S.

Thus, if I believe on the basis of what I take to be a strong case that I have an obligation to give my students fair grades and that grading their papers is indispensable to giving fair grades, then I have an obligation to grade their papers. Similarly, if I believe that I have an obligation to unite myself to God, and that firm faith in a divine message is indispensable to union with God then I have the obligation to believe the divine message. The Christian who believes there is a stronger case for than against the existence of the obligatory end and the indispensability of the means is thus obliged to undoubting belief.[22]

Of course not everyone sees it this way. But a great many do. Millions believe that doctrine is divinely revealed, and they see embedded in that revelation a command to believe every word of the Son of God with one's whole heart and mind. It follows that they are obliged to do just that.

VI. SOME OBJECTIONS AND REPLIES

Is Any Belief or Disbelief Justified?

Two obvious objections are certain to be made. The first is that principles (O) and (DO) justify any belief and none at all. The second is that the principles dispense the believer from the obligation to be objective. We consider the first objection in this subsection, the second in the next subsection.

Given that different people make positive appraisals of the cases for different religions, members of different religions are obliged to believe resolutely different things. Furthermore, since an atheist can see resolute atheism as an indispensable means to the obligatory end of truth, for some people even resolute atheism is obligatory. These results are unacceptable. So, something is wrong with either (O) or (DO) or both.

But the results are not unacceptable. After all, why should we think that in worshiping according to their lights earnest Christian, Jews, and Muslims are doing anything but carrying out their duties? We can certainly look for such principles without at the same time committing ourselves to a religious indifferentism that regards any religion to be as full a revelation as any other. What the principles (*O*) and (*DO*) support is the correctness of believing according to our lights, not the correctness of the beliefs themselves. The same holds for resolute disbelief. If we conscientiously see disbelief as an indispensable means to an obligatory end, disbelief is obligatory.

It is worth stressing how little this last concession comes to. Principles (*O*) and (*DO*) entail a conditional. *If* it is conscientiously thought that atheism is an obligatory means to the obligatory end of truth, *then* atheism is obligatory. Principles (*O*) and (*DO*) do not guarantee that anyone ever fulfills the condition. Even if some or many were to satisfy the condition, this would not show that (*O*) and (*DO*) were false. But in fact it is very hard to see how anyone *could* fulfill the condition.

Consider first *resolute* disbelief. How could one arrive at the conclusion that resolute atheism was obligatory? Asked to justify the conviction that faith is required, a Christian points to scriptural or ecclesial statements which she takes to express the mind of God. But an atheist cannot similarly point to some Bible of Disbelief to justify *resolute* atheism. An atheist can believe that truth is a necessary end, and that since God does not exist, disbelief is obligatory. But nothing in this argues *resolute* disbelief.

For related reasons, even *irresolute* disbelief is hard to justify. In his well-known essay ' The Presumption of Atheism,"[23] Michael Scriven argues that absent clear evidence to support the claim that God exists the only proper response is atheism. But Scriven also holds that atheism is proper only if the existence of God is strictly disprovable, i.e., demonstrably incompatible with the evidence or wholly unfounded, or if the existence of God is wholly lacking in general or particular support. If there is any general or particular support for theism, then the only proper attitude is a skepticism accompanied by a "recognition of a real *possibility*" of God's existence.[24] So even if there is a presumption of atheism, atheism itself is justified only if one is sure there is not a shred of evidence for God's existence. To establish this, however, one must do more than rebut all the various arguments for God's existence, as Scriven seeks to do. One must prove that Ward's "super-superabundant evidence" and Newman's "case so strong" come to exactly nothing. The immensity of that task of demolition is obvious from Scriven's own considerable efforts to refute all the relevant theistic arguments. Wide ranging as it is, his survey of the evidence is quite incomplete. For example, replying to what he calls the "Argument from Revelation," Scriven says only that "no account of their experience [those who claim to have received a revelation] by itself can contribute to the argument in any way—there must be some independent evidence of its veracity or their expertise and this is notably absent."[25] But there is independent evidence of its veracity and their expertise, and of more than this. There is, to begin with, the sublimity of the message, keenly sensed as transcending the reach of human genius—a message Divine Goodness would vouchsafe, did God vouchsafe any—conveyed at first to the world by a most unlikely collection of uneducated people, wonderfully and consistently developed over centuries, in words that attest its miraculous nativity. I am not arguing that Christianity is true, but only that the very least that can be said for Christianity is that it is not obviously false. It follows on Scriven's own principles that disbelief is the wrong attitude for anyone in the least taken with evidence favoring theism or Christianity.

And even the convinced unbeliever may be so taken. Long satisfied with the claim of rationalist exegetes that centuries of "overpainting" completely obscure the person Christ, one is suddenly struck by the primal phenomenon of Jesus and the power of a message that alone seems to answer the fundamental questions of existence, too radiantly beautiful and deep to be anything other than the manifestation of the mind of God. Accustomed to contemporary science's routine assumption of a naturalism seemingly at variance with Christianity and other religions, one suddenly senses our existence is engulfed in unutterable mystery. An article in a leading journal in the philosophy of science informs us that "modern science provides enough evidence to justify the belief that the universe began to exist without being caused to do so."[26] No cause at all? How can this be? Matters are not improved when others argue impressively that the universe began to be with initial conditions astonishingly improbable except in light of the anthropic principle that these properties are necessary if the universe is to contain carbonaceous astronomers like ourselves.[27] These are troubling thoughts for unbelief. And on Scriven's principles, if one sees in any of this a scintilla of evidence for theism or Christianity, disbelief is unjustified.

Must Not the Christian Acknowledge the Possibility of Error?

What, though, about objectivity? Is Ward's rationalist right to claim that the avowed intellectual maxims of the resolute believer place him beyond "the pale of intellectual civilization"? Can Christians do justice to the requirements of objectivity?

Well, what are the essential conditions of objectivity? Obviously one condition is that evidence be given its due. The nub of the imputation against Christians is that they cannot satisfy this condition. Faith is bias. Christians therefore cannot properly assess the evidence. In a moment we must consider this. But let us consider first a condition that must be satisfied before one can hope to weigh the evidence properly—the need to *acquire* the relevant evidence. We can scarcely claim objectivity if we give only the evidence at hand its due, neglecting to acquire other relevant evidence. Now on this point, which is the first point of objectivity, the Christian certainly meets the test as well as the rationalist. Arguably, the Christian does even better. For as the leading theologians of Christianity have held, the evidence of its truth, though deriving from many sources, is largely conveyed through the experience of living it. Among the divine aids to belief, Aquinas lists second and third the content of doctrine and confirmation by miracles. The experience of an "inner call" (*interiorem vocationem*) heads the list.[28] We are bound to believe, Aquinas argues, because "that interior instinct, by which Christ is able to manifest himself without exterior miracles, pertains to the power of the first truth, which illumines and teaches us from within" ("quae interius hominem illuminat et docet").[29] But this illumination increases as one lives the life, praying, reading Scripture, receiving the sacraments, doing Christian works of mercy. The first condition of this form of life is faith. The condition must be satisfied not only because faith is a defining ingredient of the Christian life, but also because a life of devotion requires conviction of the value of the acts. "Without certitude of religious faith," Newman remarks, "there may be much decency of profession and observance, but there can be no habit of prayer, no directness in devotion, no intercourse with the unseen. . . . "[30] Since a life of devotion is impossible without firm faith, and since a great part of the Christian's implicit evidence derives from that life of devotion, only one who enters the Christian life can claim to seek all the relevant evidence.

Does this beg the question by assuming a point no rationalist would grant—the truth of Christianity? Not at all. We are not assuming that God actually illumines and instructs the human mind and heart by an inner light. This any rationalist would indeed deny. We are rather assuming what no one denies, namely, that Christians believe this happens, and they believe it because the relevant data appears to vary with their participation in the life of One who described himself as "the Way." Though it takes a theologian to systematize the reasons for the Incarnation or the fittingness of Christ's death on a cross, the Christian absorbed in Christ's life will understand, if only tacitly, the immense power of Christian doctrine, its beauty, its coherence, and its surpassing excellence, all of which speak in favor of its divine origin. It is thus not the Christian who fails to pass the first test with respect to objectivity, not the Christian who fails to gather the data. If someone were to say that the jewel you are examining will appear brilliant and clear if you move it out of the range of the sickly yellow artificial light into daylight, the best way—maybe the only way—to see whether it is true is to make the move.

Of course this idea can be carried too far by insisting that since gaining access to some of the evidence relevant to determining the truth of a religion requires entering into its practices, you cannot objectively evaluate a religion from the outside. The argument, however, does not require any such extravagant assumption. If you are told that a religious experience will follow such and such practices and that that experience will reveal that you have no self or that you are the World-Soul or that God is a prime number, you may well believe that the religion flunks the test of coherence and that further investigation is unnecessary. And, of course, many believe just this about Christianity. They dismiss as absurdities the doctrines of the Trinity, of vicarious atonement, of transubstantiation of bread into the body of Christ. And indeed if these are absurdities, then insisting on the need for relevant religious experience before making a final judgment is pointless. But we are not considering here an argument made directly against the coherence, or the truth, of particular Christian doctrines but, rather, the general philosophical objection that purports to show that Christianity, if it requires faith, cannot be an expression of the divine mind. Faith, or resolute belief as I have called it here, is the abandonment of objective reasoning and hence of reason itself. The reply is that quite the reverse is the case, at least so far as gathering evidence is concerned, for the Christian does gather evidence. One cannot deny this by pretending that its acknowledgment is tantamount to screening off all religions from outside evaluation.

Weighing the evidence properly, the second condition of objectivity, is a bit more complicated. And this because, I think, we routinely assume that we cannot possibly give the evidence its due unless we are prepared to acknowledge at the outset that the beliefs we carry into the investigation may in fact be false. Even very able defenders of Christian belief appear to accept the assumption. Thus, Alan Donagan writes:

> When confronted with contemporary naturalism, Christian apologists should begin by disclaiming any view about nature other than that Christian doctrine, as embodied in traditional confessions of faith such as the Nicene creed, will prove to be compatible with any authentic advance in the natural sciences.

This seems exactly right. But Donagan continues disconcertingly:

> Newman's attitude to the natural sciences seems to me to be a paradigm of Christian faith, properly understood. He implicitly acknowledges that discoveries in the natural sciences could conceivably be incompatible with Christian faith by leaving no room for anything supernatural. . . . At the same time, he asserts the rational legitimacy of accepting the Christian faith without philosophical or scientific proof. Holding the Christian faith is believing something that, since it is neither philosophically nor

scientifically proved, can conceivably be scientifically (and hence philosophically) disproved.[31]

Approving Newman's contention that it is "very undignified for a Catholic to commit himself to the work of chasing what might turn out to be phantoms,"[32] Donagan seems to say it suffices to justify firm faith to recall that current arguments against Christianity rest not on science in its perfected form but only on the science of the day. Christians are thus free to ignore contemporary naturalism and even to concede that discoveries in the natural sciences could conceivably be incompatible with Christian faith by leaving no room for anything supernatural.

We need a distinction. If by "conceivably" one means "it is possible that," then the Christian cannot agree that conceivably Christianity will prove to be incompatible with authentic discoveries of science. For if it is possibly false, it *is* false.[33] But if by "conceivably" one just means that for all one *knows*, there *could* be a contradiction, then the Christian can concede that a conflict is conceivable. There is no incoherence in saying "I am absolutely certain the Christian message is true, but for all I *know*, Christianity is false." For this means only that Christian doctrine does not belong to the set of propositions that the Christian knows to be true. Christians, then, should indeed remain confident that authentic advances in the sciences will not prove incompatible with the Nicene Creed, not because they know the truth of the Creed, but because they have grounds sufficient to warrant the judgment that they have a duty to believe.

I have been arguing that the Christian meets the first requirement of objectivity—obtain the relevant evidence—in part by living the life that purports to furnish evidence of its divine origin, and that the Christian begins to meet the second requirement—give the evidence its due—by acknowledging the reasonableness of some arguments against the teaching that the Christian believes but does not know to be true.

The rationalist may protest that this acknowledgment of ignorance, while welcome, scarcely resolves the problem. It remains to be explained how the resolutely believing Christian who admits that ten years of study might leave a fundamental objection unanswered can possibly claim to give the evidence its due. If unanswered objections do not register, if they are met with a shrug, if belief is neither abandoned nor abated, if the believer is unmovable by any argument, in what intelligible sense can the resolute believer be objectively weighing the evidence?

Such questions suggest that the resolutely believing Christian is committed to the proposition that no amount of evidence against Christianity would warrant abandoning it. But this is not true. I can easily imagine circumstances in which it would be proper to relinquish belief in Catholicism. With a desire to close ranks with all Christians, a general council summoned by the pope deliberately rejects a previously defined doctrine such as the Tridentine teaching that the whole substance of the bread is converted into the body of Christ, the appearance of bread only remaining. This would prove that the Catholic church was not the infallible interpreter of the divine message. As Donagan notes, Christianity is not in principle unfalsifiable. Resolute belief is certainly consistent with acknowledging this. Moreover, it is entirely consistent with resolute belief to say I would abandon my belief if upon mature reflection the case for Christianity were to prove inferior to the case against Christianity. The key word, of course, is *if*. The faithful Christian is confident the condition will not be satisfied. This willingness to change one's mind if the condition should be satisfied is all that can be reasonably asked. To insist on more is to insist that belief be proportioned to the evidence. This is simply to fall back on the defective precept we examined earlier, and it is to ignore the first requirement of objectivity. We cannot weigh the evidence unless we acquire it. We cannot acquire it unless we live the life. We cannot live the life unless we have faith.

NOTES

I wish to take this occasion to thank Michael Degnan, Douglas Lewis, Sandra Menssen, Russell Pannier, Thomas G. Sullivan, and Linda Zagzebski for many helpful comments on earlier drafts of this paper.

1. William G. Ward, *Essays on the Philosophy of Theism*, vol. 2, ed. Wilfred Ward (London: Kegan Paul, Trench, 1884), pp. 244–246. Influenced by John Henry Newman and the Oxford movement, William G. Ward joined the Roman Catholic church shortly before Newman himself. The cited material is from an essay by Ward on Newman's *An Essay on the Grammar of Assent*, which Ward believed supplied invaluable materials for an adequate response to "the philosophical objectors."

2. John Locke, *An Essay Concerning Human Understanding*, ed. P. H. Nidditch (Oxford: Clarendon Press, 1975), bk. 4, ch. 20, n. 10, p. 713.

3. William G. Ward, "The Reasonable Basis of Certitude," originally printed in the nineteenth century (1878), reprinted in *The Ethics of Belief Debate*, ed. Gerald D. McCarthy (Atlanta: Scholars Press, 1986), p. 173.

4. See *Faith and Rationality: Reason and Belief in God*, ed. Alvin Plantinga and Nicholas Wolterstorff (Notre Dame, Ind.: University of Notre Dame Press, 1983).

5. George Mavrodes, "Belief, Proportionality, and Probability," in *Reason and Decision*, ed. Michael Bradie and Kenneth Sayre (Bowling Green, Ohio: Applied Philosophy Program, 1982), p. 64.

6. C. S. Lewis, "Obstinacy in Belief," in *Philosophy of Religion: An Anthology*, ed. Louis P. Pojman (Belmont, Calif.: Wadsworth, 1987), p. 377. St. Augustine, in *The Utility of Believing*, may have been the first to offer this defense.

7. Catholicism in particular teaches that the entire point of human existence is awareness of the truth, for the goal of existence is to see the divine essence face to face, without any creature acting as a medium of vision. Truth is the core of everlasting life, the source of the love that Scripture celebrates in varied images of the wedding meal. Beatitude, Augustine writes in the *Confessions*, is *quadium de veritate*, "rejoicing in the truth." Following Augustine, Aquinas argues "the essence of beatitude consists in an intellectual act, but to the will pertains the delight consequent upon the beatitude" (*Summa Theologiae* [hereafter *S.T.*] 1, 2, Q.3, c.). Furthermore, the norms of conduct must be consistent with the ultimate end (*S.T.* 1, 2, Q.94, a.2). Since the goal of human life is the fulfillment of the promise of Scripture to see God face to face (1 Cor. 13:12), since our beatitude is a form of knowledge, and since the norms of conduct are to be drawn from that end, there surely must be a sense in which it is correct to say that it is vicious to indispose oneself willfully to the acquisition of truth.

8. To the objection that our very perfection as rational beings consists in an attachment to the truth, and therefore it is impossible to want the truth too much, Aquinas responds: "[W]hile the human good does indeed consist in a cognition of truth, the highest human good does not consist in the cognition of just any truth, but in the perfect cognition of the highest truth, as the Philosopher makes plain in *Ethics*. Therefore it is possible for vice to taint cognition of truth, inasmuch as desire fails to be ordered to the knowledge of the highest truth, in which consists ultimate felicity" (*S.T.* 2, 2, Q.167, a.1, ad 1).

9. Ward, "Reasonable Basis," p. 185. Much the same thing can be found in recent writers. Thomas Russman makes a case for this claim in "A Faith of True Proportions: Reply to Sullivan," in *Thomistic Papers* 5, ed. Thomas Russman (Houston: Center for Thomistic Studies, 1990), pp. 81–91. "A Reply to Russman," also in *Thomistic Papers* 5 (pp. 91–95), expresses more fully my reservations about this approach.

10. In *Documents of Vatican II*, ed. Walter M. Abbott and Joseph Gallagher (New York: Guild Press, American Press, Association Press, 1966), p. 689.

11. Ward tries to meet this difficulty by invoking a distinction of Cardinal Franzelin: a truth can be absolutely "certain" without its being "evident": "Where truth is exhibited as 'evident,' doubt is impossible as in the instance of a demonstrated mathematical theorem. But where it is exhibited as 'certain' but not as 'evident' doubt is possible though most unreasonable, and belief therefore laudable" (Ward, "Reasonable Basis," p. 185). This Franzelin–Ward solution is very unsatisfactory. For surely what is praiseworthy about faith is not that one refrains from working up a doubt where it is just barely possible to do so. This is not the saving belief Christ praised as the beginning of eternal life.

12. Aquinas, *S.T.*, 2, 2, Q.5, a.2. We should not be misled on this point by the practice of Aquinas and other theologians who call faith "knowledge," even "scientific knowledge" (*scientia*). It is abundantly clear that for Aquinas such usages are justified by nothing more than the fact that faith, like knowledge, is very firm true belief. "Faith is said to be inferior to scientific knowledge because faith, unlike science, lacks vision of the data, though it has the same firmness" (*Disputed Questions on Truth*, Q.14, a.2, c. and ad 15). For Aquinas, in a strict sense of "know," *A* knows *p* only if *p* is directly or derivatively apparent to *A*. But the truths of faith are not apparent to us. Faith can be called, as Aquinas's Latin text of Hebrews 2:1 called is, an *argumentum*, for faith produces firm adhesion of the intellect to the truth.

But faith is *argumentum non apparentium*. Faith substitutes for evidence. Faith is just a habit of mind by which eternal life exists inchoately in us, making us assent to what is not apparent (*S.T.* 2, Q.4, a.1, c.). To know in the strict sense of the term that God has revealed something, then, we would need compelling evidence. But this most Christians do not have even about the existence of God, let alone about the fact that God has revealed something to someone (*S.T.* 1, Q.2, a.2, ad 1). They receive the belief on faith. The object of faith is God, the First Truth, on which all revealed truth rests, and everything else insofar as it is related to God (*S.T.* 1, 2, Q.1, a.1). Thus any proposition bearing on God, including God's existence, can be a matter of faith, though "faith" here is used in a somewhat extended sense. Obviously, one cannot accept the existence of God on God's authority, but one can accept the existence of God because one is moved by grace to accept this truth as proclaimed by others.

13. "The will, influenced by the movement of the good contained in the divine promise, proposes as worthy of assent something not apparent to natural understanding" (Aquinas, *Disputed Questions on Truth*, Q.14, a.2). This is the common doctrine of the church's great doctors. Thus, St. Frances De Sales writes: "When God gives us faith, he enters into our soul and speaks to our mind. He does this not by way of discussion but by way of inspiration. So pleasantly does he propose to the intellect what it must believe that the will thereby receives such great complacence that it incites the intellect to consent to the truth and acquiesce in it without any doubt or opposition whatsoever. A marvelous thing is seen here: God proposes the mysteries of faith to our soul amid obscurity and darkness in such wise that we do not see those truths, but only get a glimpse of them" (*Treatise on the Love of God*, vol. 1, trans. John K. Ryan [Rockford, Ill.: Tan Publishers, 1975], p. 138).

14. "[K]nowledge of faith consists in assurance rather than comprehension" (John Calvin, *Institutes*, III, ii, 14.9). For a very useful comparison of Aquinas and Calvin, see Kenneth Konyndyk, "Faith and Evidentialism," in *Rationality, Religious Belief, and Moral Commitment: New Essays in the Philosophy of Religion*, ed. Robert Audi and William J. Wainwright (Ithaca: Cornell University Press, 1986), pp. 80–107.

15. Alvin Plantinga, "Justification and Theism," *Faith and Philosophy* 4 (October 1987), p. 404.

16. More precisely: "[A] belief B has positive epistemic status for S if and only if that belief is produced in S by S's epistemic faculties working properly (in an appropriate environment); and B has more positive epistemic status than B^* for S if (1) B has epistemic status for

S, and (2) *B** does not or else *S* is more strongly inclined to believe *B* than *B**" (Plantinga, "Justification," p. 410).

17. I am inclined to say of his definition what Plantinga has said of each of the three current views of justification (Chisholmian Internalism, Reliabilism, and Coherentism): the definition gives necessary but not sufficient conditions for epistemic justification.

18. I stress *in virtue of the appraisal* because one might for special reasons fault a person for believing *p*, while praising her for disbelieving *q*, even though she appraises the bodies of evidence for *p* and *q* as equal: she may have taken proper pains to gather evidence in one instance, or she may have been more cautious in her appraisal of one case than the other, or perhaps had nonevidential reasons for believing *p* but not *q*, including obligations to persons.

19. Catherine Ward, letter to John Henry Newman, 10 October 1848, in *Letters and Diaries of John Henry Newman*, vol. 12, ed. Charles Stephen Dessain (London: Thomas Nelson, 1962), p. 289.

20. I have elaborated this point and examined Newman's various accounts of the rational ground for resolute belief in "Adequate Evidence for Religious Belief," in *Thomistic Papers* 4, ed. A. Kennedy (Houston: Center for Thomistic Studies, 1988), pp. 73–100; and "The Problem of Certitude: Reflections on Newman's *Grammar of Assent*," in *Thomistic Papers* 5, ed. Thomas Russman (Houston: Center for Thomistic Studies, 1990), pp. 81–91. Someone might object that I have misstated Catholic belief; the ground of certitude is not the human will but the unfailing Word of God and the gift of grace. Of course it is true that a complete account brings in these supernatural factors, but we here need an answer that makes sense to the rationalist challenger who would reject such a response as a patent *petitio*. We are confining ourselves here to the human side of faith.

21. John Henry Newman, letter of 12 October 1848, in *Letters and Diaries*, vol. 12, p. 289. In the same vein, Newman writes to Mrs. William Froude, 27 June 1848 (ibid., p. 227): "Faith then is not a conclusion from premises, but the result of an act of the *will*, following upon a *conviction* that to believe is a *duty*. The simple question you have to ask yourself is, 'Have I a *conviction* that I *ought* to accept the (Roman) Catholic Faith as God's word? . . . For directly you have a conviction that you *ought* to believe, reason has done its part, and what is wanted for faith is, not proof, but *will*."

22. This is not the place to pursue the actual evidence for Christianity. Still, it is worth once more citing Newman on the grounds of belief: "The Word of Life is offered to a man; and being offered, he has Faith in it. Why? On these two grounds,—the word of its human messenger, and the likelihood of the message. And why does he feel

the message probable? Because he has love for it. . . . He has a keen sense of the intrinsic excellence of the message, of its desirableness, of its likeness to what it seems to him Divine Goodness would vouchsafe, did He vouchsafe any" (*Oxford University Sermons* [London: Longmans, Green, 1898], p. 203).

23. Michael Scriven, "On the Presumption of Atheism," in *Primary Philosophy* (New York: McGraw-Hill, 1966), pp. 87–167.

24. Scriven, "Presumption," p. 106.

25. Scriven, "Presumption," p. 140.

26. Quentin Smith, "The Uncaused Beginning of the Universe," *Philosophy of Science* 55 (1988), p. 39. But see T. D. Sullivan, "Coming to Be without a Cause," *Philosophy* 65 (July 1990), pp. 255–270.

27. John D. Barrow and Frank J. Tipler, *The Anthropic Cosmological Principle* (Oxford: Clarendon Press, 1986), p. 15.

28. Thomas Aquinas, *Questiones Quodlibetales*, Q.4, a.2, c. I follow the number of the Marietti edition, ed. Raymundi Spiazzi (1956).

29. Aquinas, *Quodlibetales*, Q.4, a.2, ad 3.

30. John Henry Newman, *An Essay in Aid of a Grammar of Assent* (London: Longmans, Green, 1898), p. 220.

31. Alan Donagan, "Can Anybody in a Post-Christian Culture Rationally Believe in the Nicene Creed?" in *Christian Philosophy*, ed. Thomas P. Flint (Notre Dame, Ind.: University of Notre Dame Press, 1990). pp. 109–110.

32. John Henry Newman, *Apologia Pro Vita Sua*, critical ed. (London: Oxford University Press, 1964), pp. 272–273; cited in Donagan, "Can Anybody," p. 110. I cannot agree with Newman on this point. It can easily be one's duty to look into these matters. If no one does, it may easily appear that modern science decisively shows the falsity of Christianity.

33. This can be shown using the following abbreviations: S = the set of propositions constituting current (materialistic) science; $S*$ = the set of propositions constituting the ideal (true) science, the science of the future; C = a set of propositions constituting a central core of Christian teaching. Suppose we say, then, that though $S \Rightarrow -C$, S is possibly (probably) false. Moreover, while it is true that it is possible that $S* \Rightarrow -C$), it is only possible. So we are free to believe C.

This leads to the conclusion that Christianity is false:

1. $S*$ [Assumption: Science of the future is true; it makes "discoveries."]

2. $<> (S* \Rightarrow -C)$ Asp.

3. $W: (S^* \Rightarrow -C)$ 2
4. $W: [\,] (S^* \rightarrow -C)$ 3
5. $(S^* \rightarrow -C)$ 4
6. $-C$ 1, 5

The Christian cannot concede, therefore, that it is possible that ideal and true science will prove incompatible with Christianity.

5. Evidentialism, Plantinga, and Faith and Reason

Patrick Lee

1. HOW NOT TO ANSWER
THE EVIDENTIALIST OBJECTION TO
RELIGIOUS BELIEF

Plantinga's Answer to the Evidentialist Objection

The evidentialist objection to religious belief is this:

(1)   One ought not to believe a proposition unless one has sufficient evidence for it.

(2)   There is not sufficient evidence for religious belief.

(3)   Therefore, one ought not to have religious belief.

In a series of very instructive and incisive essays Alvin Plantinga has argued that the correct reply to the evidentialist objection is that sufficient evidence is *not* needed for the justification of belief in God because belief in God is a properly basic belief, and a properly basic belief is epistemically warranted in the absence of any evidence whatsoever.

Some other theistic apologists have replied to the evidentialist objection that, while sufficient evidence is needed, such evidence is available. Plantinga objects to this answer that it ends up, or tends to end up, *basing* one's religious belief on the evidence. And to base one's religious belief on evidence or arguments is foolhardy, for one's certainty will have to vary according to how the evidence looks at different times; and

140

believing in this way is less than complimentary to God. Referring to Calvin, Plantinga says that believing in God on the basis of argument is "whimsical at best and unlikely to delight the person concerned."[1]

Plantinga argues that not every belief can be accepted on the basis of *reasons;* some beliefs must be accepted in the absence of reasons. Such beliefs are basic. Of course, not just any belief is *properly* basic: only beliefs formed in the appropriate circumstances, or under the appropriate conditions, are properly basic. But to the question, what type of circumstances or conditions can confer epistemic warrant? Plantinga declares that particularism, rather than methodism, is the proper reply. That is, one cannot specify in advance a method by which to distinguish warranting circumstances from others. (In his latest writings Plantinga uses the term "warrant" to refer to that feature or relation which makes true belief knowledge, and he reserves the term "justification" for doing one's epistemic duty, which, of course, he distinguishes from epistemic warrant. I will follow him in this use of the terms.) Rather, one begins with the recognition that particular circumstances or conditions are in fact warranting before trying to determine what general features circumstances must have in order to qualify as providing epistemic warrant.[2] There are various circumstances, such as observing the starry heavens above, experiencing beauty, or experiencing forgiveness, which render belief in God a properly basic belief. Such circumstances are not *evidence* of God's existence but are grounds, or circumstances, that trigger the disposition for belief in God.[3]

According to Plantinga, epistemic warrant is a matter of our cognitive faculties functioning properly, that is, in accordance with their cognitive design and in appropriate circumstances.[4] I come to believe in God, says Plantinga, because God has implanted in me a tendency to believe in God in certain circumstances, and those circumstances occur. So, belief in God is the result of a reliable belief-forming mechanism operating properly in appropriate circumstances. Hence the belief is an epistemically warranted belief. So, no reasons at all are needed to render religious belief warranted.

I think Plantinga is right that religious belief should not be *based on* arguments, or evidence, or reasons, and for the same reasons Calvin and Plantinga indicate. However, I believe Plantinga's account of epistemic warrant is mistaken and therefore that he has not shown that belief in God is epistemically warranted. I argue here for an internalist constraint upon the types of circumstances that can provide epistemic warrant. With this stricter or narrower view of the requirements for epistemic warrant, I argue that we should concede that the absolute certainty of Christian belief (which I discuss in this paper, instead of just the belief that God exists) does not have epistemic warrant. But I argue that Christian belief is not *irrational*, either, and that it does have *moral* justification. I argue that for a belief to be morally justified, there must be *some* evidence for it, and evidence in this sense: something of which one is aware and which seems to indicate that the proposition believed is true, or likely to be true. (Thus "evidence," in my use of the term, as distinct from Plantinga's use, need not be propositional, although it must be in one's awareness.) How much evidence is needed or even whether a belief should have more evidence for it than against it to be morally justified cannot be specified in advance. Rather, how much evidence is needed for a particular act of belief to be morally justified varies according to the other factors—namely, how the belief might have an impact on other human goods—in the situation. Nevertheless, I will argue that some evidence is needed to insure that one's religious belief is a morally responsible act, or to make it clear to one that one morally ought to believe. Thus, evidence, in the sense mentioned above, has an important, necessary function to perform (other than being the basis) in the act of religious belief.

My objection to Plantinga's account of the epistemic warrant of religious belief concerns his theory of epistemic warrant in general. In brief, his account seems to me too externalist. On his account, God implants in me a tendency to believe in God in certain circumstances, say, on observing the starry heavens. Observing the starry heavens is not functioning as *evidence* for belief in God, but as a "triggering mechanism." More generally, God has arranged it that circumstances *C* will trigger in me

belief *p*. But *C* and the content of *p* need have no particular
relation to each other. Plantinga is not saying that in circumstances *C* God brings it about that I directly experience God,
albeit vaguely.[5] If I understand him correctly, he is not saying
that God actually appears to the believer's consciousness, or is
directly experienced, but that the belief in God is *occasioned*
by an experience of some sort. The fact that God implants in
me a tendency to believe *p* in circumstances *C* and that I am in
such circumstances, then, satisfies Plantinga's requirement for
"epistemic warrant," that is, it is a belief "produced by faculties
that are working properly in an appropriate environment."[6]
There are two questions here: a *de jure* one concerning the
nature of epistemic warrant; and a factual question, namely,
whether God has bestowed such a tendency or inclination in all
human beings.

I will address the *de jure* question. Suppose God did
implant in me a tendency to believe in God in circumstances *C*,
and *C* occurs and I "find myself" (to use Plantinga's expression)
believing in God.[7] Do these facts by themselves confer
epistemic warrant on my belief?

I think not. *With respect to my own cognitive apparatus*, it is a
matter of luck that I have arrived at a true belief, or a belief
that has warrant for people generally. I might express my point
as follows: on Plantinga's account the sole "epistemic merit,"
so to speak, lies outside the cognitive agent. What confers
warrant on a belief cannot be as extrinsic to the cognitive agent
as Plantinga's account of the epistemic warrant of religious
belief allows.

Plantinga holds, of course, that not just any belief can be
held as basic. One cannot arbitrarily start from beliefs that
just happen to suit one's fancy. While basic beliefs do not require evidence, they do require *grounds*, that is, circumstances
which render such beliefs warranted, says Plantinga.[8] A full
theory of epistemic warrant would specify restrictions on the
sort of circumstances that could render such beliefs warranted.
But concerning our ability to reach such a theory Plantinga is
skeptical.[9] I believe, however, that one of the restrictions such a
theory would need is that the cognitive agent must be *somehow*
aware of the warranting circumstances.

Yet a lot is included in the circumstances that render a belief warranted. Some factors in the circumstances are irrelevant. Other factors are essential, that is, without such factors the circumstances would not provide warrant. It seems to me that one must be somehow aware of the essential factors of the warranting circumstances.

This means that one is not epistemically warranted in believing in God from the sole facts that one finds oneself believing in God, that God implanted the inclination to believe in certain circumstances, and that those circumstances obtain. For it seems that the fact that God implanted that inclination in one is essential to the warranting circumstances. So, unless one were aware of the fact that the tendency to form that belief was implanted in one by God (or had some warranted reason to believe that), then the fact that the belief issues from such a tendency would not render that belief epistemically warranted.

Must one also be aware that one's cognitive faculties are functioning properly? And must one be aware that one's cognitive faculties are appropriately attuned to the environment? On Plantinga's account proper functioning of one's cognitive faculties and their attunement to the environment—but not the awareness of these facts—are essential to epistemic warrant. It would seem, then, that on my account the awareness of these conditions or relations would be necessary.

One reply to this problem might be to distinguish between circumstances that provide epistemic warrant on the one hand, and the nonobtaining of epistemic defeaters on the other hand. Clearly, in order to be epistemically warranted in a belief one need not be aware that conditions which would defeat one's evidence do not obtain. Nor need it be the case that in fact such defeaters of one's evidence do not obtain. To be warranted in believing that I see a tree I need not first be warranted in believing, or be aware of in any way, that no one has cleverly constructed tree replicas here. And if someone has in fact built such replicas and deceived me, my act of belief would still be epistemically warranted, though mistaken. Plantinga holds that the appropriateness of the environment to one's cognitive faculties is part of epistemic warrant. But one might want to argue that the nonappropriateness of the environment to one's cognitive faculties is an epistemic defeater. Then, it could be argued that one need not be aware of the appropriateness of the environment to one's cognitive apparatus as a prerequisite to epistemic warrant. However, one would then have to admit that no one seems to have a clear-cut criterion by which to distinguish warranting circumstances (which I say one must be somehow aware of) from the nonobtaining of defeaters (of which one need not be aware).

Although that reply is tempting, I think it is incorrect. The correct reply to this problem, I think, is that one is implicitly aware (or seems to be, since one can be mistaken) of the appropriateness of one's cognitive apparatus to the environment, in one's awareness that what one sees or understands is objective. My vision of a tree before me seems to be the revelation of an actual (objective) tree or the presence of a real tree. So my act of seeing (and thus, implicitly, my faculty of seeing) seems to be the sort of act that reveals things as they are. If my act of seeing or my faculty of seeing is not that sort of thing, then my belief that there is a tree before me is not epistemically warranted.[10] But it also seems that in the awareness that seeing is the sort of thing that is revelatory of other things there is implicit the awareness that the act of seeing and the power or faculty of seeing are apt to do that in this sort of environment.

Someone might object that perception and memory beliefs are counterexamples to such an internalist view. One might object that in sensation, memory, and other basic epistemic practices, what provides them with epistemic warrant is not something the subject is aware of. In basic epistemic practices, the argument might run, the warranting circumstances just *are* external to the cognitive agent's perspective or awareness.

However, I do not think in sensation and in memory-beliefs we have an experience that "triggers" our belief and then we simply believe in accordance with a tendency to believe and with no "reason," in any sense whatsoever, to believe. In sensation, memory, and so on, the known object itself appears to the knower, and the knower is aware (or seems to be—errors are possible here) of that fact, rather than the knower just "finding himself" having a belief. In sensation, for example, as well as having the sensation, I also intellectually have an *insight* into the nature of sensation.

I sense *X*, but I am also aware, or seem to be aware, that sensing *X* just is *X*'s being present to me. I am aware of this not in a separate propositional awareness; rather, this "second-order" awareness is precisely what occurs in any first-order affirmation. It is part of my awareness that *That tree is tall*, or that *That building is over there*, or so on. In affirming that *That tree is tall*, for example, what I am aware of is the objectivity of the tree's being tall, that is, I am aware that the content of my experience or thought is something other than my experience or thought.[11] The notion of truth, in the sense of correspondence or conformity to a distinct reality, is part of what we mean when we affirm or believe.[12] To affirm or believe something is to see one's experiencing or thinking as a recording or receiving of reality as it is. In the basic cognitive practices—beliefs formed directly on the basis of sensation or memory, for example—it is an awareness of the nature of one's experiencing or thinking that moves one to affirm or believe the relevant proposition.

This is not to say that this second-order awareness is infallible. I seem to myself to be receiving the object itself when I sense; but it remains *logically possible* that an evil scientist is systematically fooling me, or that I'm actually hallucinating rather than sensing. The point is, that in sensation—and the same with memory, reasoning, and so on—I do not just "find myself with a belief." Rather, I do have (or seem to have) an awareness of the essential warranting circumstances of those beliefs: I have an awareness, or seem to, that sensation is the presentation of the object itself. Therefore, sensation and memory beliefs do not constitute counterexamples to an internalist account.

This does not mean that I must also be aware of the adequacy or accuracy of the second-order act of awareness in a third-order act, leading then to an infinite regress.[13] The awareness I am speaking of does not occur in a distinct belief. Rather, it is part of, indeed the essential part of (in the sense of what makes it an act of affirming rather than an act of considering), the original belief. It is a reflexive awareness. One need not be aware of the accuracy of one's awareness of one's awareness—though I see no reason why one could not if one so desired—in a third-order act, because the objectivity of one's awareness of one's own awareness is not what one is affirming but, rather, the objectivity of one's awareness of a distinct object.

What argument can be presented for such an internalist account? It is difficult to find one that does not beg the question. As Bernard Williams claimed, it just seems, to many at least, that if one discovers that one has no reasons or evidence for a proposition that one has believed then that just *is* to cease believing it, or at least causes one to cease believing it. However, that is not so much an argument as an appeal to what one thinks is ideally involved in believing, and it seems that some people think evidence, in the sense I described above, is ideally involved and some do not.

There is, however, an indirect argument. Suppose that I find myself with a belief, which in fact has the features that qualify it has having epistemic warrant according to Plantinga's account. But suppose further that I reflect on this belief I happen to have and ask myself whether I have it as a quirk or as a belief I ought to retain. In this second-order reflection on my beliefs the chief aim is to determine which beliefs are true or are likely to be true. The features that provide it with epistemic warrant on Plantinga's account could be features I cannot discover in any reasonable amount of time. So, when I discover that, as far as I can tell, this belief might as well be the result of a quirk instead of a reliable cognitive mechanism, I lose confidence in this belief, and, I think we must also say at this point, this belief loses whatever epistemic warrant it previously had. (Of course, if I have reason to believe that I formed this belief by a natural belief-forming mechanism and I have a trust in my inborn cognitive mechanisms, that is another matter; I am supposing that nothing like that is occurring in our example.) So, given that when I hold this belief up to scrutiny my main concern should be how this belief is related to reality, to the truth, it follows that if Plantinga's account were right then a belief could in one moment have epistemic warrant and yet lose it the next moment with a simple act of doubt. Without evidence—in the sense of something I am aware of which seems to indicate the belief is true or likely to be true—many epistemically warranted beliefs would be such that a doubt directed on them would suffice to destroy whatever epistemic warrant they had before that doubt. But it seems to me that epistemic warrant cannot be that fragile. I would say that in the example we are discussing, before the reflection on my belief, I may not have been doing anything *im*proper (after all, my belief may not have been held with any degree of voluntariness, either direct or indirect—and the propriety, in some sense, of this belief is perhaps part of what Plantinga has in mind in his externalist account), but the belief was not epistemically warranted, and that is what I discover upon reflection. In other words, if an externalist account such as Plantinga's were correct, then some beliefs would be such that they are epistemically warranted only if they are not reflected on. That implication cannot be true, therefore the externalist account is mistaken.

Perhaps a more specific example will not belabor the point too much. Let us suppose that God has designed matters, perhaps through the mechanisms of evolution, such that a particular hormone in the blood causes a child to form a belief that her parents care for her, and this belief is generally true and having it is helpful to children's survival. (Of course, we are just ignoring for the moment all the care and nurturing that in the real order cause the child to know that her parents love her. After all, skeptical children might contest the significance of this evidence, and perhaps the child's brothers and sisters even propose disproofs of her parents' love.) One day the child begins to reflect on her beliefs, to determine which should be retained and which should not. (It is important to note, also, that reasonable people do this sort of thing constantly, or frequently.) She discovers that this belief was caused in her by a hormone. Then, she thinks to herself that perhaps this hormone was placed in her by God to produce a true belief, but just as likely, as far as she can tell, the hormone has another purpose and its producing this belief is simply a side effect and, perhaps, of no value whatsoever.[14] It seems to me that at this point her belief has lost whatever epistemic warrant it might previously have had. For as far as she can tell this belief is as likely to be false as true, and how these beliefs are related to truth is her focus in this reflection. (Of course, if she then goes further to reflect on the evidence for her parents' love, or the evidence against it, we then have a different example.) Now, I would say that the belief she forms after reflection is a warranted belief. But then it seems to follow that the belief she had prior to the reflection must have lacked epistemic warrant; its lack of epistemic warrant is precisely what she seems to have discovered in the reflection.

My point can be expressed in two ways. First, epistemic warrant cannot be the sort of thing which, for a large class of beliefs, a simple reflection or scrutiny would destroy. And that would be the case if Plantinga's externalist account of epistemic warrant were correct.

Or the point could also be expressed in this way. Epistemic warrant, according to Plantinga, is the proper functioning of our cognitive faculties (when their design is aimed at truth and in an appropriate environment). But reflecting on one's beliefs is part of proper functioning. And a belief reflected on cannot have epistemic warrant unless it has evidence for it (not necessarily propositional). Thus, proper functioning implies believing through evidence.[15]

I agree that what Plantinga describes as being "epistemically warranted" is a favorable condition: it is better to be in such a condition, or to operate cognitively in such a way, than it is, for example, to suffer from a cognitive malfunction. Indeed, I think that what he describes as epistemic warrant is part of epistemic warrant and that his clarification of reliabilism to include a teleological component is an important advance. Still, given the reflective nature of believing, I think that to have epistemic warrant one must have some assurance that one's belief is appropriately related to truth. And to have that one must have evidence, in the sense of something one is aware of which seems to indicate that the belief is true or likely to be true.

Thus, I conclude that Plantinga's account of epistemic warrant is mistaken, and that as a consequence one cannot hold that belief in God (or Christian belief, which I prefer to discuss in this context) is epistemically warranted on the sole grounds that it is a belief produced by cognitive faculties, functioning properly, designed with an aim toward truth, in an appropriate environment. Thus I also conclude that Plantinga's answer to evidentialism is not satisfactory.

Another Way Not to Reply to Evidentialism

The premises of the evidentialist argument can also be expressed as follows:

(*1*)   One ought to proportion one's beliefs to the evidence one has for those beliefs.

(2)   The evidence for religious belief by itself will not warrant firm belief in it.

I agree with Plantinga that (*1*) should be rejected. But someone might argue that (2) is not correct, that there *is* evidence for religious belief sufficient for epistemic warrant. Partly what is in question here is this: Just how good is the case for religious belief, or, specifically, for Christian belief? But there is also a psychological consideration that seems to support the position that there is sufficient evidence for religious belief.

Proponents of this position may argue that they do not find themselves now free to reject their religious belief. And so it may seem to them that their religious belief is not a matter of choice, but that the evidence, or their insight into the evidence, determines them to believe. How else can I explain why I could not right now simply choose to cease believing what the Nicene Creed says, for example?

But I think this view is incorrect. First, however, the position is right in this respect, that one usually cannot self-consciously and directly choose to believe a proposition. That is, one cannot simply and self-consciously will to believe a proposition in the absence of any evidence for it at all. My feelings or moods may move me to believe something, but only if I am not conscious of that causality. Or at least, to the extent that I *am* conscious of my feeling or mood moving me to believe something, to that extent I cease to have confidence in a belief that perhaps I cannot fully shake. Yet this point does not mean that the will does not have an important role to play in many beliefs.

I think we have a tendency or innate propensity to believe upon the awareness of even the slightest degree of evidence. But if the evidence is not overwhelming then one can choose to refrain from believing, precisely by concentrating on the gaps in the total evidence. Hence one cannot directly choose to believe, but one can choose not to refrain from believing and thus to let what evidence there is for a proposition (which may be scant) move one to believe.

Secondly, to say that I am not free now to reverse my belief is not the same as to say, nor does it imply, that it was evidence, much less an assessment of the totality of the evidence, that determined my belief, or that the evidence now determines it. Something other than evidence could determine my act. Moreover, even if I am now unable to cease believing (or begin believing), that does not mean that I am in every sense not free to cease believing (or begin believing). I may be free to do something even though doing it takes time; and even though doing it requires me to do several other things which put me in a position to do that. So, the fact that I may not be able immediately to cease believing provides no evidence at all for the position that in my religious belief the evidence for it—directly or indirectly—determines me to believe.

Thirdly, the principal reason why this position seems to me untrue is simply the character of the evidence and arguments for Christian belief (I am ignoring other religions for the moment because I do not think there is as much evidence for them as there is for Christianity). I think the "case for Christianity"—the evidence for its being a revelation from God—is very strong, strong enough to make it the more reasonable position, and even strong enough to be beyond reasonable doubt. Still, I do not think the evidence is of the sort that, even after considering it with an open mind, one is compelled to accept the belief it supports with the absolute certainty with which Christians accept that belief.[16] I think that on purely evidentialist grounds, the verdict would be: Give this a high degree of certainty, but not absolute or unreserved certainty. It does seem that the evidence just by itself is *not* sufficient to warrant the high degree of certainty which Christianity requires of its adherents.[17]

2. HOW TO REPLY TO EVIDENTIALISM

The False Presupposition of the Evidentialist Objection

The evidentialist objection presupposes several claims about what is needed for a belief to be a proper act. Of course the evidentialist objector claims that religious belief is not *epistemically* warranted. While Plantinga and many others deny this claim, I have argued that we should grant it to the evidentialist, in this sense, that the absolute certainty of Christian belief is not epistemically warranted. But evidentialism also presupposes that one ought not to accept a belief that is not epistemically warranted, in other words, that to accept a belief that is not epistemically warranted is not *morally* justified. So the heart of the evidentialist argument concerns moral justification.

The evidentialist norm for believing has been expressed in various ways: It is wrong to believe anything upon insufficient evidence. Or: One ought to proportion one's belief in a proposition to the degree of evidence that one has to support that proposition. Or: One ought not to go beyond the evidence in one's acts of believing. (I think the word "evidence" here means roughly what I used it to mean above, namely, something of which one is aware that seems to indicate that a proposition is true or likely to be true, and evidence in this sense need not be propositional.) These ways of expressing the evidentialist norm come down to the same thing, for what is meant is that evidence alone should be determinative of what and how one believes. Nothing else should affect one's acts of believing except the relationship between the proposition believed and the evidence one knows that supports it.

However, what evidence is there for this *sola evidentia* position? After all, an act of believing is a moral act, and moral acts typically relate to *several* human goods rather than just one. Why should this human act be motivated or influenced by only one human good—possession of truth—while there seems nothing morally wrong with other human acts being simultaneously motivated and influenced by several human goods?

An example frequently discussed is a mountain climber who has climbed to a dangerous spot from which he can escape only by jumping across a wide chasm. The evidence just on its own indicates that it is only probable that he will make the jump (I shall discuss the type of case where the available evidence goes *against* one's belief in a moment.) But if he believes with certainty he will make the jump then his chances are greatly increased. It does not seem immoral for him to induce in himself, or to try to induce in himself, the belief that he will make the jump. Such an act does not seem to involve a disrespect or a disregard for the basic good of possession of truth. The type of act involved here is accepting a proposition with certainty (partly) for the sake of a good which the belief of that proposition, together with its truth, if it turns out to be true, will help or enable one to realize.

Another example, more closely analogous to religious belief, is accepting a marriage proposal. Suppose George proposes marriage to Hilda. He tells Hilda that he loves her, proposes that they set up a common life, and tells her of things he has done for her—that he has, for example, bought them a house for the home they will make if she says yes. So Hilda seems to have a choice. She can accept what George says as true and sincere and accept the proposal, or not. She cannot, obviously, *prove* that his proposal is sincere. Let us suppose George is not a villainous type, that there are signs that he is a good and honest person, in other words, one would likely say his claim is "credible," worthy to be believed. Well, if Hilda decides to accept, it is likely that she will have more certainty in George than the evidence just by itself about him would epistemically warrant. But is there anything morally improper about such belief or faith?

Religious belief is analogous to acceptance of a marriage proposal. Religious belief in the full sense, according to Christians, is believing what God has communicated through the words and deeds of prophets and of Jesus. Revelation is not merely impersonal information or a set of speculative truths. It is a personal communication. It reveals, in part, who God is, his invitation and commitment to personal communion, and many of the things he has done for us.[18] To be sure, there is evidence, or signs of credibility—signs indicating that indeed it is God who is speaking here. Yet the Christian's act of acceptance and the certainty of that act are motivated not just by that evidence or "signs" but also by the desire for the personal communion offered.[19] Is such an act morally justified?

Moral justification primarily concerns basic human goods, that is, aspects of human flourishing. In acts of believing the primary good involved—although I will argue not the only good—is possession of truth, or a grasp upon reality. I believe the basic moral norm can be expressed in this way: In all of one's choices and acts of willing, one ought to respect all basic human goods, including such goods as human life, aesthetic experience, friendship, society, and so on.

This position on morality is derived from Thomas Aquinas's natural law theory and has recently been articulated and developed by Germain Grisez, Joseph Boyle, and John Finnis.[20] I can briefly clarify this view by contrasting it with consequentialism or utilitarianism. Consequentialism is correct in this sense that moral good is closely linked with the human good or the fulfillment of the whole person. But consequentialism is incorrect in basing morality on the production of goods or benefits rather than directly on how the will is related to human goods. The moral norm is not that we should maximize human goods, which would justify suppressing a particular human good for the sake of the consequences "in the long run." I do not think it morally right to choose to destroy or suppress a human good for the sake of (what one thinks will be) the balance of human goods in general. Morality does depend on how one's action is related to human goods, but the important relation is this: one's choice or will should be directed to human goods and should remain open to all of them.

From this basic principle several more specific moral norms follow. For example, one ought not to be deterred from pursuing human goods by mere lethargy or laziness; one ought not to prefer the mere experience or the mere appearance of a good to its reality; and one ought not to choose to destroy, damage, or impede one good for the sake of another. One is not required to pursue all of the basic human goods all of the time, but one is (morally) required to respect them at all times. Perhaps the central question concerning the ethics of belief, then, is: What does respect for the good of possession of truth require?

First, respect for this good seems to require that we pursue it at least sometimes. I would be less than honest if I said I had a love for truth but *never* made any effort to pursue it.

Secondly, I think respect for this good also requires that we never choose precisely against it, for example, by suppressing truth for the sale of an ulterior end.

And, thirdly, respect for the good of possession of truth requires that in any of our actions which could affect this good (in ourselves and in others), we at least take it into account, that is, that we do not disregard this good. An example of disregarding the good of possession of truth is believing in astrology because it makes me feel good or, even, believing in God (or trying to induce belief in God in someone else) solely because one thinks such belief makes people morally better.

Yet believing for the sake of a good other than truth need not include any failure to pursue truth, any suppression of truth, or any disrespect for the good of possession of truth. An action that directly bears on one good may be chosen to promote another good without slighting the good that the action most directly bears on.[21] Therefore, believing for the sake of a good other than truth need not be immoral.

In sum: (1) religious belief can be motivated by a hope for the realization of a basic human good; (2) religious belief need not include a negative attitude toward, or a disregard for, any other instance of a human good. From these points it follows that religious belief could be, in the appropriate conditions, a morally good act. More formally:

> Every act which does not negate or disregard a basic human good is a morally good act.
> Some acts of religious belief do not negate or disregard a basic human good.
> Therefore, some acts of religious belief are morally good acts.[22]

Someone might object that my account leads to approving all kinds of irrational acts. Is not the person who believes in astrology because it makes him feel good doing just what I have described, believing for the sake of a good other than truth? Is not irrationality precisely allowing concerns other than for truth to take over?

In reply, first, saying that believing for the sake of a good other than truth need not involve disrespect for truth does not mean that *every* believing for the sake of a good other than truth is respectful of truth and morally right. If we reject the evidentialist restriction on how concern for other goods can influence one's actions in relation to truth, it does not follow that we are left no restrictions at all on such influence.

Secondly, I have said that religious belief is analogous to an act of accepting a proposition for the sake of a good which the belief, *together with the truth of the proposition,* will help one realize. If the belief by itself were sufficient to bring about the good one is seeking by believing then it seems that the action would be immoral. Believing in astrology because it makes one feel good or, even, believing in God solely because such a belief makes one more moral are examples of doing that. If the belief by itself—independently of the belief's truth—were sufficient to bring about the good one hoped for, then one's choice to believe (or choice to do what leads to believing) would include implicitly a willingness or consent to believe falsely. This would violate the basic good of possession of truth. But in the type of act we are discussing there need be no implicit consent to believe falsely. That is, no doubt there are acts of religious belief that do involve a disregard for truth or insufficient regard for truth, but it is not necessary that every act of religious belief do so.

Thirdly, I believe *some* degree of evidence is needed in order for the act of belief to be a morally responsible act. I am not sure we can give an explicit criterion for determining how much evidence is needed. But I think *some* degree of evidence is required. If, for example, the man who proposed marriage to Hilda were known to be a J. R. Ewing type, then it would probably be unreasonable for her to accept his proposal as sincere. The less evidence there is, then I think the more the other factors in the situation must contribute to justifying (morally) a risk with respect to the good of possession of truth.

Fourthly, we must remember that respect for the good of truth requires at all times openness to evidence that may go to support a view opposite the belief. The will to bring it about that I believe p does not excuse suppressing evidence for not-p.

For one thing, what looks like evidence for not-*p* may turn out to be evidence for some other proposition, or it may cause us to understand more fully what it is we are understanding in the proposition *p*. It is good to remember here that our goal is, not simply to believe true propositions and refrain from believing false ones, but to have a cognitive grasp upon the real, or to have as accurate and complete a picture of what the real is as we can. The evidence for not-*p* may eventually serve to reveal important aspects of the real other than what it first seems to point to. Because of that fact and because the evidence itself is part of our possession of truth, it is never morally permissible directly to suppress evidence.

What about believing when the available evidence or, rather, the balance of the available evidence goes the other way? I do not think this is necessarily improper either. One reason why is that the *available* evidence may be misleading, and I do not see that taking a second-order view, so to speak, and holding that the available evidence must be misleading is necessarily disrespectful of truth. In other words, it is difficult to arrive at many universal rules implied by the respect due the good of possession of truth (but there is at least one exceptionless norm here—the duty not to suppress truth).

But a further point can be added. There are three ways the evidence and the situation could stack up. (1) The evidence and situation might be such that one ought not to believe. (2) It might be such that it is permissible for one to believe, but also permissible for one *not* to believe. And (3), as I shall argue in more detail in a moment, the evidence and the situation might be such that one positively ought to believe. I think that the more the evidence points in the opposite direction, the less likely it is going to be that I positively *ought* to believe. In other words, where the available evidence does point one way, it may be *permissible* to believe the opposite but not likely that one would be *obliged* to do so.

In any case, I do not think God has left us where the available evidence does point in the direction opposite religious belief. In *fact* there are signs of credibility for God's revelation. Of course, what evidence is available to reasonably intelligent and conscientious inquirers may not be readily available to my next-door neighbor, partly because I may be too indifferent to speak to him or her about my belief and partly because my life may fail to manifest any of the splendor of the Christian faith. As Christians we have a responsibility to help make the faith credible. Faith, as well as redemption and sanctification, are communal.

My argument so far has been deductive. I have appealed to ethical principles to show that concern for a good other than truth can morally justify certainty. However, a confirming argument can be added: It seems that friendship, any friendship, is a good that can be realized *only by* going beyond the evidence. One does not have to be a dualist to see that crucial aspects of the person, such as a person's commitments, are not directly seen or experienced by other persons. And yet it is especially with these aspects of the person that one unites oneself in a friendship. In a friendship each friend not only cares for the other for the other's sake but also in some way chooses, freely accepts, the friendship, i.e., the relationship itself. This could not be so unless each friend accepted the other's (explicit or implicit) claim to be a friend, the other's claim to care for that friend. But this caring, this resolve to be a friend, is an aspect of the other person that cannot be directly experienced or proved to exist. In other words, reaching out to central aspects of another self in friendship requires one to go beyond the evidence, for the simple reason that central aspects of the self *are* beyond the evidence. One must be willing to accept, without proof, that the other is sincere in his or her offer or claim of friendship.

If this is true, then belief is not a necessary means toward friendship but is a part of it. Friendship is impossible without belief, without accepting something upon insufficient evidence, without an assent (acceptance of a proposition as true) not proportioned to the evidence. Now, friendship is a morally good thing. Therefore belief, going beyond the evidence, which is part of it, must also be morally permissible. Or, to state the argument differently, if the evidentialist objection against religious belief were effective, it would also show that friendship is immoral, which, I think, we can take to be a *reductio ad absurdum*.

According to the evidentialist objection, a belief must be epistemically warranted in order to be morally justified, and the evidence for religious belief is not sufficient to provide epistemic warrant for the degree of certainty characteristic of religious belief. Plantinga denies that evidence is needed for epistemic warrant and argues that belief in God is epistemically warranted in the absence of any evidence whatsoever. Others argue that there is sufficient evidence to render religious belief epistemically warranted. I have sided, however, with those who hold that it is incorrect to assume, as the evidentialists do, that a belief must be epistemically warranted in order to be morally justified. And I argue that concern for a good which the belief plus the belief's truth would help one realize can supplement evidence in order morally to justify certainty.

Why Reasons Are Needed for Religious Belief

I have said that evidence is needed for belief to be reasonable. But one might question this. Why are reasons needed at all for religious belief? Why not just say that concern for a good other than truth can by itself morally justify a belief?

Whenever one acts one ought to be concerned with how one's action is related to the various goods that will be affected by one's action. Epistemic warrant is secondary. The purpose of epistemic warrant is solely to ensure that one is more likely to possess more of the truth than one would if one's beliefs were not epistemically warranted. So, in every act of belief—an action that necessarily bears on the good of possession of truth—one ought to be concerned with how one's action affects the good of possession of truth. Therefore, if one stops and asks oneself whether one's religious belief is a good thing, then one morally ought to examine or consider how that belief is related to the good of possession of truth before one accepts or continues to accept it. That is, one morally ought to consider how likely it is that this belief is true. So if one considered whether one's religious belief is a good thing but failed to examine how this belief is likely to be related to truth, that is, if one failed to consider the evidence, then one would act without sufficient regard for the good of possession of truth. For this reason, for those who reflect on their religious belief to believe in the absence of reasons or evidence seems objectively immoral.

What about someone—for example, a child—who does not reflect on his religious belief, someone who believes spontaneously, without asking himself whether his religious belief is a good thing? Is such belief objectively immoral or improper? I believe the answer to this question is No, for there does not seem to be any general moral duty to scrutinize every spontaneous choice, and I see no special ground for there being such a duty in the area of choices which involve how one is related to the good of possession of truth. So, for those who reflect on their religious belief evidence is necessary.

How Evidence Or Reasons Function in Religious Belief

The main function of evidence or reasons in religious belief is not to show the truth of what is believed—for then *faith* would not be required. Nor is the main function of reasons even to show the truth of the factual proposition that God has spoken. Rather, the main function of reasons in religious belief is to show the truth of the moral proposition that I *ought* to believe.

Suppose a young man has just been in a serious motorcycle accident and has almost been killed. He is lying in the hospital bed with his head bandaged so that he can only see dimly and hear vaguely. Suppose also that the hospital authorities have informed him that his treatment will be discontinued unless he proves himself able to pay the bill, and he cannot do that. Further, the boy was estranged from his family a few years back: he left home, say, after a heated argument with his parents. While he is lying in the hospital bed a man comes into his room, claims to be his brother, and claims to have a message from their father that the father is in town and would like to visit the boy and receive the boy back into the family.

Since the boy cannot see or hear well, it is not immediately evident that the person speaking to him really is who he says he is. Maybe, the boy reflects, the man is really a doctor trying to make him feel good before he dies. So, it seems that the boy has a choice; he can believe the claim or not.[23] What should the boy do?

Perhaps he would listen to the alleged brother very carefully. Perhaps he would investigate him and what he says, to determine as well as he could whether he acts like his brother would act, whether he does and says just the kinds of things his brother would say and do. Similarly, people looking into the Christian claim should look at Jesus, his deeds, and his teaching to see whether Jesus does indeed act like a messenger from God, and whether he does and says the things that only a messenger of God would and could do.

The boy might scrutinize the alleged brother's message to see if it is the sort of message his father would give, whether, perhaps, it reveals things only his father would know, whether, that is, it has the marks or signs of really being a message from his father. Likewise, people can investigate Christian teaching and ask whether it has signs of having a divine origin.

Suppose that in the boy's case the evidence is not sufficient to compel the boy's assent. Suppose that the evidence by itself does not warrant absolute certainty, but, say, only a high degree of probability. Nevertheless, at some point there might be enough evidence so that the boy *ought* to accept the claim. The basic goods of friendship (with his father) and health (his own) could require this: that is, there could be situations in which anyone who has a love for these goods would accept the claim. The boy ought not to demand absolute proof before he accepts the claim made by the (alleged) brother. Were he to do so, this would indicate an ungracious or impious attitude toward his father and perhaps an insufficient regard for his own health.

Similarly, at some point the evidence for the Christian claim might be such that it does not provide epistemic warrant for absolute certainty, but is enough so that one morally *ought* to accept the proposal as certainly true. Just as in the boy's situation, so here, to demand absolute proof, to demand proof that would be proportionate to the assent asked of one, is lacking in the virtues of gratitude and piety, and perhaps an intelligent concern for one's ultimate welfare. And this shows how evidence or reasons function. They function, not to show with absolute certainty the theoretical proposition that the claim is a fact, but to show the *moral* proposition that I ought to believe. Without such reasons or signs of credibility it may still be permissible to believe. But it seems that reasons or signs of credibility are needed to put one in a situation where one morally ought to believe.

It is worth remembering that someone may have reasons for believing something without being able to articulate those reasons. The reasons for holding that God has indeed spoken, the signs of credibility, need not be the same as what one may read in an apologetics book. The sublimity and evident sanctity of Christian doctrine, of the liturgy, and of the Church (or members of the Church), these are signs indicating that the gospel is God's message and that the Church has a divine origin and guidance.

One's ability to see this sublimity or more-than-human quality is aided, or perhaps in most cases made possible, by divine help, i.e., divine grace. The recognition of beauty and the recognition of generosity in other people require an ability or "sense" on the part of the subject. An art critic sees beauty in a painting where others without his "aesthetic sense" will see only paint on a canvas. Someone who has no generosity himself is typically unable to see generosity in others, so that such a person continually asks, "What's that person's angle?" The beauty and generosity are really there, only they require an ability or sense on the part of the subject to be recognized.

In a similar way, the presence of the Holy Spirit in a human person enables her to recognize the sublime and the holy, or really, the divine, in the words and deeds of the prophets and of Jesus, handed on to us in the Church. Thus, of the Good Shepherd, Jesus says that he calls his own sheep by name and the sheep hear his voice, "and the sheep follow him because they know his voice. But a stranger they will not follow, but will flee from him because they do not know the voice of strangers" (Jn. 10:4–6).

In sum, I argued, first, that Plantinga's account of epistemic warrant is mistaken or incomplete, and I made the case for an internalist constraint upon the circumstances that provide epistemic warrant. Second, with this stricter or narrower view of epistemic warrant, I concluded that we should probably grant that the certainty of Christian belief does not have epistemic warrant (although it is not *ir*rational either). Third, I explained that the certainty of Christian belief is morally justified, because it is morally proper to believe partly for the sake of a good other than possession of truth, in the case of Christian belief, for the sake of the personal communion offered. Fourth, I argued that to be morally justified, the religious belief of reflective believers must have evidence or reasons, for only then does such an act of belief have the morally required regard for the basic good of possession of truth. And, finally, I described the function that reasons or evidence play in a reasonable act of faith: to make it clear to oneself that one's act of belief is a morally responsible act, or that one morally ought to believe.

NOTES

1. Alvin Plantinga, "Reason and Belief in God," in Alvin Plantinga and Nicholas Wolterstorff, eds., *Faith and Rationality: Reason and Belief in God* (Notre Dame: University of Notre Dame Press, 1983), p. 68.

2. See Roderick Chisholm, *The Problem of the Criterion* (Milwaukee: Marquette University Press, 1973), passim.

3. See Plantinga, "Reason and Belief in God." p. 80.

4. Alvin Plantinga, "The Prospects for Natural Theology," in James Tomberlin, ed., *Philosophical Perspectives* 5: Philosophy of Religion (Atascadero, Calif.: Ridgeview Press, 1991).

5. Thus Plantinga's position is quite different from that of William Alston. See William Alston, "Christian Experience and Christian Belief," in *Faith and Rationality.* pp. 103–134.

6. Plantinga, "Prospects for Natural Theology." Later in this article Plantinga adds that the cognitive mechanism must be designed with an aim toward truth, instead of, say, survival.

7. Ibid.

8. Plantinga, "Reason and Belief in God," pp. 78–82.

9. Ibid, p. 76.

10. And this is so, it seems to me, even if a powerful benevolent scientist, or God, has brought it about, perhaps by a pre-established harmony, that every time I seem to see a tree before me there *is* a tree before me.

11. A classical source for this internalist position is Thomas Aquinas, *Disputed Questions on Truth*, question 1, article 9. Cf. *Summa Theologiae*, part 1, question 16, article 2; *Commentary on Aristotle's Metaphysics*, book 6, number 1236. See also my "Aquinas on Knowledge of Truth and Existence," *New Scholasticism* 40 (1986), pp. 46–71. Some may argue for a weaker internalism, arguing that one need not be aware, in sensation, that one is sensing, but only be aware of the object, that is, experience the object, in order to be epistemically warranted. But it is not the object itself, or the fact, that warrants one's belief about the object or fact; rather, it is one's awareness of the object or fact that warrants one's belief. For example, if I see a tree in my peripheral vision but believe there is a tree for a different reason, then my belief that there is a tree is not thereby epistemically warranted. Thus, I must not only see the tree but I must be aware that I am seeing the tree, to be epistemically warranted in the belief that there is a tree. The internalist view I favor is essentially the same as Paul Moser's in his *Empirical Justification* (Dordrecht: D. Reidel, 1985).

12. Cf. William Alston, "Yes, Virginia, There Is a Real World," American Philosophical Association, Presidential Address, 1979; reprinted in Paul Moser, ed., *Reality in Focus* (Englewood Cliffs: Prentice Hall, 1990), pp. 17–33. See also Bernard Williams, "Deciding to Believe," in *Problems of the Self* (London: Cambridge University Press, 1973), pp. 136–151.

13. This is the objection of William Alston to the position I am advocating, and which Alston calls "consciousness internalism," as it was articulated by Paul Moser in *Empirical Justification*. See William Alston, "An Internalist Externalism," in *Epistemic Justification: Essays in the Theory of Knowledge* (Ithaca: Cornell University Press, 1989), p. 233.

14. She may even "find herself" having this belief despite herself—the hormone continues to exert its influence. But she resists this tendency because she has the belief, on the reflective level, that the chances of this belief being true are no greater than its being false.

15. This way of expressing the point was suggested to me by Linda Zagzebski.

16. By "evidence" here I mean either direct or indirect evidence. Thus, I disagree on a matter of fact with Dewey Hoitenga (see his "Knowledge, Belief, and Revelation: A Reply to Patrick Lee," *Faith and Philosophy* 8 (1991). pp. 244–251). I hold that, as a matter of fact, neither direct understanding, nor reasoning, nor experience provides sufficient evidence to satisfy the evidentialist. Unfortunately, Hoitenga's careful and lucid article, which is a reply to an earlier article of

mine on faith and reason, came to my attention too late for me to take it into account here.

17. See the argument of Anthony Kenny: "No doubt it may be reasonably believed that Moses and Jesus did and said many of the things ascribed to them in the Bible; but can it reasonably be believed with a degree of certainty resembling that of knowledge? Unless the relevant stories can be as certain as the commitment which faith demands of the believer, the commitment is, so far forth as it is faith, irrational; and if the belief is a commitment which is rationally in proportion to the support given by the history, it is, so far forth as it is rational, something less than faith" (Anthony Kenny, *Faith and Reason* [New York: Columbia University Press, 1983], p. 83).

18. See Germain Grisez, *The Way of the Lord Jesus*, vol. 1: *Christian Moral Principles* (Chicago: Franciscan Herald Press, 1983), chapter 20. A disanalogy with cases of human belief or faith troubles some people. In other cases of belief or faith it is usually obvious that the one to be believed is indeed speaking, while what is not obvious is that the one believed is honest or knowledgeable. In religious belief it is just the reverse—what is not obvious is that the one to be believed is speaking. It is not God's veracity that nonbelievers principally doubt, but that God has spoken at all. Nevertheless, in both cases one's act of believing goes beyond the evidence: in religious belief one's certainty goes beyond the evidence regarding whether God has spoken, but in belief of a human person one's belief goes beyond the evidence regarding the veracity of the speaker. So this disanalogy between religious belief and most other instances of belief cannot reasonably be a basis for deriding religious belief. In any case, we are primarily interested in the act of accepting that God has spoken, even though the believer accepts both that God has spoken and that what God says is true in a single act. For more on this, see my "Reasons and Religious Belief," *Faith and Philosophy* 6 (1989), pp. 19–34.

19. The situation is more complicated than what I have just said indicates. One is accepting the Christian claim not only for the sake of personal communion offered but also for the sake of possessing truth. Everyone knows that there is a sense in which to understand Christianity well one must live it. If Christianity is true then there is a whole world of truth that can be delved into and appreciated only by someone who lives the Christian life. Hence the good of possession of truth itself can call for assenting to propositions with more certainty than the evidence by itself would seem to warrant. It is as if there were a hypothesis that could only be tested by someone who believed in it 100 percent. Suppose to test a hypothesis in biology one had to live

many years on an isolated island, but that to survive on the island one had to believe the hypothesis with absolute certainty. The analogy is not exact, but the point is that there is, as it were, a short-run view of possession of truth and a long-run view. One's commitment to Christianity is motivated not only by the desire for the personal communion offered but also by the desire for truth, truth not in the narrow sense of this or that proposition conforming to reality, but truth in the sense of as deep and complete and true a picture of reality as possible.

20. Cf. Germain Grisez and Russell Shaw, *Beyond the New Morality,* 3rd ed. (Notre Dame: Notre Dame University Press, 1988); John Finnis, Joseph Boyle, Germain Grisez, *Nuclear Deterrence, Morality, and Realism* (Oxford: Claredon Press, 1987), pp. 175–197.

21. Cf. Grisez and Shaw, *Beyond,* chapters 11–14.

22. Perhaps the ethics of belief can be clarified by comparing it with the ethics of sex, although of course there are also important differences. The sexual power is naturally oriented to the procreative good, while the cognitive power is naturally oriented to the possession of truth. But just as it does not follow that the sexual power must be used *only for* procreation (no one argues this) so also it does not follow that one's cognitive acts, one's acts of believing, must be influenced only by the goal of truth. What follows is that all of the basic goods that could be affected by the action carrying out one's choice must be respected. Just as one ought not to negate the procreative good, so one ought not to negate the good of possession of truth. But just as the choice to engage in sex for the sake of expressing marital communion is morally good if it is a choice that does not disregard the procreative good; so it would seem that the choice to believe for the sake of a basic good which the belief, together with the truth of the belief, will help one realize, could in some instances be morally good, i.e., in those instances where truth is not disregarded. In neither case does there seem to be a choice to impede or destroy an instance of a basic good; in neither does it seem necessary that one disregard an instance of a basic good. The two areas seem to be similar in this respect. Yet there is this significant disanalogy. In sex, failing to procreate is only not realizing a good that could have been realized. With the intellect, if one's belief fails to attain truth, it is false, which means one's cognitive grasp upon reality is harmed (in an important matter) instead of simply not being realized. For this reason, while one need not intend or try to bring it about in every sexual act that conception result (it is enough that one's sexual act be open to conception, I would argue); in every act of belief one ought to hope and, if necessary, make an effort to bring it about that

one's belief is true. Still, in both sex and belief there seems to be nothing wrong in one's act being influenced simultaneously by more than one good.

23. I believe it is easy to see in such a case how someone can have a choice bearing on his belief even though it is not a bare choice to believe or to disbelieve. It is easy to imagine someone in the situation described having a choice to let the evidence he sees move him to assent (or dissent), to continue the inquiry, or to dismiss the claim on the grounds of lack of evidence.

6. Is Natural Theology Necessary for Theistic Knowledge?

John Greco

Reformed epistemologists argue that natural theology is not necessary for theistic knowledge. In the following passages, Alvin Plantinga cites Hermann Bavink and John Calvin approvingly.

> According to Bavink, then, a Christian's belief in the existence of God is not based upon proofs or arguments. By 'argument' here, I think he means arguments in the style of natural theology—the sort given by Aquinas and Scotus and later by Descartes, Leibniz, Clarke and others. And what he means to say, I think, is that Christians don't *need* such arguments. . . . [1]
> Here the subject for discussion is not belief in the existence of God, but belief that God is the author of the Scriptures; I think it is clear, however, that Calvin would say the same thing about belief in God's existence. The Christian doesn't *need* natural theology, either as the source of his confidence or to justify his belief.[2]

In a more recent work Plantinga writes:

> Hence natural theology is not needed for belief in God to have warrant; the natural view here, in fact, will be that many people *know* that there is such a person as God without believing on the basis of the arguments of natural theology.[3]

Finally, the same position is suggested by Nicholas Wolterstorff.

168

Could a person be justified in believing that God exists (or some other affirmative theistic proposition) without the justifying circumstance consisting in the fact that he believes it on the basis of other beliefs of his which he judges to be good evidence for it? Could a person whose belief that God exists is one of his immediate beliefs nonetheless be rationally justified in that belief? . . . I see no reason to suppose that holding the belief that God exists as one of one's immediate beliefs always represents some failure on one's part to govern one's assent as well as one ought.[4]

In this paper I shall argue that the Reformed claim about natural theology is incorrect. In other words, I will argue that natural theology *is* necessary for attaining knowledge regarding one's theistic beliefs. But to make this point it will be necessary to undertake an investigation into the nature of epistemic justification and knowledge. Both Plantinga and Wolterstorff defend theories of epistemic justification that make the Reformed claim about natural theology plausible. In other words, each philosopher defends a theory of epistemic justification such that, if it were correct, it would lend considerable force to the claim that natural theology is not necessary for attaining theistic knowledge. I will argue, however, that the conditions for justification defended by Plantinga and Wolterstorff are in both cases too weak. Further, I will argue that once the conditions for justification are appropriately strengthened, it becomes plausible that natural theology *is* required for theistic knowledge.

Before turning to the theories of Plantinga and Wolterstorff, it will be helpful to make some general remarks toward clarifying the Reformed claim concerning natural theology. First, theistic knowledge is here understood as knowledge regarding one's theistic beliefs. Theistic beliefs, in turn, are to be understood as beliefs involving propositions about a theistic God, the belief that God exists being the paradigm case. Other examples of theistic belief would be the belief that God created the universe and the belief that God loves me.

Secondly, I propose the following understanding of natural theology. Natural theology is the use of natural reason for the purpose of justifying the belief that God exists, or for the purpose of justifying other theistic beliefs. By "natural reason" I mean to include all and only those cognitive faculties that are typically thought to give us knowledge of the natural world. Thus natural reason includes sense perception, logical intuition, introspection, and memory, as well as deduction and induction.

Following the above remarks, we may state the Reformed claim about natural theology as follows.

(R)　　Natural theology, or the use of natural reason, is not necessary for acquiring knowledge regarding one's theistic beliefs.

I shall argue that (R) is false. More specifically, I shall consider two theories of epistemic justification that make (R) plausible but I shall reject each theory as too weak. Further, I shall argue that once the conditions for justification are appropriately strengthened, it becomes plausible that the use of natural reason is necessary for the justification of theistic beliefs. Since the argument is somewhat extended; it will be helpful to have the following outline.

1.　　Plantinga's theory of positive epistemic status is considered. The main idea is that epistemic justification is a result of properly functioning cognitive faculties in an appropriate environment.

2.　　Plantinga's theory is rejected as too weak. Specifically, there are cases where a belief B and a believer S satisfy Plantinga's conditions for positive epistemic status, but where S is epistemically irresponsible in believing B.

3.　　Wolterstorff's theory of rational belief is considered. The main idea is that a belief B is epistemically rational for S so long as S does not violate any epistemic obligation in believing B.

4.　　Wolterstorff's theory is also rejected as too weak. Wolterstorff's theory is credited with recognizing the importance of epistemic responsibility for knowledge, but it is argued that Wolterstorff is wrong about what such responsibility involves. Specifically, there are cases where S does not violate any epistemic obligation in believing B, but where S's believing B does not manifest the sort of internal excellence, or virtue, or praiseworthiness required for knowledge.

5.   A distinction is drawn between "S's not being blameworthy in believing B" and "S's being praiseworthy in believing B". It is argued that knowledge requires praiseworthiness rather then mere lack of blameworthiness. It is suggested that one source of epistemic praiseworthiness is coherence among one's beliefs and experiences, as well as among one's various cognitive faculties.

6.   Several kinds of coherence are distinguished, including social coherence, or coherence with one's epistemic community. It is argued that several important kinds of coherence are often lacking for theistic beliefs, and that only natural reason can provide the most important of these. I do not argue that coherence is always required for knowledge. Rather, I argue that it is required in "epistemically hostile conditions" and that the typical theist in the twentieth century is in such conditions regarding her theistic beliefs.

7.   Some further considerations are offered in favor of the requirement for coherence in epistemically hostile conditions. Specifically, such coherence is needed in order to meet potential defeaters of one's grounds for believing.

It is concluded that natural theology plays a necessary role in the justification of theistic beliefs. More specifically, the use of natural reason is necessary to provide the kind of coherence required for knowledge in epistemically hostile conditions.

1. PLANTINGA'S THEORY OF POSITIVE EPISTEMIC STATUS

Let us use the terms "epistemic justification" and "positive epistemic status" to designate whatever property it is, enough of which turns true belief into knowledge.[5] According to Plantinga, the core idea behind epistemic justification is proper function. A belief B has positive epistemic status for a person S if and only if B is the result of S's cognitive equipment functioning properly, i.e., working in the way it ought to work in producing and sustaining B.[6] This core idea must be qualified, however, in several ways. .

The first qualification arises because proper function is valuable only in the right sort of environment. Plantinga imagines that you take a trip to a planet revolving around Alpha Centauri. Conditions on this planet are epistemically different from conditions on earth. Specifically, cats on this planet are invisible to human beings. Moreover, Alpha Centurian cats emit a particular kind of radiation which, when it interacts with the human brain, causes the owner to believe that a dog is barking nearby. At some point during your trip an Alpha Centurian cat slinks by, and you form the belief that a dog is barking nearby. It is obvious that in this situation, your belief does not have positive epistemic status for you. Even if a dog actually is barking nearby (perhaps in a soundproof room), you certainly do not know that a dog is barking nearby. But now as Plantinga points out, there is nothing wrong with your cognitive faculties here. The problem is not with your faculties but with your environment. These considerations lead Plantinga to add a further condition for positive epistemic status. A belief B has positive epistemic status for S only if S's cognitive faculties are working properly in an appropriate environment.

The next qualification Plantinga makes concerns degrees of epistemic status. It is widely agreed that epistemic justification comes in degrees. Thus a belief B might be somewhat reasonable for S, or very certain for S, or something in between. Furthermore, we should agree that knowledge requires a very high degree of justification. How does Plantinga's theory account for these considerations? According to Plantinga, his belief in *modus ponens* has more positive epistemic status for him than his memory belief that forty years ago he owned a second-hand 16-gauge shotgun. Yet both beliefs result, it is presumed, from properly working faculties in an appropriate environment. What makes the difference in degree of epistemic status, Plantinga suggests, is that the first belief is held much more firmly than the second. When S's cognitive faculties are functioning properly, a belief has positive epistemic status to the degree that S finds herself inclined to accept it. Accordingly, S knows B only if S accepts B very firmly.

Finally, we should consider three additional points concerning the idea of proper function. First, proper function should not be confused with normal function. It might be perfectly normal, in some statistical sense, for human beings to form beliefs out of wishful thinking, or jealously, or low self-esteem. But one's faculties would not be functioning properly here, in the relevant evaluative sense.

Secondly, Plantinga distinguishes proper functioning from reliable functioning. A faculty might function reliably, even if it is not functioning as it was designed to function. But it is the *latter* concept, Plantinga thinks, that is essential to positive epistemic status. Plantinga makes the point by introducing the idea of a design plan, or specifications for design. When something is functioning properly, Plantinga explains, it functions so as to fulfill a particular purpose. But more than this, it functions so as to fulfill that purpose *in a particular way*. Thus a car is designed to provide transportation, and it is designed to do so in a particular way. There will be a complicated design plan, a set of specifications, which determines *how* the car is to fulfill its purpose. A similar point can be made with respect to our cognitive faculties. Such faculties are designed, at least in part, to provide us with true beliefs about ourselves, our environment, abstract objects, etc. But this does not happen in just any old way; our faculties are designed to perform their function in a particular way, according to a particular design.

This stipulation is important because it allows us to distinguish cognitive processes that are reliable by design from cognitive processes that are reliable *by accident*. Thus consider an example commonly offered against simple versions of reliabilism. By cruel coincidence, S has a brain tumor that reliably causes him to believe that he has a brain tumor. Imagine also, however, that S has no other evidence for his having a brain tumor, or imagine that he has evidence against this belief. Obviously S's belief that he has a brain tumor does not have positive epistemic status, even though, by hypothesis, it is reliably caused. The reason for this, Plantinga tells us, is that S's belief is reliable by accident. Although S's cognitive faculties are functioning reliably, they are not functioning in the way they are designed to function.

Finally, proper function is to be understood in relation to the purpose of producing true beliefs. It could be the case, and probably is the case, that our cognitive faculties are designed for *other* purposes than producing true beliefs. For example, we sometimes remember a painful experience as less painful than it really was. Similarly, we sometimes have more optimism in a difficult situation than is warranted by the evidence. This kind of cognitive functioning can be extremely useful, but for different purposes from obtaining true beliefs. Since this is so, we cannot say that positive epistemic status is the result of proper functioning in general. Positive epistemic status attaches to properly functioning faculties, or faculties working according to the design plan, insofar as that segment of the design plan is aimed at producing true beliefs.

The above considerations result in the following conditions for positive epistemic status. According to Plantinga, a belief B has positive epistemic status for S if and only if B is produced in S by his epistemic faculties working properly in an appropriate environment and insofar as the relevant segment of the design plan is aimed at producing true beliefs. Furthermore, B has more positive epistemic status than B^* for S if and only if B has positive epistemic status for S and either B^* does not or else S is more strongly inclined to believe B than B^*.

2. CRITICISM OF PLANTINGA'S THEORY

Plantinga's account of positive epistemic status has much to recommend it. It explains nicely why knowledge arises from the normal use of perception, memory, introspection, and deduction, but not from wishful thinking, neurotic worrying, or hasty generalization. As was noted above, the theory also constitutes an advance over simple versions of reliabilism and so avoids counterexamples such as the person with the brain tumor.

Moreover, Plantinga's theory of positive epistemic status serves the Reformed claim about natural theology embodied in (R). If Plantinga is correct, then the Reformed epistemologist is well on his way to the conclusion that natural theology is not needed for knowledge. The central idea is that we are endowed with a cognitive faculty for knowing God directly. One way to conceive such a faculty is as a kind of religious perception. According to this model, theistic belief is grounded by a religious experience of God or God's creations. Looking at the stars, the theist *feels* the presence of the Creator. While praying the theist *senses* that she is in communication with her Lord. Such perceptions then act as grounds for the theist's belief that the Creator is present, or that the theist is communicating with her Lord.[7] Alternatively, the faculty could be conceived on the analogy of logical intuition. Upon contemplating certain theistic propositions, the theist simply "sees" that they are true.[8] In either case, the relevant theistic beliefs qualify as properly basic. Such beliefs have positive epistemic status but do not owe this status either to inference or to any other faculty of natural reason.

Plantinga cites Calvin as holding just such a view of our cognitive faculties.

> "There is within the human mind, and indeed by natural instinct, an awareness of divinity." This we take to be beyond controversy. To prevent anyone from taking refuge in the pretense of ignorance, God himself has implanted in all men a certain understanding of his divine majesty. . . .[9]
>
> Therefore, since from the beginning of the world there has been no region, no city, in short, no household, that could do without religion, there lies in this a tacit confession of a sense of deity inscribed in the hearts of all. . . .[10]
>
> [There] is abundant testimony that this conviction, namely, that *there is some God,* is naturally inborn in all, and is fixed deep within, as it were in the very marrow.[11]

If such a cognitive faculty exists, and if Plantinga's conditions for positive epistemic status are correct, then clearly the relevant theistic beliefs will have positive epistemic status. Relevant beliefs that are both true and firmly believed will amount to knowledge. Finally, both positive epistemic status and knowledge will have been achieved without the use of natural reason.

As I have said above, Plantinga's theory has much to recommend it. I think it is clear, however, that Plantinga has not provided sufficient conditions for positive epistemic status. There are cases where a person S and a belief B satisfy the conditions laid down by Plantinga's theory, but B does not have positive epistemic status for S.

Consider Mary, who is in most respects a normal human being. The relevant difference is that Mary's cognitive faculties produce the belief in her that there is a tiger nearby whenever there is a tiger nearby, and even when Mary does not see, hear, or otherwise perceive a nearby tiger. Mary's brain is designed so as to be sensitive to an electromagnetic field emitted only by tigers, thus causing her to form the relevant belief in the appropriate situation. We can imagine that this cognitive feature was designed by natural processes of evolution, or that it was literally designed by a beneficent creator who realizes that tigers are dangerous to beings like Mary and therefore wishes to equip her with a reliable warning device. Now suppose that a tiger is walking nearby, and that Mary forms the appropriate belief. Add that Mary has no evidence that there is a tiger in the area, nor any evidence that she has such a faculty. Rather, she has considerable evidence *against* her belief that there are tigers in the area. Clearly, Mary's belief that there is a tiger nearby does not have a high degree of positive epistemic status in this situation, even though the belief is caused by properly functioning faculties in an appropriate environment. Mary does not *know* that there is a tiger nearby. In fact, in the situation described, Mary's belief is epistemically irresponsible. Given the way things look from Mary's point of view, she *ought not* believe that there is a tiger nearby.

Someone wishing to defend Plantinga's view might respond to the example as follows. Given that Mary has evidence against there being a tiger nearby, it is true that she ought not to believe that there is a tiger nearby. But this only shows that Mary's cognitive faculties are not working properly, since they are not sensitive to the relevant evidence. If her faculties were working properly, she would believe according to the evidence. The above example, therefore, is not a counterexample to the theory.

I think that there are two adequate responses to this line of reasoning. First, it seems to me that the counterexample does not depend on Mary's having evidence against her belief that there is a tiger nearby. If we were to revise the case so that Mary has no evidence either way, the revised case would still constitute an effective counterexample to Plantinga's theory. When Mary finds herself believing that there is a tiger nearby, but she has no grounds for her belief whatsoever, Mary clearly does not know that there is a tiger nearby.

But if this is not convincing to the defender of Plantinga's theory, we can consider a third scenario. Imagine that things are as in the first example above—Mary finds herself believing that there is a tiger nearby despite the fact that she has no evidence in favor of this belief and despite the fact that she has considerable evidence against it. Now add that Mary's creator knows that tigers are very very dangerous to beings like Mary. For this reason, he has designed Mary's cognitive faculties so that her tiger-warning faculty always overrides her evidence-gathering faculties whenever the faculties conflict. In this case we shall have to say that Mary's belief is the result of properly functioning faculties. But because Mary's belief is contrary to all the evidence she has, her belief cannot be considered knowledge. From Mary's point of view, she ought not to have the belief she does.[12]

In my opinion, the principle behind the above examples is this. It is possible for a belief to be caused by properly functioning faculties, but for that belief to be entirely irresponsible. Knowledge, however, requires epistemic responsibility. Here is another way to put the same point: The examples show that it is not enough for knowledge that S's cognitive faculties are *in fact* working properly. A requirement of knowledge is that things be working properly *from S's point of view*. A strong interpretation of this requirement would be that S know that her faculties are working properly. A weaker interpretation, and I think a more plausible one, is that it must not be the case that S ought to believe that her faculties are *not* working properly.

Of course Plantinga might deny that knowledge requires epistemic responsibility, and in fact he does deny this when "epistemic responsibility" is interpreted in terms of "fulfilling one's epistemic obligations." But it is important to note that Plantinga cannot avoid the above counterexamples simply by denying that knowledge requires epistemic responsibility. This is because it remains counterintuitive that Mary has knowledge in the above examples no matter how one interprets the principle behind the counterexamples. I have interpreted the examples as instances of epistemic irresponsibility, but I take it that the examples are counterexamples whether one accepts this interpretation or not.

Secondly, epistemic responsibility need not be understood in terms of fulfilling one's epistemic obligations. The more central point is that knowledge requires, in some important sense, that things be right from S's point of view. Whatever this sense may be, it seems plausible to say that things are importantly not right for Mary. According to Mary's point of view, there is no reason to think that there is a tiger nearby, and in the worse cases there are reasons against this belief. I have said that this state of affairs makes Mary's belief irresponsible. But we need not talk that way. And if we do talk that way, we need not understand that talk in terms of fulfilling one's epistemic obligations. The important point is that Mary does not have knowledge in the cases above, but she does fulfill Plantinga's conditions for positive epistemic status.

We may conclude that Plantinga's theory does not provide sufficient conditions for positive epistemic status. I have suggested that the reason is the Plantinga's conditions for positive epistemic status leave out any requirement concerning epistemic responsibility. But now we begin to see an opening for natural theology. It might be argued that natural theology is required for achieving epistemic responsibility regarding one's theistic beliefs, and it is for this reason that natural theology is required for knowledge. Or, to put it another way, we might argue that natural theology is needed to make things right from S's point of view. Wolterstorff, however, is one philosopher who has resisted this line of reasoning. Wolterstorff agrees that epistemic responsibility is required for knowledge, but he disagrees that natural theology is needed to achieve it. We may now turn to Wolterstorff's theory of rational belief, and his arguments that natural theology is not required for epistemic responsibility.

3. WOLTERSTORFF'S THEORY OF RATIONAL BELIEF

According to Wolterstorff, there is an analogy between epistemic justification and moral justification. Just as moral justification is a function of how well we do concerning our moral obligations, epistemic justification is a function of how well we do concerning our epistemic (or "noetic") obligations. In a nutshell, for Wolterstorff, rationally justified belief is belief that does not violate our noetic obligations.[13]

Several points regarding Wolterstorff's understanding of rational belief are worth mentioning here. First, Wolterstorff thinks that noetic obligations are obligations in a strong sense. Specifically, S has a noetic obligation not to believe B only if S can refrain from believing B. Secondly, rational belief, or belief that violates no noetic obligations, is a mark of epistemic *blamelessness* in the believer. Irrationality, on the other hand, is a mark of epistemic *blameworthiness*. According to Wolterstorff, a belief is rationally justified because the believer has governed her belief in an epistemically blameless way. Finally, we should point out that epistemic blamelessness is an "internal" virtue of the believer, a virtue that is grounded in the way things look from the believer's point of view. For this reason, Wolterstorff's theory avoids the main objection that was raised against Plantinga. It will be remembered that we faulted Plantinga's theory for not recognizing the importance of epistemic responsibility, or for not recognizing the importance of how things look from the believer's point of view.

According to Wolterstorff, to say that a belief is rational is to say that it is believed in a way which is epistemically blameless. Wolterstorff's next step is to formulate a criterion for rational belief. In other words, he wants to formulate necessary and sufficient conditions for a belief's having the status described above. What he ends up proposing, however, is not a criterion for all rational belief. Rather, he restricts his account to beliefs that are both "eluctable" and "innocently produced."

An eluctable belief is one that, in the relevant sense, S could have refrained form believing. An innocently produced belief is one that is not the result of S's culpably tampering with her cognitive faculties. Wolterstorff's proposed criterion for the relevant beliefs is as follows.

(C)   A person S is rational in his eluctable and innocently produced belief Bp if and only if S does believe p, and either:

(i) S neither has nor ought to have adequate reason to cease from believing p, and is not rationally obliged to believe that he *does* have adequate reason to cease; or

(ii) S does have adequate reason to cease from believing p but does not realize that he does, and is rationally justified in that.

According to Wolterstorff, the principle behind the above criterion is that a belief is innocent until proven guilty. Whereas the evidentialist proposes that a belief is rational only if one has adequate reason for believing it, Wolterstorff's proposal is, roughly, that a belief is rational unless one has adequate reason for not believing it. It is only this weaker criterion, Wolterstorff argues, that is demanded by the concept of blameless belief, or by the idea of not violating one's epistemic obligations.

As I have already suggested, the conditions for rational belief defended by Wolterstorff would serve the Reformed position well. If Wolterstorff's (C) is correct, then it is plausible that natural theology is not necessary for having rationally justified theistic beliefs. More specifically, it seems perfectly reasonable that there could be some person S, such that S has a theistic belief B, S does not believe B on the basis of natural reason, and S neither has nor ought to believe she has an adequate reason for ceasing to believe B.

Wolterstorff puts the case as follows.

What our criterion instructs us to consider is whether it is possible that there be a person who believes *immediately* that God exists, and at the same time has no adequate reason to surrender that belief. Or more precisely, whether there is a person who at the same time neither has nor ought to believe that he has any adequate reason to surrender that belief. Might a person's being in the situation of believing immediately that God exists represent no failure on his part to govern his beliefs as well as can rightly be demanded of him with respect to the goal of getting more amply in touch with reality? . . . I see no reason to suppose that people who hold as one of their immediate beliefs that God exists always have adequate reason to surrender that belief—or ought to believe that they do.[14]

4. CRITICISM OF WOLTERSTORFF'S POSITION

But has Wolterstorff given us an adequate account of positive epistemic status? Let us grant that there is some concept of rational belief, such that (C) represents an adequate criterion for the application of that concept. Has Wolterstorff also given us an adequate account of what it is that turns true belief into knowledge? That is the question which is relevant to (R) above, and which I want to investigate now.

Several considerations show that Wolterstorff has not given an adequate account of positive epistemic status. The first two considerations are pointed out by Wolterstorff himself, although he does not take them to count against his position. (This fact suggests that Wolterstorff does *not* take his theory to be about positive epistemic status.) First, on Wolterstorff's account, all ineluctable beliefs come out rationally justified. In other words, all beliefs that are such that S can not refrain from believing them are rationally justified for S. This is because, on Wolterstorff's account, rationally justified belief is blameless belief. but if S cannot help but believe B, then S cannot be blamed for believing B—it cannot be rightly demanded of S that she not believe B. But this leads to absurd consequences. Consider, for example, the case of poor Michael. Despite all evidence to the contrary and because of a severe neurosis, Michael cannot help but believe that his mother hates him. Add to this that it is in fact true that Michael's mother hates him, although she has never let on in any way. Certainly Michael's belief does not have a high degree of positive epistemic status for him. Michael does not *know* that his mother hates him.

Secondly, Wolterstorff's position entails that small children and idiots are rationally justified in all their beliefs. This is because they do not have the cognitive tools to recognize adequate reasons for giving up their beliefs and so are never obliged to recognize that they have such reasons. Clause (*ii*) of (*C*) ensures that children and idiots never fail to have rationally justified belief. But surely, small children and idiots do not know everything that they truly believe.

Thirdly, consider the following case. On the basis of wishful thinking, Jack believes that Jill is secretly in love with him. Jack has no evidence whatsoever in favor of this belief, but neither does he have any evidence against it. Add that Jack's not having evidence against his belief is not due to any epistemic wrongdoing on Jack's part. It is not the case that Jack ought to have reasons for giving up his belief, nor is he rationally obliged to believe that he does have such reasons. Jill simply does not let on about her feelings, one way or another. According to Wolterstorff's criterion for justified belief, Jack is rationally justified in believing that Jill is secretly in love with him. But this seems obviously wrong, considering that Jack has no evidence *in favor* of his belief. And this seems so even though Jack has no adequate reason for giving up his belief either.

Wolterstorff responds to this kind of example by claiming that Jack *does* have adequate reason for giving up his belief. Namely, any normal adult knows (or ought to know) that wishful thinking is an unreliable process for arriving at one's beliefs. But this being so, Jack has (or ought to have) an adequate reason for giving up his belief.[15] Wolterstorff's response, however, does not diffuse the kind of counterexample under consideration. This is because the response assumes, implausibly, that Jack can correctly identify the source of his belief in wishful thinking. But as a matter of fact, epistemic agents seldom have second-order beliefs about the sources of their beliefs. In the typical case we simply do not consider, nor ought we to consider, what cognitive processes are causally responsible for believing what we do. But if Wolterstorff disagrees on this point, we may simply stipulate that *Jack* does not consider the source of his belief in this case, whether the typical believer does so or not. Secondly, we may stipulate that Jack is not epistemically blameworthy for this, since he lacks the capacity to consider the source of his belief. But then it is false that Jack either has, or ought to have, a reason for giving up his belief that Jill secretly loves him. Yet clearly Jack does not know that Jill secretly loves him, even if Jill does secretly love him.

So far I have argued that both Plantinga and Wolterstorff fail to identify sufficient conditions for positive epistemic status. This suggests that the situation might be remedied by combining the conditions offered by each philosopher. The new suggestion is as follows. A belief B is justified for S if, and only if, S's believing B is the result of properly functioning cognitive faculties in an appropriate environment *and* S violates no epistemic obligation in believing B. We would then have the following revised conditions for innocently produced eluctable beliefs.

(C')   An eluctable and innocently produced belief B has positive epistemic status for S if both:

(i) S's faculties are functioning properly in an appropriate environment; and

(ii) S neither has nor ought to have adequate reason to cease from believing p, and is not rationally obliged to believe that he *does* have adequate reason to cease, or S does have adequate reason to cease from believing p but does not realize that he does and is rationally justified in that.

We should agree, however, that even this new suggestion offers conditions for positive epistemic status which are too weak. We may see this by considering the tiger examples brought against Plantinga's theory above. Although (C') deals nicely with the first version of our tiger example, it rules incorrectly on the second version. You will remember that in the first version of the example Mary had evidence against her belief that there is a tiger nearby. (C') therefore rules correctly that Mary's belief about the tiger does not have positive epistemic status. But (C') rules incorrectly in the second version of the example. In that version Mary finds herself with the belief that there is a tiger nearby, although there is no evidence either for or against this belief. It seems to me that Mary does not have positive epistemic status in this case, but according to (*C'*) she does.

Consider one last example. Suppose Mary *does* have substantial evidence against her belief that there is a tiger nearby, but that the belief is ineluctable. Further, we may imagine that the belief is ineluctable *by design,* perhaps to guarantee proper evasive action on Mary's part. If positive epistemic status is a function of proper function plus blamelessness, then Mary's belief has positive epistemic status in this case. But it is clear that her belief does not have such status, since Mary has substantial evidence that it is false and no evidence that it is true.[16]

These last examples show that we cannot save Wolterstorff's position by combining it with Plantinga's, or vice versa. Even if we combine the conditions offered by Wolterstorff and Plantinga, the resulting position would still be too weak. The next question is What is lacking? What is it that positive epistemic status requires, but that the believers in the above examples do not have? This question can be answered, I think, if we go back to something Wolterstorff says about rational belief. At one point in "Can Belief in God Be Rational If It Has No Foundations?" Wolterstorff says that rational belief is a mark of epistemic *praiseworthiness* in the believer.[17] But if we consider the examples concerning Mary, we see that there is nothing especially praiseworthy about her belief that there is a tiger nearby. This suggests that Wolterstorff is correct that knowledge requires praiseworthiness, but wrong about what is required for praiseworthiness. I want to investigate this contention below.

5. POSITIVE EPISTEMIC STATUS AND PRAISEWORTHINESS

Wolterstorff comments suggest the following definitions for the concepts of epistemic praise and blame.

> (*D1*)   *S* is epistemically praiseworthy for believing *B* if and only if *S* does not violate any noetic obligation by believing *B*.

(D2)   S is epistemically blameworthy for believing B if and only if S does violate some noetic obligation by believing B.

According to (D1) and (D2), someone who violates no noetic obligations in believing B is necessarily both praiseworthy and blameless regarding B. But then the above definitions miss an important distinction between "S's being praiseworthy in believing B" and "S's not being blameworthy in believing B." Specifically, we can not say that S is praiseworthy in *every* case where S violates no noetic obligation, for it might be the case that S does not *have* any noetic obligations, or if she does, that she has very few of them. I believe that this is the case with small children and idiots, as well as with people with ineluctable beliefs. Such persons violate no noetic obligations, in Wolterstorff's strong sense of "obligation," only because they fail to have noetic obligations. But this does not make these people praiseworthy, although it does make them not blameworthy.

Let us agree that positive epistemic status requires that a person be praiseworthy in her belief, and that being praiseworthy amounts to more than not being blameworthy. What does praiseworthiness amount to? We may approach an answer by noting that knowledge requires several kinds of excellence, or virtue, or merit. Some of these are more "objective" and "external," while others are more "subjective" and "internal." Let us consider this distinction in more detail.

The first kind of objective merit that knowledge requires is truth. In order for a belief to be knowledge, it must have the distinction of being true. A second kind of objective excellence has to do with de facto reliability. It must be true that, as a matter of fact, one's beliefs are a reliable indication of how things are. I believe that this is the kind of excellence that Plantinga is trying to explicate in his theory of positive epistemic status. But we noted that Plantinga's theory fails to capture a different requirement of knowledge. i.e., that things seem right from one's own point of view. This is a more subjective kind of virtue which is required by positive epistemic status, and which we try to capture by saying that one must be epistemically praiseworthy in one's beliefs. It is not enough that one's beliefs are in fact true, or even reliably tied to the truth; it must also be that they have merit from one's own point of view. Furthermore, such merit involves more than freedom from blame. Even if freedom from blame is a kind of subjective (internal) virtue, there are other kinds of subjective (internal) virtue which knowledge requires and which go beyond mere freedom from blame.[18]

At best, the above remarks about epistemic praiseworthiness are groping and vague. What we need is a better understanding of what such internal excellence or virtue amounts to, and why natural theology is necessary to get it regarding theistic beliefs. But in what follows I will not attempt to offer a full account of epistemic praiseworthiness. Rather, I want to suggest that there are many finds of internal excellence which are important for knowledge, and I want to focus on one of these that seems particularly relevant to the present topic. My suggestion will be that an important kind of internal excellence is constituted by coherence among one's beliefs and experiences, as well as among one's epistemic faculties. Further, in order to achieve such coherence for theistic beliefs, natural reason must play a crucial role. If both of these contentions are correct, then the Reformed claim about natural theology embodied in (R) is false. It will turn out that the use of natural reason is necessary for knowledge regarding one's theistic beliefs.

6. COHERENCE AND NATURAL REASON

I have suggested that knowledge requires various kinds of epistemic praiseworthiness in one's belief, and that one important kind of praiseworthiness is constituted by a coherence among one's beliefs and experiences, as well as among one's cognitive faculties. In order to understand better what I have in mind, let us consider some examples in which such coherence is lacking.

First, we may consider the examples involving Mary. In each of those cases Mary's special tiger-detecting faculty was out of sync with her other cognitive faculties. In the worst of those cases Mary's faculties gave conflicting information about the presence of tigers. In the best cases the faculties merely failed to support each other.

But we do not need recourse to such unusual cognitive apparatus in order to see cases of incoherence. Consider Henry, who is perfectly normal regarding his faculties for detecting tigers. Consider the case where Henry has an auditory experience as if there were a tiger nearby but, due to unusually good camouflaging, he has no visual experience of a tiger. Or consider the case where Henry is part of a group of people, some of whom report that they hear a tiger nearby, others of whom report that they do not. In the first case there is a sort of incoherence among Henry's own faculties, while in the second case there is an incoherence with the faculties of others.

The above examples show that coherence comes in many kinds. Below I want to define several of these kinds, some of which are more epistemically valuable than others. I shall then argue that natural theology is necessary to provide the most valuable of these for theistic beliefs.

A1. A belief *B* has negative coherence for *S* with respect to a group of beliefs and experiences *G* = the beliefs and experiences in *G* do not support not-*B*.

A2. A belief *B* has positive coherence for *S* with respect to a group of beliefs and experiences *G* = the beliefs and experiences in *G* support *B*.

B1. A belief *B* has intrafaculty coherence for *S* = *B* is produced by cognitive faculty *F* of *S*, and *B* has negative or positive coherence for *S* among the beliefs produced or sustained by *F*.

B2. A belief *B* has interfaculty coherence for *S* = *B* is produced by cognitive faculty *F* of *S*, and *B* has negative or positive coherence for *S* among the beliefs produced or sustained by faculties other than *F*.

C1. A belief *B* has personal coherence for *S* = *B*'s coherence of kinds *A1* through *B2* involves beliefs and faculties of *S*.

C2. A belief *B* has social coherence for *S* = *B*'s coherence of kinds *A1* through *B2* involves beliefs and faculties of other believers in *S*'s epistemic community.

D1.   A belief *B* has narrow coherence for *S* = *B*'s coherence of kinds *A1* through *C2* involves few faculties and beliefs.

D2.   A belief *B* has wide coherence for *S* = *B*'s coherence of kinds *A1* through *C2* involves many faculties and beliefs.

It should be evident that it is better to have positive coherence than merely negative coherence. Likewise, it is better to have interfaculty coherence than merely intrafaculty coherence, social coherence rather than merely personal coherence, and wide coherence rather than merely narrow coherence. In each case, to have the former kind of coherence for one's belief is to be in an epistemically more praiseworthy position than to have merely the latter kind of coherence.

Let us agree that having *A2, B2, C2,* and *D2* coherence is in each case preferable to having merely *A1, B1, C1* or *D1* coherence, meaning that in each case having the former constitutes a greater degree of internal epistemic excellence than having merely the latter. Two questions remained to be answered: (1) Is having the type-2 virtues for one's belief necessary for having knowledge?; and (2) Is natural theology, or the use of natural reason, necessary for achieving such virtues for theistic beliefs?

I will not argue that having all of the type-2 virtues is always necessary for a belief to be knowledge. I think that many philosophers have thought that having all these virtues is always necessary for knowledge, although it is not clear to me that they are right about this. Fortunately, we do not have to settle that issue here, for it will be sufficient for our purposes to argue the following weaker thesis: at least some type-2 virtues are needed for knowledge in some situations. More specifically, I want to argue that the kind of praiseworthiness provided by type-2 coherence is needed in "epistemically hostile conditions," defined as conditions where one has grounds for doubting the reliability of one's cognitive faculties.[19]

In support of this view we may reconsider the example of Henry. Remember that Henry has an auditory experience as if there were a tiger nearby, but he has no visual experience of a tiger, due to unusually good camouflaging. Moreover, while some of the people in Henry's group are reporting similar auditory experiences, others are reporting that they do not hear a tiger. We should agree that in those circumstances, Henry does not know that there is a tiger nearby, even though it is true that there is a tiger nearby. A plausible explanation for this is that Henry has grounds for doubting that his auditory faculty is reliable here. He is in what we have called epistemically hostile conditions. In order for Henry to have knowledge, this situation must be corrected. In other words, Henry needs the kind of coherence manifested by the type-2 virtues. He cannot rely on his auditory faculty alone but must bring it into coherence with his other cognitive faculties and with those of others in the group. Against Plantinga, this is so even if Henry's auditory faculty is in fact functioning properly. Against Wolterstorff, this is so even if Henry is not capable of correcting the situation, and even if Henry cannot be blamed for not correcting the situation.[20]

I want to argue now that the theist is in epistemically hostile conditions regarding his theistic beliefs, and that natural theology is necessary for the kind of coherence that is required for knowledge in such conditions.

First, when we say that the theist is in epistemically hostile conditions, we must qualify that statement by acknowledging that not all theists are created equal, or are placed in equally advantageous circumstances. In what follows I have in mind the typical theist, in typical conditions for this time (meaning late twentieth century) and this place (meaning the Western world). Secondly, let us agree with Plantinga that the typical theist is endowed with a reliable cognitive faculty for ascertaining a certain range of theistic beliefs, so that the typical theist in typical conditions does believe in God as the result of properly functioning cognitive faculties in an appropriate environment. Finally, we must imagine a theist who is in no way depending on the use of natural reason in the justification of his theistic belief. The point here is to ask whether theistic belief can be knowledge *without* the use of natural reason. What are the epistemic conditions like for such a theist, and what kind of internal virtues do his theistic beliefs have?

One important point is that such a theist, call him T, will have prima facie grounds *against* his theistic beliefs. This is because T's faculties of natural reason provide him with evidence of evil, as well as evidence of a lack of belief by others. Moreover, this latter evidence may be broken down into two kinds. First, many people in T's epistemic community do not believe that God exists, or believe that God does not exist. Secondly, many in T's community share his belief that God exists, but differ with T in other of their theistic beliefs. And now the important conclusion to draw is this: All of these considerations will amount to prima facie grounds for doubting the reliability of T's cognitive faculties for forming theistic beliefs. The average theist is in what we have called "epistemically hostile conditions" regarding his theistic beliefs.

What internal virtues do T's theistic beliefs have in these conditions? First, T's theistic beliefs do not have positive interfaculty coherence for T, and this is so by hypothesis. For by hypothesis, none of the grounds which T has for his theistic beliefs are provided by T's faculties of natural reason. Secondly, T's theistic beliefs do not even have negative interfaculty coherence since, as noted above, his faculties of natural reason provide him with evidence *against* his theistic beliefs. Thirdly, T's theistic beliefs have little social coherence for T, since there are many others in the Western world at this time who do not share T's theistic beliefs; there are in fact many who accept the denial of those beliefs. Finally, to the extent that T's theistic beliefs lack these various kinds of coherence, the coherence which T's theistic beliefs do enjoy is narrow rather than wide. T's theistic beliefs have little coherence with T's natural beliefs and faculties, or with the beliefs and faculties of the wider community. For the most part, the only coherence which T's theistic beliefs do enjoy is narrow, personal, intrafaculty coherence.

We may note at this point the T's situation is not very unlike Henry's. Henry's belief that there is a tiger nearby also enjoys only narrow, personal, intrafaculty coherence, such coherence being provided by his auditory faculty, but by no other cognitive faculty of his. Now we agreed that Henry does not know that there is a tiger nearby. The meager coherence which his belief enjoys does not amount to the epistemic excellence required for knowledge, or at least not in such adverse circumstances. I believe that the same should be said about our theist, *T*.

Can natural theology improve *T*'s epistemic position regarding *T*'s theistic beliefs? It looks as if the use of natural reason is the only thing that *could* improve *T*'s position. For it is only by bringing in natural reason that *T* could build the sort of coherence that the situation requires. Let us consider how a natural theologian would do in *T*'s circumstances. Assuming that she is successful in her natural theology, we could say the following.[21]

First, by constructing counterarguments to natural evidence against her theistic beliefs, the natural theologian could use natural reason to build negative interfaculty coherence between her nonnatural theistic faculty and her faculties of natural reason. This could be done either by constructing arguments which undermine or eliminate the evidence against her theistic beliefs, or by constructing arguments which outweigh that evidence. Secondly, by using natural reason to construct arguments in favor of her theistic beliefs, the natural theologian could build positive interfaculty coherence. Thirdly, success by the natural theologian in the previous two tasks could also improve social coherence for her theistic beliefs. This will be so to the extent that her arguments are convincing to others in her epistemic community. Where natural theology is successful, there will be fewer atheists in the epistemic community, and fewer theists with conflicting beliefs, than there otherwise would be. Finally, to the extent that the natural theologian is successful in building coherence as outlined above, narrow coherence for her theistic beliefs will be turned into wider coherence. Unlike those of our theist *T* above, the theistic beliefs of a successful natural theologian would enjoy wide coherence with her natural beliefs and faculties, and at least wider coherence with the beliefs and faculties of others in her epistemic community.

In sum, successful natural theology would provide exactly the kinds of coherence that I have argued are necessary for knowledge in epistemically hostile conditions. Further, it is hard to see what else could provide the kinds of coherence that are needed.[22] We may therefore conclude that natural theology is necessary for theistic knowledge, at least in epistemically hostile conditions.

7. SOME FURTHER CONSIDERATIONS IN FAVOR OF TYPE-2 COHERENCE

I said above that I wished to defend the importance of type-2 kinds of coherence without defending a full-blown theory of epistemic praiseworthiness. Nevertheless, in this final section of the paper I would like to go a little deeper. Again, these considerations will not require, or lead me into, a complete theory of either epistemic praiseworthiness or positive epistemic status. Rather, I want to argue that any adequate theory of positive epistemic status will ground the requirement for type-2 coherence in epistemically hostile conditions.

In order to make the argument, it will be helpful to introduce a stipulative definition. Let us define a "potential defeater":

> d is a potential defeater of S's grounds for believing p = (i) S believes that d is true; (ii) S's grounds for believing p support p to the degree required for knowledge; and (iii) if d were added to S's grounds for believing p, those grounds would no longer support p to the degree required for knowledge.

The notion of a potential defeater is relevant to our topic in the following way: When one is in epistemically hostile conditions, one is thereby in a situation where there are potential defeaters for one's knowledge.

Consider for example the situation where Henry believes that there is a tiger because he seems to hear a tiger, but where this belief is contradicted by sight and by others in Henry's group. In this situation, the fact that Henry does not see a tiger where he would expect to see one counts as a potential defeater of his grounds for believing that there is a tiger. In other words, even though seeming to hear a tiger would normally support one's belief that there is a tiger nearby, such grounds for one's belief can be undermined. By adding to Henry's grounds that he does not see a tiger where he would expect to, it is plausible that this widened evidential base no longer supports the belief that there is a tiger nearby. The fact that others in Henry's group do not hear or see a tiger also counts as a potential defeater of Henry's grounds.

But these considerations do not entail that Henry can never have knowledge that there is a tiger nearby. This is because potential defeaters can be defeated. In other words, Henry can further widen his grounds so that they again support his belief to the degree required for knowledge. This could be done by eliminating a potential defeater, or by undermining it, or by gathering evidence which outweighs it.

For example, consider the potential defeater that others in Henry's group do not hear a tiger. Henry might be able to look closer, so that his sight does clearly reveal an initially well-camouflaged tiger. This new evidence, I presume, would *outweigh* the potential defeater under consideration. If Henry can clearly see that there is a tiger nearby, this would outweigh the defeater that not everyone can hear a tiger. Or suppose that other members in the group cannot hear a tiger, but that Henry has grounds for believing that their hearing is not reliable under the present conditions. These grounds would tend to *undermine* the potential defeater that others in the group cannot hear a tiger. Finally, consider the potential defeater that Henry does not see a tiger where he would expect to. If Henry were to take a closer look, so that he does clearly see an initially well-camouflaged tiger nearby, this would *eliminate* the potential defeater in question.

But now all of this can be applied to theistic belief as well. For if the theist is in epistemically hostile conditions regarding his theistic belief, there are potential defeaters of his grounds for believing. This is because, by definition, epistemically hostile conditions are conditions where one has reasons to doubt the reliability of one's cognitive faculties. So even if Plantinga is correct that we have a religious faculty which spontaneously gives rise to a belief in God, and even if this faculty would be sufficient for providing positive epistemic status where all things are equal, in epistemically hostile conditions all things are not equal. Specifically, in epistemically hostile conditions there are reasons to doubt one's cognitive faculties, and so there are potential defeaters of one's grounds for believing.

As was the case with Henry, the theist can have knowledge concerning his theistic beliefs only if she can defeat the potential defeaters which mark epistemically hostile conditions. But this is exactly what successful natural theology would do. Depending on the particular defeater in question, and the particular kind of natural theology, successful natural theology would either undermine or outweigh potential defeaters, or eliminate them altogether. For example, natural theology that addresses the problem of evil tries to undermine or eliminate potential defeaters arising from the existence of evil in the world. Positive natural theology, or natural theology that attempts to establish that God exists, tries to outweigh potential defeaters by adding strength to the grounds in favor of theistic belief. As I have argued above, building type-2 coherence for one's theistic beliefs amounts to performing exactly these kinds of tasks.

But the issue might be pressed. Why is it necessary for knowledge that one's grounds meet potential defeaters? In order to answer this question, we may consider that there have been two main traditions in epistemology regarding positive epistemic status. One of these main traditions understands positive epistemic status in terms of epistemic responsibility, while the other understands positive epistemic status in terms of de facto reliability. Either tradition, I will argue, provides a rationale for why the grounds for one's knowledge must meet potential defeaters.

According to the first tradition, being able to meet all potential defeaters is simply a requirement of epistemic responsibility. According to this tradition, positive epistemic status is essentially a matter of epistemically responsible belief formation, and epistemically responsible belief formation is largely a matter of having good grounds for one's beliefs. But having *good* grounds means having grounds which are good enough to meet potential defeaters. Put another way, epistemic responsibility is essentially a matter of things being right form one's own point of view. But if one's cognitive perspective contains undefeated defeaters, then things will not be right from one's own point of view. From within one's own perspective, there will be reason to doubt the adequacy of one's grounds for belief.

According to the second main tradition, positive epistemic status is essentially a matter of de facto reliable belief formation. Understanding positive epistemic status in this way does not directly give rise to the requirement of meeting potential defeaters, but it does give rise to such a requirement indirectly. We may see this if we consider some facts about human belief formation. It is just a fact of our human condition, for example, that we are not very reliable when we cannot meet potential defeaters of the grounds for our beliefs. In general, when we form our beliefs on the basis of grounds that do not eliminate or outweigh potential defeaters, we are often wrong about what we believe. According to this line of reasoning, the requirement that we can meet potential defeaters acts as a kind of guarantee of general reliability. Of course we might be able to describe some belief-forming processes very narrowly, so that they are reliable even when they do not satisfy the requirement of meeting potential defeaters. but it is plausible that knowledge requires a more general kind of reliability, and that this more general kind of reliability requires being able to meet potential defeaters.[23]

Therefore, either of the two main traditions in epistemology provides a rationale for the idea that knowledge requires meeting potential defeaters. In ny own view, positive epistemic status requires both reliability and responsibility, and so the need for type-2 coherence in epistemically hostile conditions is twofold.

In conclusion, natural theology, or the use of natural reason, is necessary for knowledge regarding one's theistic beliefs, at least in epistemically hostile conditions. This is because only natural theology could build the kinds of coherence required for knowledge in such conditions. Put another way, knowledge in epistemically hostile conditions requires a range of internal epistemic excellences or virtues to meet potential defeaters, and the use of natural reason is required for achieving at least some important kinds of these excellences or virtues.[24]

NOTES

1. Alvin Plantinga, "The Reformed Objection to Natural Theology," *Proceedings of the American Catholic Philosophical Association* 54 (1980), p. 50.

2. Ibid., p. 53.

3. Alvin Plantinga, "The Prospects for Natural Theology," in *Philosophical Perspectives* 5: *Philosophy of Religion*, ed. James Tomberlin (Atascadero, Calif.: Ridgeview Press, 1991).

4. Nicholas Wolterstorff, "Can Belief in God Be Rational If It Has No Foundations?" in *Faith and Rationality*, ed. Alvin Plantinga and Nicholas Wolterstorff (Notre Dame, Ind.: University of Notre Dame Press, 1983), pp. 175–176. I say that the position is "suggested" by Wolterstorff because it is not clear that Wolterstorff thinks that justified true belief is knowledge.

5. Plantinga suggests the term "proper epistemic status" because it is neutral between internalist and externalist theories of knowledge. For aesthetic purposes, however, I will use "positive epistemic status," "epistemic justification," and "justification" interchangeably, all to designate whatever property it is that, in sufficient degree, turns true belief into knowledge.

6. Alvin Plantinga, "Positive Epistemic Status and Proper Function," in *Philosophical Perspectives*, vol. 2: *Epistemology*, ed. James Tomberlin (Atascadero: Ridgeview Press, 1988), p. 32. The following exposition of Plantinga's theory of positive epistemic status is drawn from his "Positive Epistemic Status"; "Epistemic Justification," *Nous* 20 (1986); and "Justification and Theism," *Faith and Philosophy* 4 (1987).

7. This model is implied in Alvin Plantinga, "Reason and Belief in God," in *Faith and Rationality*, ed. Alvin Plantinga and Nicholas Wolterstorff (Notre Dame, Ind.: University of Notre Dame Press, 1983). See also William Alston, "Christian Experience and Christian Belief," in *Faith and Rationality*, ed. Alvin Plantinga and Nicholas Wolterstorff (Notre Dame, Ind.: University of Notre Dame Press, 1983); and William Alston, "The Perception of God," *Philosophical Topics* 16 (1988).

8. This model is suggested in George Mavrodes, "The Stranger," in *Faith and Rationality*, ed. Alvin Plantinga and Nicholas Wolterstorff (Notre Dame, Ind.: University of Notre Dame Press, 1983).

9. John Calvin, quoted in Plantinga, "Reason and Belief," p. 65.

10. Plantinga, "Reason and Belief," p. 66.

11. Ibid.

12. The present example does not violate Plantinga's condition that the relevant segment of the design plan be aimed at producing true beliefs. For although the design plan is here aimed at Mary's preservation, that goal is achieved by means of producing true beliefs about tigers.

13. Wolterstorff, "Can Belief in God Be Rational?" p. 144. Here Wolterstorff is explaining Locke's view, but later he agrees. It is not clear that Wolterstorff identifies rational belief with what we have been calling "positive epistemic status." However, other authors *have* made this identification. For a discussion of responsibilist theories of epistemic justification, see my "Internalism and Epistemically Responsible Belief," *Synthese* 85 (1990). In any case, such a position seems worthy of investigation.

14. Wolterstorff, "Can Belief in God Be Rational?" p. 176.

15. Ibid., p. 172.

16. Once again, the example cannot be avoided because it violates Plantinga's condition that the design plan be aimed at producing true belief. For in the example, the plan *is* aimed at producing true belief, although it is also aimed at Mary's preservation. These two aims are not inconsistent.

17. Wolterstorff, "Can Belief in God Be Rational?" p. 145; he contradicts this at p. 186, n. 19.

18. Plantinga argues against internalist theories of positive epistemic status in his "Epistemic Justification" and "Positive Epistemic Status and Proper Function." But there his arguments are directed against the claim that internal virtues are by themselves sufficient for positive epistemic status. Since this is not my claim, the present position is not vulnerable to Plantinga's objections.

19. The need for type-2 coherence in such conditions can be accounted for in terms of traditional ideas about justification. First, it could be argued that coherence is necessary to defend prima facie justification against grounds for doubt by either undermining the force of such grounds or providing grounds which outweigh their force. Alternatively, it could be argued that coherence is needed to boost a low degree of justification to a higher degree required for knowledge. I shall say more about this below.

20. It would be too strong to require that Henry achieve all the coherence that is logically possible, so that all his cognitive faculties be brought into positive coherence, with everyone in the group agreeing that there is a tiger. What is needed is that "enough" coherence is achieved, although I shall not attempt to turn this platitude into something more informative.

21. It is, of course, beyond the scope of this paper to inquire whether or not natural theology can be successful in the ways required. This paper is restricted to the question of whether natural theology is required for theistic knowledge and does not investigate the question of whether there is theistic knowledge.

22. William Alston and Keith De Rose have suggested to me that several theistic faculties would do the same job. But as far as I know, no Reformed philosophers have argued that we have such faculties in the required number or variety.

23. The requirement of this more general kind of reliability is closely connected with the generality problem for reliabilist theories of knowledge. For a statement of that problem and its relevance to Plantinga's position, see my "Virtue Epistemology," in *The Blackwell Companion to Epistemology*, ed. Jonathan Dancy and Ernest Sosa (Oxford: Basil Blackwell, 1991).

24. It will be obvious that in this paper I am greatly indebted to the work of Alvin Plantinga and Nicholas Wolterstorff. Also, I would like to thank Linda Zagzebski, Dean Zimmerman, Brian Leftow, and James McBride for their helpful comments on earlier drafts of the paper.

7. Religious Knowledge and the Virtues of the Mind

Linda Zagzebski

1. SOME FEATURES OF REFORMED EPISTEMOLOGY

Since the publication of *Faith and Rationality* a lot of attention has been focused on the claims of Alvin Plantinga, Nicholas Wolterstorff, and George Mavrodes that religious belief can be rational or justified without evidence and without foundations in other justified beliefs. This position has important negative implications for epistemic theory, in particular, the consequence that certain forms of evidentialism and classical foundationalism are false. More recently, Plantinga has proposed a set of positive criteria for epistemic justification and knowledge and has argued that his proposal is preferable to those of other contemporary epistemologists such as Chisholm, Goldman, Nozick, and Dretske.

Plantinga uses the terms "positive epistemic status" and, more recently, "warrant" to refer to that normative quality that a true belief must have enough of to be a case of knowledge.[1] He prefers either term to "justified" since he says the concept of justification is a deontological one, implying the fulfillment of duty, whereas it ought to be an open question whether or not the quality that converts true belief into knowledge is deontological. In this paper I shall argue that the quality that converts true belief into knowledge is not a property of the belief at all, but a property of the believer, so neither "justification" nor

199

"warrant" is an appropriate term for this property. I will, however, speak derivatively of beliefs being "justified" or "warranted," and will use the terms interchangeably, although I agree with Plantinga that such a property involves more than fulfilling a duty.[2]

Plantinga's proposed criterion for warrant is as follows:

> A belief B has warrant for S if and only if that belief is produced in S by his epistemic faculties working properly (in an appropriate environment); and (in those circumstances) B has more warrant than B* for S if and only if B has warrant for S and either B* does not or else S is more strongly inclined to believe B than B*.[3]

Plantinga has argued that on the above criterion theistic belief has warrant for many people and, in fact, has a fairly high degree of such status. Wolterstorff speaks approvingly of Plantinga's criterion,[4] and Mavrodes has used an approach similar to Plantinga's in defending the justification of religious belief based on revelation.[5]

So in these and other recent works by Reformed Epistemologists a positive theory of knowledge and justification has begun to take shape. The theory has a number of interesting aspects, but I would like to call attention to three of its features that I think are important if we want to compare it to other current epistemic theories, on the one hand, and to traditional Catholic theology, on the other.

First, like almost all contemporary American epistemology, Reformed Epistemology focuses on individual beliefs—where by a "belief" is meant a particular state of believing, not the proposition believed—and it searches for the properties of a belief that convert it into knowledge. We already saw this feature explicitly in Plantinga's criterion for epistemic warrant. So just as most contemporary moral theory is act-based, most contemporary epistemology is belief-based, and Reformed Epistemology is no exception. The property of being justified or warranted or having positive epistemic status is a property of a belief, just as being right is a property of an act, and as long as a belief has the right properties, it is a case of knowledge. Of course, it may be recognized that certain properties of the believer are relevant to the status of the belief, just as it is often recognized that certain properties of the agent may be relevant to the rightness of an act; nonetheless, the analysis focuses on the individual belief and the most important epistemic concepts are analyzed in terms of properties of an individual belief.

Second, Reformed Epistemology is largely externalist. The distinction between internalism and externalism has become important in recent epistemology and the distinction is not precise. The basic idea is that a theory is internalist as long as the criteria for justification or warrant are accessible to the consciousness of the believer. Since there are stronger and weaker forms of accessibility, there are stronger and weaker forms of internalism. Internalism has dominated modern epistemology until recently, its primary contemporary exponent being Roderick Chisholm. Externalist theories, such as the reliabilism of Goldman, Nozick, and Dretske, define justification in terms of the relation between a belief and features of the world that typically are not accessible to consciousness, such as the causal process generating the belief. There are also theories that combine internal and external features in the criteria for justification, such as Alston's "internalist externalism."[6]

On internalist theories, if a belief is justified, the believer is in a position to be aware of its justifying feature and, on most internalist theories, is in a position to be aware of the justifying feature as justifying. It cannot happen that two believers are with respect to a certain belief in exactly the same mental state as far as they can tell, and yet one is justified and the other not. On externalist theories the believer will often have no awareness of those properties of the belief that make it justified and consequently will not be in a position to know or justifiably believe that it is justified. Two believers could be relative to a certain belief in exactly the same mental state as far as they can tell, and yet one would be justified in the belief and the other not.

Generally, internalist theories hold that whether a belief has justification or warrant is within the control of the believer. This, of course, does not automatically follow from the claim that the conditions for justification are accessible to consciousness, but in the most historically important versions of internalism, including Chisholm's, the motivation to make justification something within our voluntary control is so strong it could plausibly be maintained that the internalism follows from the position that we control justification and warrant rather than the reverse.

Externalist theories, in contrast, present criteria for justification that we do not control, and again, although no necessary connection exists between externality and lack of control, the belief in lack of control tends to be associated with the belief in externalism. Because of the sense in which those features of us and our beliefs that we do not control are a matter of luck, we can say that the more externalist a theory is, the more room is made for epistemic luck.

An important motivation driving externalist theories is the desire to avoid skepticism; in fact, this is one of its most attractive features. As long as nature has insured that we respond to stimuli from the external world in a way that reliably leads to truth, our beliefs are warranted, and if they are true, as they often are, we have knowledge. Indeed, Plantinga began to develop his epistemic theory as a response to religious skepticism. His work demonstrates that the generous optimism about knowledge that we find in this school of epistemology can be rather easily extended to religious knowledge.

Now in what way is Reformed Epistemology externalist and nonvoluntarist? The heart of Plantinga's criterion for warrant is that a believer's cognitive faculties are working properly in the appropriate environment. But this operation is not typically accessible to her consciousness, at least not directly or immediately so, and sometimes it may not be even indirectly accessible. The second component of the criterion—the fact that she feels more inclined to believe B than $B*$—is accessible yet is not within her control, according to Plantinga. So neither component of Plantinga's criterion for warrant is within the control of the believer. Theistic believers whose faculties are working properly are heavily blessed with good luck. Nontheistic believers whose nonbelief is due to the fact that their faculties are not working properly are cursed with epistemic bad luck. The fact that the presence or absence of warrant is very heavily, if not totally, a matter of luck does not, however, alter the fact that warrant is intended on this theory to be a normative concept.[7]

Plantinga's rejection of cognitive voluntarism is both central to his positive theory and is offered as one of his chief grounds for rejecting Chisholmian internalism. Plantinga stresses that we do not *decide* what to believe.[8] Typically, he says, I simply *find myself* with the appropriate belief. Mavrodes also routinely uses the expression "I find myself believing *p*." This way of expressing the matter suggests that not only do we not voluntarily control the process of coming to believe a proposition *p*, but also we are typically not even *aware* of the process, only of the outcome. Plantinga thinks the nonvoluntary character of belief formation in typical cases is an important asymmetry with typical cases of actions, many of which are voluntary. This asymmetry makes impossible Plantinga's taking very seriously the structural similarity between good believing and good acting that I want to defend.

Nicholas Wolterstorff's early view of justification does not seem to be externalist and nonvoluntarist.[9] In recent papers, however, there are indications that he is sympathetic with an externalist and nonvoluntarist view. He says, for example, that "fundamentally, it is not our volitional but our dispositional nature which accounts for our beliefs."[10] In the case of religious belief, he explicitly accepts the Calvinist explanation that God has implanted in human beings a natural disposition to believe in God, a disposition that can be, and has been, thwarted by sin of all kinds. The dispositional process leading to belief is largely outside both the control and the consciousness of the believer. In addition, Wolterstorff at least hints that he might go further and accept the justifiability of beliefs that are implanted by God in a more direct way than by disposition: "Is not God's power and freedom such that he might well reveal something to some person without providing good evidence for his having done so? Might he not simply effect in the person the firm conviction that he has said such-and-such? . . . Why would God speak to us if he did not want us to *believe* that he was speaking to us? And if he wants us to believe, are we not at least *permitted* to believe?"[11] The implication here is that a person would be justified in believing in such a case, at least in the weak sense that he is violating no epistemic duty.

As far as I know, George Mavrodes does not explicitly endorse Plantinga's criterion for warranted belief, nor does Mavrodes propose a criterion of his own, but his analysis of religious revelation is clearly externalist and nonvoluntarist. He argues in "Enthusiasm"[12] that there is no way to tell from the inside the difference between the genuine revelations to Abraham, Moses, St. Paul, the prophets, and mystics, on the one hand, and the ravings of "enthusiasts," on the other hand. Mavrodes is clearly willing to say that the prophets, saints, and mystics have knowledge and consequently that their beliefs have justification or warrant. The enthusiasts, however, seem not to have justification even though the recipients of the alleged communications themselves cannot tell the difference. Whether a belief has justification or not, then, is not accessible to the consciousness of the believer. Another example that shows the extent of Mavrodes's externalism comes from his book, *Revelation in Religious Belief.*

> Suppose that we think of God as being powerful, perhaps even omnipotent. And suppose that we think of God as being the creator of the world. It would seem plausible to suppose that an agent of that sort would probably be able to produce psychological effects in human beings. In fact, it might well seem plausible to think that God could produce some such effects directly. Suppose, for example, that someone who has had no discernible theistic belief throughout his life goes to bed one night, and he wakes up in the morning with the firm conviction that there is a God who is the creator of the world. Could it be the case that God has caused him to have this belief, inserting it, we might say, into his mind overnight? It looks like the answer to that question should be "yes." At least, if we think only of the divine power, it seems as though an effect of this sort ought to fall within the scope of that power. This would be one example of what I am calling the causation model of revelation.[13]

A third example from Mavrodes appears in a reply to a paper by Stephen Wykstra:

> Suppose, as may easily happen on my own campus, that a student hears in a single day a vigorous proponent of atheism in a classroom and a Christian evangelist outside on the central

"diag." And suppose too that it is the Gospel which attracts the student and to which he commits himself that day. Suppose finally, that it is in fact the secret and inward testimony of the Spirit of God confirming the words of the evangelist which draws the student in that direction. . . . If it really is God who draws the student to believe the Gospel, and if God . . . is not lying to him, then in what way is the student's hookup with reality defective? What better agent of such a hookup with reality could there be, a better connection with reality than God himself? Why should we not suppose that the student I describe, though he is not a sensible evidentialist in Wykstra's sense, is nevertheless in full possession of epistemic adequacy?[14]

Now clearly, if the student was moved in his heart by the workings of the devil or the weakness of his own nature to go the other way and to accept the atheist's argument, there would be no discernible difference from his point of view. So either Mavrodes must conclude that the former belief has justification or what he calls "epistemic adequacy" and the latter belief does not, in which case the criterion for having justification is clearly externalist, or, he must say both beliefs have justification, in which case the concept of justification becomes empty since the student has fulfilled no epistemic duties whatever. He has merely followed his inclination. Either way, all the work of giving him justification is outside his control; in fact, outside his consciousness.

A third feature of Reformed Epistemology is its individualism. Justification or warrant is person-relative. Warrant is a property a belief has for an individual believer, not a community. Notice first the way Plantinga sets up the criterion for warrant: "A belief B has warrant *for* S if and only if . . . ." In the ensuing discussion, Plantinga focuses on the structure of an individual person's beliefs. The relevant hookups are between each belief, the person's faculties, and the world outside— things causing the belief—but there is no significant sense in which there is a community doxastic structure.

Furthermore, there is no interesting sense in which the warrant of an individual's belief depends on the warrant that belief has for other persons in the community. True, on the

Plantinga criterion, an investigation of the proper functioning of faculties may happen to unearth certain social conditions for such functioning. For example, in Plantinga's discussion of testimony he mentions that his belief can fail to have warrant because someone else lies to him.[15] Even so, no social conditions of which we must be conscious have any impact on our beliefs' having warrant. In fact, some recent suggestions on social conditions for justification or defeaters of justification have been explicitly rejected by the Reformers. For example, Wolterstorff is suspicious of any view, such as Gary Gutting's, that links the justifiability of a person's religious beliefs to those of his "epistemic peers."[16] In addition, Plantinga and Mavrodes have both rejected Stephen Wykstra's support of "sensible [social] evidentialism."[17]

The individualistic character of justification is very clear in the work of Mavrodes, who analyzes revelation as either a communication from God, a manifestation of God, or a way in which God causes a belief *in* a particular individual; and as far as I know, all his discussions of justified beliefs are relativized to the individual person. The recipient of divine revelation is not the community or the Church; rather, the recipient is an individual, and the justifiability of the beliefs of other individuals based on such revelation is derivative from the justifiability of the revealed beliefs of the original recipient. Never suggested is that perhaps religious beliefs are held by a community and that the conditions for justification or warrant are conditions that the community must satisfy.

Reformed Epistemology has the first feature I have identified because it is a contemporary American epistemic theory, not because it is Reformed. I assume that this theory focuses on individual beliefs rather than on qualities of the believer because that is current practice, not because of any religious constraints. The second and third features of the theory, however, clearly relate to its Calvinist origins. Calvin's view on theistic belief is that it is a natural disposition implanted in us by God but corrupted by sin. A person whose faculties are working the way they were designed would believe in God automatically, the way we believe in an external world, other minds, and the past. Such a person's theistic belief would not be the result of a conscious process, much less would belief be the result of using the higher cognitive faculties. It is not surprising, then, that Reformed Epistemology is more at home with externalist theories. The nonvoluntarist aspect of the theory is connected with the Calvinist view on the Fall. According to Calvin, original sin has had a corrupting effect both on human cognitive faculties and on the human will, as well as on the natural, nonvoluntary human disposition to theistic belief. Left to our own devices, we have very little control over our belief-forming mechanisms, especially as they relate to the formation of religious beliefs. Reformed Epistemology, then, is uncomfortable with cognitive voluntarism.

In contrast, traditional Catholic theology has had a more moderate view of the effects of original sin on our cognitive faculties and consequently is more inclined to see such conscious processes as potent instruments in the justification of religious belief. The traditional Catholic respect for natural theology, then, makes Catholic theories more inclined to see internalist features of our epistemic states as desirable, though whether they are necessary is another matter. More importantly, even though the Catholic tradition would agree with Calvin that belief in God is natural but corrupted, its naturalness is closer to the naturalness of moral behavior than to the naturalness of the belief in other minds. The will has been more damaged by the Fall than the cognitive faculties, and grace is needed both for good moral behavior and for faith in God, but the consequences of the Fall do not eliminate the voluntary aspect of both morals and faith. Since on the Catholic view religious faith includes religious belief, we can see that Catholic epistemology is more at home with some form of cognitive voluntarism.

I have noted a contrast between Calvinist epistemology, which is basically externalist and nonvoluntarist, and Catholic epistemology, which tends to be internalist and voluntarist. This contrast is only rough, of course. There are other considerations in the choice between internalism and externalism than the religious aspects I have mentioned. Nonetheless, I believe that part of the motivation behind the choice of either externalism or internalism is theological and that differences between Catholics and Calvinists affect this choice.

The individualism of Reformed Epistemology is also connected with its Calvinist origins. The epistemology of Plantinga, Wolterstorff, and Mavrodes stresses personal religious experiences as the ground for religious faith and consequently de-emphasizes social relationships as the basis for the evaluation of religious beliefs. Catholic philosophy, on the other hand, is more inclined to focus on the social aspects of human activity, including beliefs, in evaluating them. This difference is particularly marked in the evaluation of beliefs based on revelation. Catholics are much more inclined to evaluate these beliefs communally rather than individually since the primary recipient of revelation in the Catholic tradition is the Church, and the validity of revelation does not depend on the validity of any particular case of personal revelation or religious experience. The possessor of warrant is fundamentally the Church, not the individual, so the conditions for justification of a belief are conditions that the Church must satisfy, not Francis or Jane or Edward. The criteria for justification of key religious beliefs and the conditions for knowledge in these cases are not primarily a matter of an *individual* believer satisfying certain criteria independently of the Church.

Catholic philosophy casts a wider social net than does Calvinist philosophy. Apart from revelation, Catholic philosophy tends to think of the criteria for both epistemic and moral evaluation as accessible to nonbelievers. So in moral theory the Catholic tradition has stressed natural law, while in epistemic theory the Catholic view might be considered the cognitive equivalent of natural law. Calvinists, on the other hand, stress that the effects of the Fall make the judgment of other persons untrustworthy, and so we have good reason not to regard nonbelievers as either our epistemic or our moral peers. The basic evaluative principles are not necessarily accessible to everyone. These differences in approach within the Christian tradition have interesting consequences for epistemic theory as well as for moral theory.

2. THE CONCEPT OF EPISTEMIC VIRTUE

Epistemological Methodology

Traditional Catholic moral philosophy has had a high regard for virtue theories. Since believing is, if not quite a form of acting, at least strongly analogous to it, I propose to use a virtue theory of morality to identify the normative aspect of knowledge. I suggest that if we think of the normative component of knowledge as a virtue and take seriously what we know about virtue from moral theory, we can learn a lot about the conditions for good cognitive activity. Although the theory I will outline in this section is inspired by some of the features of traditional Catholic philosophy, the theory is my own; I do not claim any authority for it from Catholic theology.

It is my position that knowledge is true belief grounded in epistemic virtue. In this section I want to outline an argument that epistemic virtue is the normative component of knowledge and that epistemic virtue cannot be understood apart from the believer's relationship to a social community. Then I argue that the normative element in knowledge is not adequately captured by the current versions of Reformed Epistemology that are too externalist, insufficiently voluntarist, and insufficiently social.

Before making my proposal on the normative component of knowledge, I wish to make some comments on epistemological method. It seems to me that in formulating a theory of human knowledge we ought to take certain things about human nature for granted, just as we should do in moral theory. An attempt to discuss the conditions under which a human being has knowledge is an attempt to understand something about the mental states of *human persons.* We should expect the norms of rationality and justifiability to be what they are because humans have human nature. If there had been no humans, but another species of earthly knowers instead, the norms might very well have been different, as they no doubt are different for angels or any extraterrestrial knowers there may be. There are, of course, different philosophies of human nature and we have seen some differences in the understanding of human capacities even within the Christian tradition. Still, these differences are not serious enough to preclude our taking certain things about human beings for granted in the present inquiry: I will assume that human beings are knowing creatures, that we are generally rational in the formation and maintenance of our beliefs, and that the world cooperates with our cognitive faculties much of the time. What I take for granted means that we can trust our reason, our senses, our memory, and, at least to some extent, our common sense. Our nature itself determines that we receive knowledge in these ways. A being with different cognitive faculties would not be human. Of course, this is not to say that these faculties are infallible, only that they are generally reliable or, at least, not radically defective. They lead to the formation of true beliefs often enough to make the pursuit of knowledge a realistic goal.

I will also assume that humans are social by nature, and that this means the process of acquiring knowledge depends on complex interactions with other people—in learning the language, in learning the rules of reasoning, in keeping knowledge in the collective memory, and in interpreting and explaining human experience. The epistemic norms that apply to human persons, then, are not what they would be if we lived in isolation from others of our kind. There is plenty of evidence for this assumption about our social nature, but I will not argue for it here. Furthermore, this assumption is perfectly compatible with Calvinist theology, in spite of the Calvinist tendency towards cognitive individualism.

Finally, I will assume that human beings are self-reflective creatures and that self-reflectiveness extends to an awareness of our own nature. Here I understand self-reflectiveness as both a descriptive and an evaluative property. It is a property that is vital to human nature but also admits of degree and is a property that we usually associate with maturity. No doubt the property is one we ought to have to a fairly high degree if we are to be evaluated positively. So I conclude that the evaluation of our beliefs rests both on the fact that we have a nature of a certain kind and on the fact that we ought to know that it is of that kind. I have described, of course, a very thin view of human nature, but as obvious as it may be, it is remarkably easy to ignore.

Virtue theorists claim that it is a mistake to begin an investigation in moral philosophy with the question of when an act if right or wrong. I accept this position and think that for the same reason it is a mistake to begin an investigation in epistemology with the question of when a belief is justified or unjustified. To be justified is a way of being right. "Justified" applies to individual instances of belief, just as "right" applies to individual acts. Justified beliefs are like right acts. Epistemic virtue, on the other hand, is a quality of persons, and I believe it cannot be reduced to a disposition to have justified beliefs any more than moral virtue can be reduced to a disposition to perform right acts. The concept of justification is derivative from the concept of epistemic virtue; I believe it is important that the concepts not be conflated.

The Components of Knowledge

Belief. Belief is a much easier state to acquire than knowledge. It happens easily, sometimes automatically, and an investigation of knowledge almost always begins with an investigation of belief. Some philosophers have denied that belief is a component of knowledge, but even they would agree that knowing involves thinking with assent. As long as believing just *is* thinking with assent, as Augustine says,[18] knowing has believing as a component.

In the history of philosophy the extent to which our believing processes are subject to voluntary control has been a matter of considerable disagreement. That is because beliefs are typically the outcome of processes which are either instinctive mechanisms or so habitual that they are part of our intellectual character. We have seen that the Reformers have made a point of calling attention to the questionable voluntariness of our beliefs. If beliefs really are involuntary, that would make them inappropriate subjects of evaluation in anything like the moral sense.

To respond to this point, I think it is important that we do not think that the only element of the voluntary is a distinct act of choice occurring immediately before an act. True, we rarely if ever *choose* to believe something, but then, the roles of deliberation and choice in human action are often exaggerated anyway. Acts that follow a process of deliberation and choice are in a very select category, and if morality and the realm of the voluntary applied only to that class of acts, morality and the voluntary would not apply to very much. Furthermore, even acts resulting from deliberation and choice are based on prior nondeliberative processes of belief, attitude, and value acquisition. So the element of the voluntary cannot be limited to the element of choice that *some* acts exhibit.

Aristotle himself did not limit the voluntary to the chosen, and although his account of the voluntary is notoriously difficult, I think we might find something in his discussion that is useful to the question of the voluntariness of beliefs. It seems to me that believing is in general at least as voluntary as acts done out of passion or while drunk for which Aristotle rightly says we are responsible. Consider also such acts (or omissions) as not noticing someone else's distress, taking out one's anger on an innocent bystander, laughing at someone's misfortune, impulsively making an envious remark. Each act or pattern of acts exhibits faults—insensitivity, meanness, envy—which are all moral faults, yet such acts and omissions are no more voluntary than typical cases of believing. I maintain, then, that even though there is rarely if ever an act of choice immediately preceding the formation of a belief, beliefs are nonetheless in the realm of the voluntary.

Truth and the motive to attain truth. A noncontroversial component of knowledge is truth. Truth is an external component as long as we think that the world must be a certain way for a belief to be true and that the truth of a belief is not necessarily guaranteed by the phenomenological qualities of the mental state of believing itself. It is possible for two people (or the same person on two different occasions) to be in mental states of assenting to a proposition that are qualitatively identical from the inside, and yet the proposition assented to by the one is true and the one assented to by the other is false. This means that the phenomenological quality of a mental state alone is not sufficient to determine that a particular state is one of knowing rather than of mere believing. It follows that there is some degree of independence between the external and the internal components of knowledge.

So far we can see that knowledge includes true belief, or true thinking with assent. I wish to discuss, however, another internal component of knowledge in somewhat more detail, and that is the motive for truth.

Aristotle begins the *Metaphysics* with the pronouncement, "All men by nature desire to know." If this is more an expression of ingenuous hope than a statement of plain fact, it is true enough to describe a good many of our fellow human beings. If we are going to evaluate our success in attaining knowledge, asking *why* we want it seems reasonable. An obvious answer is that we want to possess the truth, and knowledge is partly the possession of truth. The desire for truth is so deeply built into our nature that no attempt to thwart that desire, or even to weaken it, has lasted for long. And we desire truth not merely for its instrumental value. We cannot, of course, deny that true belief aids in the attainment of other goals. In fact, we cannot attain much of anything we want without a healthy proportion of true beliefs to help us out. Nonetheless, I doubt that instrumentality of truth is the most basic reason we want to possess it. Truth is valued as an end in itself, and our nature determines that we value it in that way. So the motive for truth is important in knowledge and in evaluating us epistemically, just as the motive for good is important in moral evaluation.

The motive for truth involves both the desire to obtain truth and the desire to avoid falsehood, and this can be roughly expressed as the desire to balance obtaining as much truth as we can get with as little risk of falsehood as we can manage. This motive leads us to guide our epistemic processes in certain ways. For example, we do not think of the lucky guess as a case of knowledge, for one reason that guessing is something we should not do if we want truth. I should not form a belief by guessing partly because guessing permits too great a risk of falsehood, which is incompatible with the motive for truth. Further, my belief comes from an unsound intellectual procedure, unsound because guessing is not a reliable procedure for obtaining truth; in fact, a guess could be considered the *lack* of a procedure. But I ought to use a good procedure, and, what is more, I ought to know that. If there is any doubt about this, consider the fact that a guesser will almost always *agree*, upon reflection, that he should not have guessed. We have used here one of the constraints I claimed we should put on any acceptable theory of knowledge. Our nature determines both that we ought to use reliable procedures for forming true beliefs and also that we are responsible for being aware that our nature is of that kind. So believing by guessing is defective both because guessing is an unreliable procedure for getting the truth and because I should have known that guessing is unreliable.

Furthermore, if I do not use a good procedure in one instance, I shall more easily not use a good procedure in others; I may eventually acquire a very unreliable intellectual habit that I should have known better than to let myself acquire. Beliefs are produced by processes, but there are probably only a limited number of such processes and I tend to use the same ones over and over again. So these processes soon become habits. In guessing, then, a third reason we think of the belief as defective is that guessing in one instance can lead to guessing in other instances and may lead me to form a bad epistemic habit—an epistemic vice.

The epistemic deficiency of guessing is primarily a deficiency in the motive of the guesser. Motive is an important component in the evaluation of what we do in aretaic theories. Aristotle argued that a virtuous person both has a clear view of the end of human life and acts from the motive of reaching that end. If this is right it seems reasonable that an epistemically virtuous person has a clear view of truth as the ultimate end of belief, values truth as such, and forms and maintains her beliefs from the motive of reaching that end. The guesser fails in her motive because guessing is not something a person who values the truth and wants to obtain truth and avoid falsehood would do.

It follows that reliabilist theories are inadequate because the relation between cognitive processes and reliability in such theories is merely a means–end relation. Just as moral virtues are not valuable only because they reliably lead to producing good, epistemic virtues are not valuable only because they reliably lead to true beliefs. Just as a person who fulfills the goal of the moral life not only produces good consequences but also does so through a motivational structure directed towards good, a person who fulfills the goal of the cognitive life not only obtains many true beliefs and few false ones but also does so through a motivational structure directed towards truth.

The social component of knowledge. There is another way in which believing is like acting: much of it is cooperative. The fact that we are suspicious of the *person* who uses incorrect methods of acquiring beliefs such as guessing is connected with the cooperative character of our beliefs. We do not just feel sorry for such a person, we do something similar to blaming him; and I think one reason for this is that so often our own beliefs depend upon those of others. The justifiability of my beliefs often depends on the procedures other people use, so someone else's using bad procedures can affect the justifiability of my own beliefs. And even if I am careful not to hook up my beliefs to his in a way that would affect the justification of my own beliefs, I cannot count on him in my epistemic pursuits. But I should be able to count on him, and so I can blame him.

Social relations have important implications for good believing in another way, too. If I am right that epistemic virtue is structurally very similar to moral virtue, and if virtues ought to be understood in roughly Aristotle's way, then Aristotle's concept of *phronesis,* or practical wisdom, would be as important for epistemologists to analyze as for moral philosophers. Aristotle says that we acquire virtue by modeling ourselves on persons with *phronesis* and we learn what to do in specific circumstances by imitating their behavior. *Phronesis* involves not only good judgment but also the feelings and motives that support good judgment, and, if I am right, such good judgment applies not only to what to do but also to what to believe. Identifying clear instances of *phronesis* is not difficult, but it no doubt cannot be defined with any precision.

An aspect of *phronesis* that makes it particularly difficult to analyze is that it is not strictly rule governed. The person with *phronesis* uses no one identifiable decision-procedure in all circumstances, nor can a moral theorist describe the behavior of a person with *phronesis* by appealing to a set of rules or principles that invariably fits his behavior. This means, of course, that if good believing, like good acting, is determined by the behavior of a person with *phronesis,* there will be a degree of built-in vagueness in the criteria for justification and warrant. I suggest that this lack of precision in epistemology is something we should accept.

Notice that as just described, *phronesis* is a concept which makes no sense apart from social relations. It is acquired by a process of imitating those who have it, and a person can follow no set of rules or principles as a substitute for acquiring *phronesis*. So our epistemic virtuousness is dependent on other people—the people who raise us and teach us. If *phronesis* is lacking in a community, it is unlikely that anybody in that community will be praiseworthy in either beliefs or actions. Epistemic virtue, like moral virtue, is less a matter of the health of individual faculties than of the health of the community.

Both the social character of knowledge and the connection of knowledge with habits shows that beliefs cannot be evaluated singly. As long as a component of knowledge is an intellectual habit, such a habit will result in my believing many propositions, and the evaluation of my success or failure in attaining knowledge in all the cases resulting from that habit are interdependent. Further, the social character of belief formation shows that knowledge rarely depends on facts about myself alone. The fact that I succeed at attaining knowledge depends on facts about other people, including the epistemic virtues and vices they possess and the knowledge they have attained.

From what has been said so far, I conclude that knowledge is not only the possession of true beliefs but also the possession of them in an admirable way that comes from either an instinct or an intellectual habit worthy of our aspiration. Such a habit is in part a process that reliably leads to the truth. This process must also be generated by a certain motive—briefly, a passion for truth.

We have seen that knowledge comes partly from my side, in that I supply the virtue. But it comes partly from the outside, in that the world supplies the truth. What I supply cannot be isolated to any particular belief since I supply my intellectual character. Knowledge, then, depends partly on who has the belief, and it depends on who that person knows, who taught her, and whose work she reads or hears about.[19] Knowledge requires a delicate balance of effort, skill, and luck. I supply the effort and skill; the world supplies the luck.

Summary. I have argued that believing is like acting because it is the outcome of habitual processes, many of which may not be under my immediate control but are part of my character and for which I can be held responsible. This suggests that intellectual virtue is a component of knowledge, and that such virtue is related to beliefs as moral virtue is related to acts. Since believing is an activity that can be done either properly or improperly, it is reasonable to think that believing has a proper virtue. What we have said so far suggests that we may think of epistemic virtue, like moral virtue, as a habit, enough within our voluntary control to be subject to praise and blame, and which is admirable. As a rough approximation, we might say that whereas moral virtues are habitual processes that reliably lead to the good and that are consciously motivated by a love of the good, epistemic virtues are habitual processes that reliably lead to the formation of true beliefs and that are consciously motivated by a love of the truth.

3. OBJECTIONS TO REFORMED EPISTEMOLOGY

If epistemic virtue is roughly as I have described it in section 2, and if it is an element of knowledge, as I believe it is, then there are problems with all of the features of Reformed Epistemology that I identified earlier, in section 1.

I have argued that the quality that a person must have in addition to true belief in order to have knowledge has an internalist and voluntarist aspect, although the Reformed theories are externalist and nonvoluntarist. Let us begin with one of the most extreme examples of this in Mavrodes's work on revelation. Consider again the case mentioned by Mavrodes as an example of the causal model of revelation. In that example God inserts the belief that there is a God into the mind of the believer while he sleeps. Such a believer has no idea where the belief comes from; in fact, he is not aware of any process of coming to believe at all. He simply wakes up with the firm conviction that there is a God. Mavrodes clearly thinks there is nothing epistemically wrong with such a person if he maintains his conviction, and one could argue that the example passes Plantinga's criterion for warrant. After all, there is really nothing wrong with the believer's faculties *per se*, although credulity is undoubtedly a defect. The Plantinga criterion, then, may be vague enough that it could be interpreted either way. Also, we have seen in a remark by Wolterstorff that he might accept the belief produced in this scenario as justified as well. As an aside, the belief no doubt passes the test of the reliabilist since God's direct production of a belief is reliable if anything is.

But surely the man described by Mavrodes is not justified in the belief that there is a God. He is not justified because he has contributed nothing to the process generating the belief. No habits or processes within him, much less any such habits within his control, direct or indirect, have had anything to do with his acquiring the belief. It is impossible to ascribe to him anything like an intellectual or epistemic virtue in this case. His getting the truth is pure luck from the epistemic point of view, and though, as we have said, an element of luck no doubt attends epistemic virtue just as it does moral virtue, pure luck is not enough for justification or warrant. The same point applies to the other case described by Mavrodes in his answer to Wykstra.

The Mavrodes case violates one of the strictures on epistemological methodology mentioned at the beginning of section 2 by not giving sufficient weight to the self-reflectiveness of human nature. A self-reflective person ought to worry if he wakes up with a firm belief of some sort with no memory of how he got the belief or how it might be justified. If he continues to believe, he is suffering from a deficiency of motive. He is lacking in the desire for truth that ought to motivate our cognitive activities insofar as this is within our power. Even if he cannot help believing at that moment, he ought to rethink the matter later and worry about it.

The problem with motive is related to another feature of Reformed Epistemology identified in section 1: the fact that this theory evaluates beliefs singly. To see more clearly what is wrong with such a case, consider how we would respond if the Mavrodes belief were combined in a certain way with other beliefs. Suppose that God causes me to have many true beliefs by inserting them into my head overnight on Mondays, Wednesdays, and Fridays, but the devil also causes me to have many false beliefs by inserting them into my head overnight on Tuesdays, Thursdays, and Saturdays. Let us suppose that phenomenologically the cases are identical, so that I cannot tell the difference from the inside. Am I justified in believing the ones produced by God? Even if half of the beliefs I wake up with are true, it seems to me that I am not justified in believing any of them any more than I am justified in believing half of the beliefs I acquire by flipping coins.

What is wrong with the Mavrodes view is that it comes dangerously close to reducing knowledge to true belief. Beliefs put into the head by God are epistemically on a par with guesses that are always true. The believer has not done anything to contribute to the truth of his belief. He has used no procedure to obtain true beliefs. God has done all the work in the Mavrodes case, just as the world has done all the work in the guessing case. So there is nothing admirable about the Mavrodes believer and we would not want to be such a person. We might, of course, envy him the way we might envy the lucky guesser. Someone might even envy him exactly for the *reason* that he would not have to do any cognitive work. But that is like saying it would be nice if good always came of our acts, no matter what we choose to do. Our responsibility would be taken away, and that can at times sound appealing. But given that our nature is human and not some other nature, given that we have certain capacities, and given that those capacities have norms for their proper use, epistemic virtue will be a state to which we contribute through our own efforts, both in the particular case and in the formation of the habits that make up our intellectual character. And if so, the person described by Mavrodes lacks epistemic virtue and his belief is not justified. If epistemic virtue is a condition for knowledge, as I have claimed, he will also lack knowledge.

In section 1, I showed how Reformed Epistemology focuses on individual beliefs and identifies justification and warrant with a property of a particular belief of a particular person. We have just seen one of the peculiar consequences of doing so. Even apart from the externalism of Mavrodes's example of the believer waking up with a conviction that there is a God, it will not be a convincing case of revelation in the presence of a phenomenologically identical mechanism for producing false beliefs. So this belief cannot be evaluated without examining other belief mechanisms of the believer.

There are other problems with evaluating beliefs singly and looking for justification in a property of the belief-producing mechanism of a single belief. Since a belief is acquired in a social context, it cannot be evaluated separately from the beliefs of others in the community who may, or may not, have *phronesis*. This is a serious problem for beliefs based on visions or voices, explicitly addressed by Mavrodes.[20] Mavrodes admits that on his view the difference between beliefs arising from genuine religious experience and those arising from possibly dangerous delusion cannot be reliably distinguished either by the person herself or by others. Since he analyzes revelation as based on personal religious experiences, Christians are not in a position to tell the difference between revelation and putative revelation. Mavrodes is apparently willing to live with this result. But suppose, as Catholics have traditionally believed, that the primary recipient of revelation is the Church rather than, say, Abraham or Moses or Paul. If so, it would be a mistake to look for warrant as a property of a belief of a particular person. This approach not only avoids the problems of distinguishing revelation from "enthusiasm" but also recognizes the high degree of cognitive interdependency among human beings. Such cognitive interdependency no doubt reaches across religious and confessional lines and may indicate that to the extent it does so, criteria for rationality and good believing must be both accessible and applicable to nonbelievers. This shows an important function of natural theology, I think, but that is a topic for another paper.

The individualism of Reformed Epistemology may distort the conditions for knowledge in yet another way. In section 2, I stressed the importance of *phronesis* for good believing as well as for good acting. We act well when we act in a way that imitates a person with *phronesis,* and we believe well when we believe in a way that imitates a person with *phronesis.* If this is right, we cannot be too sanguine about either our cognitive well-being or our moral well-being if our social environment is unhealthy. The presence of persons with *phronesis* in the community is vital to doing well, and this suggests that there are rather extensive social conditions for knowledge. I am unlikely to have knowledge about anything other than those states of affairs very close to me, nor will I learn the right way to form beliefs, if I do not from an early age have close and rather frequent exposure to people who already know how to do these things well. The conditions for knowledge partly depend on criteria other people in my community must satisfy.

Finally, let us look again at the criterion for warrant proposed by Plantinga. In what way does Plantinga's idea of proper functioning differ from my idea of epistemic virtue? After all, in classical Greek philosophy, virtue is actually *defined* in terms of the function of beings of a kind. If so, Plantinga's theory may not be very far removed from mine. In fact, he does mention as examples of the lack of proper functioning the formation of beliefs in a way caused by such moral vices as pride, jealousy, lust, contrariness, desire for fame, wishful thinking, and self-aggrandizement.[21] Clearly, Plantinga thinks that in each case the belief's lack of warrant is due to the fact that the believer's mechanism for generating beliefs is not functioning properly. One might conclude from this that Plantinga thinks of a vice as a type of improper functioning of human faculties, in which case our theories would be very similar.

Although I hope that this is the case, it seems to me that Plantinga's idea of the properly functioning cognizer is quite different from my idea of the epistemically virtuous cognizer. In Plantinga's discussions the primary image that comes to mind is the well-oiled machine—a machine whose functioning is not primarily accessible to its consciousness at all, much less to self-reflective control, and where the functioning of such a machine is unaffected by the functioning of the machines around it. I suggest that this does not allow adequate room for the responsibility we have for our epistemic virtues; nor does it allow adequate room for the social conditions for good believing, particularly the place of *phronesis* in our epistemic evaluation. Just as it would be odd to speak of a morally good person as a person whose faculties are properly functioning with little or no conscious awareness or control, it seems to me equally odd to speak of an epistemically good person in that way. Of course, we have seen that Plantinga denies the symmetry between the processes leading to acts and the processes leading to beliefs upon which my theory of epistemic virtue rests. He stolidly maintains that we have voluntary control over the former but not the latter, so we are more like machines in our cognitional processes but conscious and free agents in our actions. But if my argument in section 2 is correct, we are no more machinelike in our cognitional processes than in our actions. Both the processes leading to the formation of beliefs and the processes leading to action are governed by habits that come under the category of the voluntary. I have suggested that we ought to be guided in our cognitional activity by the motive for truth, just as we ought to be guided in action by the motive for good. If so, the normative element in knowledge will include this motive.

4. CONCLUSION

In this paper I have called attention to three features of Reformed Epistemology that I find problematic. The first is not specific to the Reformers but is common to almost all American epistemic theories: the fact that these theories are what I call belief-based rather than person- or virtue-based. This feature has no relation to religion or doctrine, as far as I can tell. On the other hand, the second and third features are connected with aspects of Calvinist Christianity that are usually not associated with Catholic Christianity. These are the externalism—nonvoluntarism and the individualism of these theories. In both cases, however, the doctrinal constraints the Reformers must respect seem to me to be only weakly associated with their epistemic theories. So even though the religious background of these philosophers makes it very understandable that they would be predisposed to the type of theory they advocate, I do not see that they are actually prevented by Calvinist doctrine from modifying their views in the directions I have defended. The final choice of theory will no doubt be much more influenced by philosophical considerations than by religious ones.

In spite of the objections I have given to Reformed Epistemology, it is nonetheless clear that the work of Calvinist philosophers has opened up promising strands of philosophical inquiry. I wish to mention just one of these. Until recently, philosophers have tended to be obsessed with argument as the model of rationality. Plantinga and others have called attention to the fact that rationality in belief is not always the result of argument. This point is important and I have no quarrel with it. I have suggested that rationality is a form of virtue, and that the test for rational belief, as for moral behavior, is the *phronesis* test. But persons with *phronesis* do not act by following a specifiable procedure, and I suggest that typically they do not form beliefs by following a specifiable argument. Plantinga is right that rational belief is a matter of behaving in accordance with our nature. My suggestion is that an account of that nature will show that our cognitive behavior is much more like our moral behavior than is recognized by the Reformers.

NOTES

1. Alvin Plantinga, "The Prospects for Natural Theology," in *Philosophical Perspectives* 5: *Philosophy of Religion,* ed. James Tomberlin (Atascadero, Calif.: Ridgeview Press, 1991).

2. Unlike Plantinga, I believe that knowledge involves *at least* the fulfillment of epistemic duty to the extent that epistemic duty applies. Plantinga now claims that justification is neither necessary nor sufficient for warrant in "Justification in the 20th Century," *Philosophy and Phenomenological Research,* vol. 50, supplement (Fall 1990); and in *Warrant and Proper Function* (New York: Oxford University Press, 1992).

3. Plantinga, "Prospects for Natural Theology." An almost identical definition appears in Alvin Plantinga, "Positive Epistemic Status and Proper Function," in *Philosophical Perspectives* 2: *Epistemology,* ed. James Tomberlin (Atascadero, Calif.: Ridgeview Press, 1988), p. 34, although the *definiendum* of that definition is "positive epistemic status" instead of "warrant," and the parenthetical condition about the appropriate environment is taken from the preceding page. In

Plantinga's book, *Warrant and Proper Function*, the definition is amended further. There he says that *B* has warrant for *S* if and only if *B* is produced in *S* by *S*'s epistemic faculties working properly in an appropriate environment according to a design plan successfully aimed at truth. The amendment does not affect what follows in my paper.

4. Nicholas Wolterstorff, "Once Again, Evidentialism—This Time Social," *Philosophical Topics* 16, 2 (Fall 1988), pp. 54–55.

5. George Mavrodes, *Revelation in Religious Belief* (Philadelphia: Temple University Press, 1988), and several papers.

6. William Alston's view is largely nonvoluntarist, yet it contains what he calls "an internalist constraint." This theory has been called "internalist externalism." Lately, however, Alston has suggested that the disputes about the nature of justification indicate that there is no unique concept of justification about which the various accounts are differing but that the concept of justification cannot be abandoned (William Alston, "Epistemic Desiderata," unpublished).

7. Note that this is not necessarily paradoxical if one accepts the concept of moral luck, made popular by Bernard Williams and Thomas Nagel. Williams's paper, "Moral Luck," originally appeared in the *Proceedings of the Aristotelian Society*, supplementary volume 50 (1976), pp. 115–135, and is reprinted in his collection, *Moral Luck* (Cambridge: Cambridge University Press, 1979). Nagel's paper, "Moral Luck," appears in *Mortal Questions* (Cambridge: Cambridge University Press, 1979).

8. Plantinga, "Positive Epistemic Status," p. 37.

9. Nicholas Wolterstorff, "Can Belief in God Be Rational If It Has No Foundations?" in *Faith and Rationality*, ed. Alvin Plantinga and Nicholas Wolterstorff (Notre Dame: University of Notre Dame Press, 1983), pp. 135–186. This paper is devoted to a discussion of justification in the sense of what a person is rationally permitted to believe, rather than on what it takes for a true belief to be a case of knowledge. In this paper Wolterstorff maintains that we have at least indirect control over many of our beliefs, and the account of justification he offers is not externalist.

10. Wolterstorff, "Once Again, Evidentialism," p. 55.

11. Nicholas Wolterstorff, "The Migration of Theistic Arguments: From Natural Theology to Evidentialist Apologetics," in *Rationality, Religious Beliefs, and Moral Commitment: New Essays in the Philosophy of Religion*, ed. Robert Audi and William J. Wainwright (Ithaca: Cornell University Press, 1986), p. 42.

12. George Mavrodes, "Enthusiasm," *International Journal for Philosophy of Religion* 25 (1989), pp. 171–186.

13. Mavrodes, *Revelation in Religious Belief*, pp. 37–38.

14. George Mavrodes, response to Stephen Wykstra's "Until Calvin and Evidentialism Embrace," pp. 6–7 (unpublished).

15. See Plantinga, *Warrant and Proper Function*, chapter 4.

16. Wolterstorff, "Once Again, Evidentialism."

17. Wykstra, "Until Calvin and Evidentialism Embrace."

18. Augustine, *Predestination of the Saints*, 5.

19. This may be another way in which justifiability is like morality. What makes an action good may be a matter, not only of what a person does, but also of who does it.

20. Mavrodes, "Enthusiasm."

21. Alvin Plantinga, "Justification and Theism," *Faith and Philosophy* 4, 4 (October 1987), p. 408.

8. Cognitive Finality

James Ross

1. INTRODUCTION

Reformed Epistemologists made a break with the evidentialist-foundationalist tradition by holding, as Alvin Plantinga phrased it, that "under widely realized conditions it is perfectly rational, reasonable, intellectually respectable and acceptable to believe there is such a person as God without believing it on the basis of evidence—propositional evidence."[1] Their reason, basically, is that one's convictions are warranted if they are the products of a "properly functioning" cognitive system, that is, a system whose behavior meets an original design for producing true beliefs ("of that sort," I add). That position is the outcome of Reformed Epistemologists' trenchant criticisms of various modified evidentialisms (see below) and is buttressed by the idea that an account of knowledge has to suppose our cognitive powers are "properly functioning" according to an original (divine) design.

Reformed Epistemology is more agreeable in outline than I find it in detail. The critiques (see "Agreement and Divergence") are impressive; it gets the right result: that belief in God does not have to have an evidential underpinning. And, it does seem rational to accept beliefs that are products of a properly functioning cognitive system that meets an original design biased towards truth. But there are three deficits, I think: (1) the foundationalist sympathies of Reformed Epistemology make it get the right result for the wrong reasons; (2) it seems

226

to fall into an epistemic circle; (3) most basically, it seems to mis-
describe our cognitive powers by omitting the *positive* role of the
will in warranted belief. Yet, once the role of the will is adequately described, one does not have to be a foundationalist
anymore or hold that any beliefs are properly basic. Besides,
Reformed Epistemologists belong to a tradition that ascribes
certain false believing and unbelief to misuse of the will (e.g,
sin, prejudice, and recalcitrance), so, in principle, even for
them some believing for profit is possible and, furthermore,
warranted—perhaps even belief in God. The will's being *aimed*
at our good (its finality) must have something to do with the
truth of beliefs that the will causes, but that whole dimension of
our commitments is left unexplained.

By not acknowledging that the will causes belief in the
most common and typical cases of knowledge from experience,
the Reformed Epistemologists do not explain that we make
cognitive commitments (in our beliefs and reliances) to advance
our own good, do not analyze how feelings function cognitively,
and, especially, do not make clear how refined feelings support
refined convictions even in our knowledge of God. Consequently, they do not assign any particular cognitive status in the
rationality of religious belief to *rational reliance* on a practicing
community of faith. Nor do they take note that the people of
God are a community of judgment and discernment in which
one is nurtured from childhood through confirmation to adult
mastery. The believing community has an *internal rationality* by
which practice and belief are evaluated, just as do the arts and
crafts and intellectual practices; and, like music, the relevant
data for judging the community's commitments are *inaccessible*
from outside the community.[2] Put simply, the confirmation,
vindication, or adequacy of a religious commitment is a function of its fitting and working out in the religious life for which
the commitment is developed and of its being ratified by the
other believers in their own lives, with its conformity to Scripture and to the proclaimed doctrines of grace, sin, salvation,
and redemption being inaccessible cognitively from outside the
community of faith.

Of course, some of my remarks do not apply to the simple
belief that God exists, what the Reformed Epistemologists seek

primarily to explain. Belief that God exists, 'thin' theism, can exist apart from Christian or Judaic belief *in* God (the God of Abraham, Isaac, and Jacob, to use an ancient contrast), which involves much more, getting its larger content from Scripture and its community of believers. An adequate psychology must be able to explain the rationality of the larger, richer commitment, as well as of 'thin' theism, one result of which is that a different account of 'thin' theism obtains as well.

The Christian's theistic commitment has its capillaries fed from the common faith and from natural reliances motivated by love. Both are sources of rational commitment by way of the distinctively human habits of reliance. Paying particular attention to the rationality of reliance, the cognitive psychology of rational belief has to be much more multifaceted than Reformed Epistemology allows so far. Warranted belief without evidential underpinnings is the product of rational reliance, explained by the cognitive functions of the will.

So, I will continue with broader observations to indicate what an adequate cognitive psychology will contain. For instance, it will explain how there is an internal rationality to religious life (Jewish, Christian, etc.). Religious living is a dynamic system of commitments and shapes of life in which the satisfaction attained from the way of life confirms the commitments by which it is lived, and where the very form of life (e.g., a life based on divine revelation) warrants the willing commitments of such a life while also precluding any access for judging it from outside the circle of commitment. Such hermeneutically insulated commitment is at the heart of Christianity, Judaism, and Islam, and also typifies all the highest arts, crafts, and sciences, including philosophy, that humans have attained. Rather than being a source of unjustified belief, the inaccessibility of the commitments combined with the internal rationality of the form of life restricts cognitive access to "insiders" without losing rationality or providing any basis for skepticism.

Not mentioned by Reformed Epistemologists who are concerned with the narrower subject of 'thin theism' and yet central to religious commitment's being rationally warranted, is that a life in accord with such commitment satisfies the highest human aspirations,[3] no matter what events occur in one's life.[4] That sort of satisfaction, as Augustine recognized, cannot be claimed by any of the pagan philosophies and is a distinctive evidence of the rationality of living with such commitments.[5]

Furthermore, a religious life is not a mere aggregate of personal commitments. Instead, Scripture as understood by the believing community, publicly taught, is the inspiration for, and even the norm of, private life. The same sort of analysis that explains how an artistic or sports community can develop and improve its excellence and retain its rational objectivity while refusing to submit to any external appraisal explains the rationality of developing religious belief.

Reformed Epistemologists do not account for the authority and warrant of tradition (just as tradition has authority, though defeasibly, in the arts) and, especially for the proclaimed faith of creeds and councils, the liturgy (*lex orandi, lex credendi*), and even the ritual as rational grounds for personal commitment. Yet those sources are evidently normative for belief. The very notion of norms for belief makes no sense unless the will has a role in our cognitive design. It is the individual will to believe that has to conform to the proclaimed faith. If an ecumenical council declares "The Son is of one substance with the Father," you do not come to *see* that is so but must willingly believe that is so. Thus for a faith to be rational the will has to have a suitable cognitive function.

By failing to undertake inquiries into these elements, the Reformed Epistemologists look too much like their opponents, too much like a "repaired evidentialism," with foundationalist leanings still attached to much narrower conceptions of human knowledge than are required now. They seem still stooped over by the evidentialist burdens they have thrown down.[6]

The Fall presents a special problem for Reformed Epistemologists, namely, an epistemic circle. A properly functioning cognitive system is supposed to be able to produce belief in God not based on evidence, in accord with its original design. But in order to know the cognitive system is functioning according to its original design, one has to know that it is designed to yield belief in God without needing a propositional–evidential basis.

Given the "darkening of the intellect" from the Fall of humankind, and even worse, the total depravity into which the Reformers believed human nature fell, how do we know about the
proper function and design of the cognitive system? This is
analogous to the Cartesian circle but made worse by the
premise that because of the Fall, human cognitive systems do
not function properly and even with grace (short of beatitude)
are not restored to their original integrity. So how do these
writers get access to the original design? Why should a properly
functioning cognitive system produce belief in God without an
evidential basis? Especially when to the uncorrupted understanding, the reality of God is supposed to be displayed throughout creation: "The heavens declare the glory of God and the
firmament his power."

Even without appeal to revelation, we can see how we can
misappraise our powers because we are prone to errors and un-
certainties when we turn to important matters like what is
valued, and how to act with rightly ordered values, and how
to understand ourselves—or even know our real motives or
what is really good for us. If we are obviously error prone in
central matters for living, why should we be less so about the
being of God?

If Reformed Epistemologists were to adopt the ancient
Christian position that knowledge as well as error can come
from commitment, which is caused by the will, just as saving
faith comes by willing cooperation with divine motivation, then
they could more easily explain, as I propose to do, that reliances of various kinds are rational and are means of knowing—
perhaps not as sensitive and reliable as before the Fall but still
part of our uncorrupted natures. Thus, we could arrive at the
same results: that belief in God (and a lot more) is fully warranted without an evidential basis, and we could explain why.

In brief, evidentialism foundered; it cannot be patched up
to carry the freight of Christianity. Yet Reformed Epistemology
is so cautious in its alterations that it offers us an impaired cognitive psychology, too much like what it rejects, and leaves out
the volitional elements of our cognitive powers and their being
aimed at truth by being aimed at our own good—the very features we need (reliance and the will) to explain not only the ra-

tionality of (non-evidenced) belief that God exists but also the rationality of the Christian faith.

2. PARTICULAR AGREEMENTS AND DIVERGENCES

Protestants and Catholics share two revelant religious commitments: that there is an impairment of human cognition as a result of the Fall, and that cognitive integrity is restored only by grace, and then only partly. The two confessions diverge as to how great the original impairment is, how much or little integrity is restored, and how much the disorders of the will exacerbate disorders of understanding.[7] There is, however, agreement that to some extent unbelief is voluntary and responsible, especially whatever unbelief justifies damnation, though the Reformers do not, as far as I know, present the will as a positive cause of cognition, as Aquinas does.

That there is not a religiously neutral, reliable, and comprehensive appraisal of human cognitive faculties, especially of their original design is also largely indisputed because Protestants and Catholics both are committed to the doctrine of the Fall as revealed and recorded in Scripture and as inaccessible in detail by human inquiry alone.[8] Besides, the fact that the will (and feeling) functions cognitively and is aimed at human completion, which is supernatural, places a full assessment of our cognitive powers beyond the limits of unaided rational inquiry. We can find out that human cognition is unreliable and limited in various respects, but we cannot find out why, or how extensively such limitations affect the truth or the rationality of our commitments, apart from reflections on revelation.[9]

I think Alvin Plantinga effectively criticized Chisholm's deontological conception of warranted belief, and all the forms of coherentism ("Coherentism and the Evidentialist Objection to Theistic Belief"), the reliabilisms of Nozick, Dretske, and Alvin Goldman, and virtually every other recent position because they all suppose, indeed rest on, but fail to give content to, the idea of "properly functioning cognitive abilities." Demented, demonized, drugged, and deceived humans are not able to believe as they "ought," or with processes that are reliable, or to satisfy the conditions of "being warranted," or "coherent," because their cognitive powers are not "working properly." Yet the theories being criticized cannot give an account of the proper functioning of such powers.

Similarly, both Catholics and Protestants reject nowadays the idea that the rationality, the warrant, or the permissibility of a belief is proportional to the amount of evidence one has for it. Thus, although I give a different explanation of why belief in God can stand without evidential underpinnings (see below, 4. Natural Faith), the spirit and effect are similar to the idea that if there are any properly basic beliefs, belief in God may be one of them; and the underlying idea that what issues from proper functioning cognitive powers is rationally believed (even if in error) is something also to be shared. I go further, though, to say that belief held by rational reliance often amounts to *knowledge* (cognition), in accord with what I take to be found in Augustine and Aquinas, that faith is a means to cognition, just as reason is.[10] Moreover, in what follows, I will sketch a different explanation of the roles of reasoning and "proof" and of rational inquiry into divine matters,[11] and a different account of the psychology of our convictions in the absence of compelling evidence,[12] particularly of the will's place in our "original cognitive design" and the role of feeling in cognition. My analysis of our "original design" and of the "targeted finality" of human cognition leads to a different account of the damage that occurred to human cognition in the Fall (see below), of the effects of actual sin, and of the extent and nature of our responsibility for having certain wrong beliefs and falling short in our knowledge of God. So we begin to diverge.

Even Lockean evidentialism makes axiomatic that you are to be blamed, justly, for some of your beliefs, for your unbelief, and for your credulity, incredulity, blindness, and willfulness. Locke wanted to restrain credulity and superstition and irresponsible sureness that resisted the "new" corpuscularian science because the science conflicted with old certainties, prejudices, and even with naive piety. Evidentialists wanted us to recognize that we can by will restrain belief within the scope of the evidence. (That had the anomalous result, see "Believing for Profit," that many nineteenth-century Anglican clergymen found themselves morally prohibited from affirming the Creed because they lacked sufficient evidence for its statements.) The Calvinists also wanted to restrain incredulity, rationalization, and hostile unbelief masked as rational objectivity, and to explain how something so obvious as the reality of God could be overlooked by so many educated and supposedly open-minded humanists; so Calvinists emphasized that unwarranted belief and stubborn unbelief are products of the will opposed to God, and they said you can be damned for what you fail to believe. Thus, a paradoxical agreement emerges: both evidentialists and Reformers insisted that the will is the cause of false or unwarranted belief and even of unbelief. Nevertheless, they neglected giving an account of the will as an element in true and warranted belief, especially for science, even though they knew that there are virtues of believing (e.g., judiciousness), just as there are vices (credulity). That neglect continues, and distinctively marks, their intellectual descendants today.

For instance, Roderick Chisholm speaks of one's "duty qua intellectual being" (*Theory of Knowledge*, 2nd ed., 1976), though he seems to be thinking more on the model of a worker who does the job right, or fails to do it right ("You ought to lift the plane near the end of the board"), rather than directly in moral terms.[13] Still, Chisholm does not explain, as he needs to do, the steps of cognitive psychology by which believing, or not believing, comes under the control of the will. For if there is *no* choice involved as to what and whether to believe, how can there be a *right* way of believing or any duty in response to indirect and noncompelling evidence? Reformed Epistemology has a parallel deficit in not assigning and explaining a positive role for the will when it is obvious that dutiful believing of matters proposed for faith cannot be an activity of the understanding all alone.

We also need to change the units under examination from sentence-like propositions or beliefs to habit-like commitments.[14] We are being tricked, by the passing fashions of linguistic analysis and first order logic, into treating our commitments as if they were discrete in the way sentences are, whereas evidential support and fulfillment of expectation do not typically attach to such units one by one. Justifications and evidence do not line up, like premises for a conclusion, belief by belief; instead, commitments cluster together and stand or fall in groups.

My commitment to what I see in the sunlight on my desk can be decomposed, sententially, into a very long list of "beliefs," some more nearly conscious to me than others, and some that lie entirely outside my awareness (e.g., that I do not see infrared; that there are no spaceships in sight) but which, if you mention them, I will see that I know. Thus, to suppose that "justification" segments along the lines of the sentences used for expressing our true beliefs, so that my overall commitment is justified by the justification of its sententially formulated parts, is, on reflection, without any basis at all, as if Michelangelo's *David* were great art only if arbitrarily, or even carefully, smashed up into marble parts, each being very good or great.

Rather, commitment, say, to what I see, is to the whole, or to most of it, and is sustained by continued reliance, the way I rely on the steering wheel of a car. You could segment every grip or pull on the wheel into a particular belief about the position of the front wheels in relation to road and car, each belief being formulated by a distinct (long) sentence that I am certainly not thinking of, and being justified by the high probability that the "feel" of the steering wheel is proportionate to, and caused by, something like the position of the tires. Instead, my believing is seamless, and willingly maintained by the satisfaction of reliance, until something disturbs it.[15] Whether the reliance works out in fulfilled expectations is, in perceptual matters and matters of appetite, more important to whether we know than what reasons (beliefs noticed consciously and expressed sententially) we had in taking up or maintaining the conviction. Moreover, the relevant kind of working out that is aimed at, and by being aimed at makes a commitment warranted, varies with content and has far less to do with verification, confirmation, or even prediction than it does with getting the good that we aimed at, a good as simple as keeping in our lane, or as ultimate as attaining eternal life. The commitment is warranted by its being made, from rational appetite, as a means to our good and is vindicated by the good attained, if it is. Vindication, of course, is additional to warrant or rationality of commitment. (Further qualifications are needed that I shall postpone for now.)

We also have to realign the explanatory conceptions. "Rational commitment" should be made the central notion with "warranted belief," and "justified belief" made derivative. For it is the inner workings by which commitments are made rational that we need to understand, since so many commitments depend, not on some evidential balancing, but on whether the commitment fits our bias toward what is good for us and issues from rational reliances.[16] In contrast, Alvin Plantinga and others (like A. Kenny in *Faith and Reason*) seem to maintain "justification" or "warrant" as the encompassing notion, with the result that leads to a different description of the proper functioning and original design of our cognitive powers.

3. COGNITIVE VOLUNTARISM

Consider an alternative: our cognitive powers exist and operate to serve our final good and, thus, have a "targeted finality." They are *aimed* so that we are able, circumstances being favorable, to attain our flourishing as rational animals and, further, are enabled, enlightened, and invited by grace to be happy, to reach fulfillment in a common everlasting life with God. "God made us to know, love, and serve him in this world and to be happy with him in the next" (*3rd Baltimore Catechism*). "Thou has made us for thyself alone . . ." (Augustine, *Confessions*).

The rational appetite, the will, is the aimed impulse by which we are locked on to those targets as the objectives of our cognitive abilities. The rational appetite is the constant impulse to immanent action (belief and consent) and to transient action (everything we do affecting the world, from perception to writing to farming) toward our own good. The proper act of the will is to execute, immanently or transiently, the impulse towards the good. Thus there is a constant impulse to particular cognitive commitments[17] insofar as such a commitment is understood to advance our good, in the absence of evidence that compels (or prohibits) assent. We therefore believe in the reality of physical objects; that we live on the earth from moment to moment; that the stars still shine in the daytime; that people can understand what I write; that other people think, love, and act; that our insides are still working, our hearts and breathing continue—without any need to consider or consult evidence or reasons, as long as reliance is undisturbed. Further, willing commitment comes about by reliance; in fact, reliance is the normal and main explanatory factor in ordinary empirical knowledge, in knowledge and belief by natural faith, and in knowledge and belief by divine faith;[18] reliance is a central element in the fabric of scientific certainty as well.[19]

Hume is thought to have drawn skeptical conclusions from the fact that assent is not, in ordinary matters, compelled by the evidence, with the result that you would not be said to know such things as that there are physical objects, animals, and other minds.[20] Evidentialists like Chisholm tried to find principles of "indirect evidence" that are themselves compelling and will bridge the gap from self-validating appearances to judgments of physical reality, principles that would at least causally preclude one's being in error, or put one's conviction beyond reasonable doubt. Both the skepticism and the efforts to bridge the directly evident to the indirectly evident are unconvincing. Cognition does not require a "manifest vision of truth" or compelling evidence or connection to a basis for belief that either logically or even causally precludes error. Such an idea is just a rationalist, Platonic hangover, even though it can be found in Descartes and among the many "foundationalists" in recent centuries. Instead, to explain both ordinary empirical and scientific knowledge and our knowledge by faith, we have to notice that we willingly commit to situations where something is to be gained from thus committing ourselves (e.g., comfort, lack of worry, simplicity of belief, a product of practical value or use, coherence of our views, ease in getting something done, and, often, a tight reinforcement among several such objectives). So we take the bank's word for the balance in our account unless there is a cognitive dissonance; we are willing to get on a plane we are not competent to certify for flight. The tendency to assent, especially implicitly, for the good to be gained is a result of the "targeted finality" of the rational appetite (the impulse that drives the understanding and all actions involving understanding). Whether we are doing science with instruments whose calibrations we accept, or driving on roads guided by a map, or researching economics with tax reports, we are enmeshed in a system of reliances. Even to read Hume we have to rely on the integrity of texts, about which we may never even have wondered. Reliance is warranted, even if not based on evidence, provided our own knowledge does not defeat it, when we rely in order to gain our own good, compatibly with divine grace.[21] In a phrase, evidence permitting, we are warranted in reliances on what is apparently for our own good. (To be sure, so broad a claim may have many qualifications.) That explains many broad commitments (e.g., to the continued solidity of the floor) and thus much of what we believe.[22] Furthermore, what we accept by reliance need not be the truth in order to be warranted.[23]

The kernel of the position, with roots in Augustine, Thomas Aquinas, and William James is this: On the whole, we believe willingly because we want some good to be gained by believing (allowing both for compulsion by evidence and compulsion by extreme want), where our wanting goods to be gained is part of a cognitive system that has a *targeted finality* (the survival-then-fulfillment of the active person, in a basically hospitable environment). So "believing what you want to" is not the pathology of religion and madness but the engine of adapted cognition.[24]

Believing, not at will, but willingly, according to a constant impulse to action for our good that produces a constant satisfaction, is both the *form*[25] of empirical knowledge (like the software for such knowing) and also of induction, of all patterns of discernment, as well as of abstraction and genuine conception and *the form* of reliance on others, which involves the additional element of personal trust. Thus religious faith, even strictly divine faith, is not structurally deviant among cognitive states; it builds on a natural tendency to rely on goods expected from commitment.

4. NATURAL FAITH IN GOD: A CASE OF COGNITION BY RELIANCE

We need to explain why habitual, willing commitment to the reality of things seen and heard (defeasibly by experience), as well as to what we are taught or figure out (including the

reality of God), needs no direct evidential justification to be
"rational" and "reasonable." *The key, I think, is that we are biased,
by design, to our own good (even our animal well being), and rely on
what promises (at first by mere association, then by experience) our
good, gradually refining reliance toward understood goods and expectations our experience shows to be fulfilled.* Natural medicines, like
birchbark, later understood to involve aspirin, are instances in
point. In a word, the paradigm of a warranted belief is a habitual conviction arising from a loving reliance (on persons,
community, and feeling) that is fully rewarded by satisfactions
in our responses to our patterns of experience.[26]

For many people, belief in God belongs to the fabric made
by their natural faith. They *rely* on the world's being the way
they found it and were taught to say it is (on the whole), with
the earth (mostly flat, though a globe when thinking in a
schoolish way) lit by the sun, held in place invisibly,[27] under an
endless canopy of stars, all made by God "out of nothing." The
reliance is strengthened by the fit between their experience and
community expectations. Most people never attain a vantage
from which to nitpick over the worldview they accepted as children and had modulated by collective consciousness. The conviction that God exists functions along with the sunrise and
sunset and the seasons as part of the undoubted, and usually
unconsulted, "ways things are," background that gives meaning
to what happens and offers a measure of one's well being. Theistic conviction is typically unshakeable alongside convictions
that democracy is just, that family is the primary social and personal value, and that what one is minimally to avoid is set forth
by the Ten Commandments and the criminal law. None of
those commitments are adhered to with consistency. Consistency of adherence is distinct from permanence of commitment. Besides, such commitments can fade from vividness,
loose causal force, and even desiccate and disappear if we move
into a community of value in which they have no function; but
typically, they just fade into the background and remain, im-
pervious to any evidence, even when non-functional, apart
from the resentment that one feels if the belief is attacked.

It seems that belief from will is analogous to animal assurance from appetite. That is, an animal, if it wants to eat some-

thing, on the whole eats safely (if it is in its natural habitat) and, so, survives. What it wants to eat, on the whole, is good for it to eat. One could say it "knows" what to eat, that its assurance, coming from its desire, is "justified." In fact, its appetite is aimed, in a hospitable environment, at what is good for it. So too, the will, as rational appetite, is the constant impulse to act aimed at our good; commitments that fit the expected good are "correct," "justified," "warranted." Commitments vastly exceed what are typically called beliefs, because they need not be conscious and may involve technical conceptions of which we are unaware. We can project what they are from scenarios in which such convictions are defeated (e.g., the foundation of my house begins to sink three feet a minute), as well as real potential failures (e.g., a car engine suddenly stops).

Belief that God exists, 'thin' belief, is not belief in the supernatural, not in the technical sense in which the doctrines of the Trinity and Incarnation are said to be mysteries involving the supernatural, and not in the sense in which some theologians say there cannot be natural faith in supernatural truths.[28] Belief that God exists, even faith *in* God, is as fitting for natural faith, even with grace sometimes supervening, as is belief that one's parents love one, so that a person cannot tell whether his conviction originated in his loving reliance on his parents or came from a transformation of the "sense" of the world by a divine invitation. Furthermore, Plantinga, I think, unnecessarily confuses things by suggesting that belief that God exists, by divine gift, may be exchanged for a less valuable product (knowledge) and a less valuable state (seeing rather than believing) should we somehow succeed in proving that God exists. For 'thin' belief does not require a divine gift; and robust belief, even from natural faith, would have grace supervening; it is the 'thin' belief that a demonstration would displace with insight, clearly a better state, just as the faith of the blessed is fulfilled by knowledge.

Natural faith, that is, reliance from love, is the starting point of all knowledge from experience. All the rest, the so-called sense data, sensations, "appearings," incorrigible or self-evident elements, are inventions of the philosophers forced on them by the ancient idea that if you really know, then you

couldn't have been wrong under the circumstances of your believing, an idea we find in Plato, Augustine (*Contra Academicos*),
and Descartes, and even as recently as Chisholm's foundationalism. As a result they searched for an inerrant, incorrigible
basis for knowledge, particularly fundamental units of "ap-
pearing" about which no error is possible. The fact is that in a
lot we know, we could have been committed that way, when reality was otherwise, though by no means as extensively as skeptical philosophers have claimed.[29] The ancient requirement of
an inerrant foundation is simply unnecessary. Our cognition is
made out of commitments gained by reliances—not out of incorrigible units strung together by necessary truths or other
principles of indirect evidence.

Besides, Christians who believe in infant baptism can acknowledge that the normal fabric of reliance, where the *content*
as well as reliance comes from humans, is transformed by sanc-
tifying grace, and that a child's conviction may grow in content
up through adolescence or even later life, supported by a divine
"inner invitation" as well as by the satisfaction from the solidar-
ity with one's community. Nature cooperates with grace.

One can be habitually convinced, even aware, of the reality
of God with varying degrees of vividness, just as one can vary-
ingly recoil, more or less repelled or fatigued, from the waste of
war or economic brutality. Holy people pray, meditate, and
work for God and thereby feed their feelings with new experiences that keep conviction vivid, the way lovers talk, write, and
meet. The constant conviction that God is real may not have
come about through any experience of "finding out" that God
exists, but may always have been there, or have dawned gradually. These are normal cases for persons whose family or community are believers. It is like our conviction that we are part of
the world, earth dwellers. No one has to say so. Commitment
gained by reliance does not need a personal "source": some
people remember a mother's fervent faith (Augustine), and
others do not remember anyone's in particular; that may be especially true about physical reality, the future, or money. If
everyone (one knows) *acts* as if God exists or money is important, or as if the cars, stones, grass, and rain are real, one relies
collectively and needs no source.[30] Normally, one "just finds

out," most times quite accurately, but with notable errors, whether "we are well off or not well off," whether education is worthwhile, whether acting rightly is crucial, sometimes being conflicted in feeling and resolution because families give conflicting signals and confusing directions. The same holds for the reality and, even more so, the attributes and intentions of God.[31]

Why can't belief in God be properly basic? (if anything can). I ask, analogously, Why can't one's assurance that God exists (and more) be *fully warranted* because it is the product of a properly functioning cognitive system, operating by natural faith, according to its original (divine) design? The nature of human cognition is to operate, *inter alia*, by rational reliances; we can determine that fact from examining the system. It is perfectly rational, in the absence of trumping knowledge, for a child to believe what we are led, by our senses and our rearing, and even by our common prejudices, to believe. Children rationally believe their parents, even such silly tales as "there's a hundred mile per gallon carburetor that was suppressed by the oil companies" or "Dark races are inferior," just as rationally as they believe the Christian story or the gospel. The rationality of the reliance does not, item by item, assure the rationality of the content, much less, the truth. We have to learn to do that. But, overall, given that the function of natural faith to cause knowledge without the necessity of finding out for oneself, a function by which having communities become capable of culture and civilization as well as survival, natural faith is directed at truth, not mere conviction, even though it cannot assure truth, item by item.

Consequently, it does seem that what we believe by rational reliance that is not convincingly challenged and is also true, is knowledge. That seems to be the only sensible thing to say about "other minds," "free choice," our knowledge of our self-worth, that the earth will continue to exist indefinitely, that we will, usually, get where we are going, that food offered for sale is edible, that doctors do not deliberately poison us, and almost everything else that we know. How do I know I will die? Not inductively; I have not seen many cases. Not by demonstration; the evidence I can mention certainly does not compel belief.

Yet I know. How? By relying upon the universal fear, avoidance, grief, guilt, talk, and behavior that conveys that *everyone* dies, along with the startling quality of Jesus' saying "If you believe in me, you will not die forever." How vivid is that constant conviction? It intensifies with age; with a certain pain, it lights up, but not as vividly as an insult. But it could get as vivid as sunlight. So too with conviction about God.

5. TWO COGNITIVE FUNCTIONS OF FEELING

I mention these points because they are so clearly tied to the role of the will in belief and so noticeably unmentioned by epistemology, both traditional and Reformed. First, commitment is sustained and stabilized by feeling. Powerful feeling settles one's conviction solidly "against one's ribs," as it were.[32] Just how settled the conviction is can roughly be measured by the alertness of our emotional response to challenges, dismissals, and by the warmth of fellowship in conviction, and by where, bodily, the feelings appear (in head, chest, abdomen, gut, and elsewhere, too). When someone, in an academic setting, openly insults religion as intellectually fraudulent or says it is only a means of repressing others and excusing evil, the shock may be visceral; the reaction, smoldering anger, even contempt. Exaggeration about the Inquisition arouses resentment; neo-Nazi denials of the Holocaust are repellent. The strength of our conviction and its importance are correlated with the potentiality of feeling.

Our deepest, most rational, and cognitively important convictions are the stable convictions that are linked directly with our most refined and profound feeling. I say "refined" to contrast feeling that responds to the *real* merits (or horror or evil) of situations, with the superficial, sentimental, trivial excitement of a rustic at the Dayton Holiday Inn, thrilled by "the most beautiful place in the world." I say "profound" because importance of conviction is marked by its linkage to feelings aroused by the objectives of our cognitive powers: life, beauty, mystery, innocence, intelligibility (e.g., J. S. Bach's *St. John Passion*), death, and everlasting life. That human life is of sacred importance and worthwhile, that every human is a suitable recipient of love and forgiveness, that cruelty to the innocent is especially unworthy of humans—all are convictions that are stable and supported by profound feelings that reflect real merits.

Secondly, feelings function to connect commitments into continents of awareness (the way Jung thought maturation knits up islands of consciousness). One's theistic conviction can progress in maturity of feeling towards awareness of God that connects with other attachments to deep feelings, love, family, study, and understanding (even country), and everything that is personally most important: the basis of one's self-esteem, one's love of other individuals, and, of course, the inevitable experience of failure, loss of persons loved, and one's own destiny to age and die. Some attain Augustine's ideal to come "to love all creatures in the one love in which no one is ever taken away"; some have formed life into one familiar continent of commitment and feeling. But most, even the devout, live in a shifting compromise, an evolving conflict on the matters of ultimate evaluation, despite the firm repetition of the words of faith.

"Believing for your own good"

One might regard natural faith, rational reliances and even the stabilization and unification of conscious commitment by refined feeling as nothing very dramatic, because the reliances are caused by a constant impulse whose aim we have by nature (though it is transformed by grace). But our commitments for the good to be gained can be dramatic indeed, as St. Paul, St. Augustine, and St. Thomas Aquinas had in mind: Jesus offered a *reward* for accepting him—eternal life. Aquinas acknowledged that a sufficient and rational motivation for believing that Jesus was as he said he was and did as the Evangelists report is that one wants the reward for so living and believing, namely, life with God, "never to die forever," as Jesus promised. The New Testament tells us that the reward of *faith* is eternal life, resurrection to life with God; the *hope* of the faithful is confidently on the fulfillment of the promises; the *aim* of persons committing themselves to life according to the New Law is to gain eternal life (life with God).

Some will say the order of trusting is reversed, because you ought not to trust the promise unless you believe Jesus is the Messiah. But as Aquinas says, because you *want* what is promised (along with "interiori instinctu Dei invitantis [*Summa theologica* IIaIIae, 2, 9, ad 3]), you commit to what Jesus claims, which you cannot otherwise *see* to be so. Such commitment seems not only in accord with nature but also divinely motivated by grace. Such commitment is what is praised in Scripture about those whose faith is rewarded with miracles and is, further, what we do to gain any sort of mastery that requires initiation, apprenticeship, discipleship, or qualification, whether in a conservatory, a graduate school, a medical school, pilot training, or a monastery. One finds masters, does what one is told, even when one cannot see how the exercise will lead to the ability desired, and eventually displays, if fortunate, the ability originally sought and its enjoyment. We often speak of having one's faith fulfilled or rewarded.

6. TARGETED FINALITY AND DAMAGE FROM THE FALL

We can do more than merely speculate about our "original design."[33] Scripture reports we are made in God's "image and likeness" by, of, and for the Creator. We know we are creatures—animals at that. We also know that we alone on the earth can ask "What are we?" and that every major non-religious answer is either outright wrong (as is Plato's and Augustine's dualism) or falls short (as does Aristotle's *zoon logicon*), and that what we are most sure of, we are most mistaken about, as Shakespeare warned,[34] and as Descartes so aptly illustrates with his "clear and distinct" idea that he was *res cogitans* really distinct from matter and capable by divine power of having existed disembodied. At the very least, something mysterious attends humans.

More particularly, we know that insofar as we are animals we have cognitive powers adapted to animal survival and flourishing (within the tolerances of nature for individual losses while preserving the species in hospitable environments). Our abilities to understand and to will enormously increase our powers of survival and flourishing, since the body—especially the hands, eyes, vocal powers, and facial expressions—is especially efficient for intelligent living. Nevertheless, we have to have some additional objective or attainment because these powers go far beyond the demands of animal satisfaction. The ancients thought our fulfillment was happiness or the like. I think Scripture presents that it is "life with God." *From their original design, humans are animals with understanding, aimed at everlasting life with God.* The cognitive powers of humans, especially natural faith, are aimed at the good peculiar to humans, usually supervenient on animal flourishing but, in principal, independent: a shared life with God. Thus, even the humans worst off, the victims, and the aborted, have the same fulfillment, life with God. Right from the start, humans, though materially evolved,[35] are only incidentally "natural" dwellers in the physical order; in the last evolutionary step, they are inspirited by God.[36]

Now what humans are *for* tells us what the cognitive system, in its intelligent aspects, including the rational appetite (the constant impulse to action for our apprehended good) is for. What humans are for also tells us how to gauge the cognitive system's functioning. If humans were designed for a bodily life shared with God, then there must have been an active divine enablement of the understanding and of the will right from the creation of the first human. For, given that the natural mode of understanding is by abstraction from *material* things, humans have to be supernaturally enabled to experience God so vividly as to amount to a shared life. Such enablement is lost with original sin, as are the clarity of understanding, self-understanding, and ease of will that mark freedom from wrongdoing.

Even the natural powers of understanding are dulled and the resolution of the will becomes infirm. Whether we describe the so-called corruption of human nature entirely in terms of the consequences of lost freedom (the lost active ability to live a shared life with God), or speak more definitely of damage to humankind's natural powers, as if human eyesight were damaged as well, has to be a matter of emphasis. That is because an essentialist reading of the Reform notion of "corruption of human nature," "total depravity," would be contradictory: what it is to be a human cannot change, not even by corruption. But, of course, all the things of a certain sort can be defective, damaged, or lack something "fitting" and be prone to breakdowns; and those features can be more or less extensive. Historical and sectarian perspectives are likely to disagree in their estimates of impairment.

Still, the will, in our original design, is aimed at our good and stays that way by nature; the will is the constant impulse toward our apprehended good by any form of action involving understanding, whether it be assent, consent, agency, or causation; and by the will we maintain convictions because we want to. Because of the Fall, the finality of the cognitive system became opaque rather than transparent. That is, without grace, the will is still a constant impulse to action toward our apprehended good, but the apprehension is opaque (e.g., a search for happiness or fulfillment, whose particular content, life with God, is no longer supplied along with the urge). So *what* the final good is, either as human flourishing or as human fulfillment, is not accessible by the study of our nature but can only be made clear to us when we cooperate with grace.

Integral humans would, on my account, have both a supernatural awareness of an encounter with God, something like one's constant self-awareness, and a natural awareness, probably of God as that active cause by which they exist, understand, and love, the way we can be aware of the light by which we see. After the Fall, humans lack both awarenesses. Mere faith does not restore either. The habitual awareness of the reality of God that we can attain falls far short of those original states; it is more like the difference between seeing someone you love and merely knowing the he or she is in the house. Calvin was probably right that those whose wills are opposed to God live their lives as if in a thunderstorm, a chaos of wild darkness, faint images, swaying specters, and mistakes, in which occasionally in a flash of lightening God is glimpsed by our natural awareness, lost to sight, and then willingly denied, damnation resulting. But I do not think that explains typical cases of unbelief.

Unbelief from Unrighteousness?

I doubt that unbelief in God, in the 'thin' sense that God exists, is typically the result of unrighteousness, in the sense of a will opposed to God or a conviction that what is really wrong to do is the path for living ("supposing truth in unrighteousness"). I have less trouble with the idea that unbelief comes from a failure of the proper functioning of our cognitive powers, that is, because of the Fall, and involves bad luck for the individual. For one thing, many people are brought up in faithless, even immoral homes, or are given such bad example that they reject belief in God and have no interest in any story of redemption. In others, the natural ability to find out that God exists is defeated by natural faith in the opposed testimony and actions by persons respected or loved. A good deal of unbelief is caused by honest misunderstanding on the part of good parents who want their children shielded from prejudices and made able to "decide for themselves"; that seems to be unbelief caused by mistaken righteousness.

But it is a harsh view that those who do not believe that God exists (and accept revelation) are caused not to do so by their unrighteousness and that by that unrighteousness have wills opposed to God so as to deserve damnation. That seems totally implausible, especially when a kind of atheistic naturalism can be as well warranted by the means of rational reliance (natural faith) as the right belief, since warrant from the aims of the rational appetite can extend to what is not true as well as to what is true. It might be another matter if the unbelief in question is a refusal to accept Christ after the gospel is properly brought to a person, in the innocence of fortunate rearing that does not create prejudice. Still, whether one's unbelief amounts to a will opposed to God cannot be determined from the externals of unbelief alone but only from the inner heart visible to God. So we are not entitled to attribute unrighteousness to unbelievers from their unbelief.

In fact, I think the basis in St. Paul, Romans 1, that unbelievers "suppose truth in unrighteousness" is that certain of those whom Paul contrasts with the faithful did suppose that a manner of life that is actually unrighteous is how a person ought to live. That was particularly shocking to Paul and a lesson to be emphasized to the faithful: that one can become so opposed to God as to suppose that the right way to live lies in the very action that God forbids. And all of us, to some extent—even Christians—are prone to believe that certain actions are right that are unrighteous. How else can we explain killing by Christians in the name of God and the truth? Yet, I see no reason to take the passage from Romans as a universal psychological truth about unbelievers, and certainly not as a general truth revealed.

The implicit supposition (if the Reformed Epistemologists even contemplate such a thing) that sincere unbelievers are more deeply mired in sin than sincere 'thin' theists, or even sincere Christians, seems most unlikely. Certainly no general behavioral pattern by which unbelievers appear more immoral than believers can be identified. To the contrary, unbelievers do not typically embrace the license and riotousness and power-madness that a world without God might seem to invite, though many go far enough to horrify other unbelievers; and believers, even professedly ardent ones, are virtually indistinguishable from unbelievers in their injustice, oppression, hypocrisy, intolerance, greed, murder, and lies, except that they sometimes compound their acts into scandal by claiming God's authority to do them, or divinely sanctioned motives. *Then* we see cognitive powers run amok, when the very faith is used to facilitate and authorize the evils that faith in God, and adherence to the Old or New Law, give us the freedom to avoid. So, while the will has an important function in explaining how belief in God without evidential underpinnings can be natural and rational, I conjecture that "bad" will has far less role in explaining religious unbelief than bad luck, and the general condition of mankind.

7. CONCLUSION

In broad terms, I agree with Plantinga not only in his critique of the theories of knowledge mentioned, but also in his insistence both that belief in God does not need to rest on a framework of other supporting beliefs that are supposed to be sufficient "evidence for it," and that warranted belief can issue from "properly functioning" "cognitive faculties" insofar as they are aimed at that sort of truth. However, I think natural faith is a proper function of our cognitive system that makes such theistic commitment, that typically leads to knowledge (as well as to prejudice and error), that is rational, and that is without an evidential framework. Further, I am quite uneasy with the idea that unbelief is from unrighteousness, in the sense of a will opposed to God, as I have explained.

The key difference about cognition concerns the "original design" and the role of the will in knowledge. I propose that the aimed rational appetite, which amounts to a constant impulse toward action to attain our apprehended good (most notably causing the internal actions of assent [commitment], absent compelling evidence, and consent [to doing]) is part of, and essential to, our cognitive powers, and is the source of a variety of rational reliances, enriched and stabilized by refined feeling. Such reliances are the source of belief that is warranted without evidential underpinning and, when true, can amount to knowledge.

With the Fall, the *aim* of the will has become opaque; our real good remains life with God, but it is no longer transparent to the understanding as the object of our choices. We aim transparently at the good but, if at all, only opaquely at our divine good, absent grace. Thus, we have lost freedom, defined as Augustine and Anselm did as the "ability to act rightly" and the "ability to keep uprightness of will for its own sake," as an ability to come to life with God. Even with freedom restored by grace, our cognitive system is damaged. Part of the damage is that the will is aimed only opaquely at God, as if at a figure through frosted glass illumined from behind, whose identity we know only by faith. Thus, we can easily aim actions at what is not our real good but only attractive pretenders: pleasure, pride, power, excitement, comfort, contentment, and the like.

If we explain belief in God that is not evidentially based to be a product of natural faith, or even rational reliance on our own construal of the world, we do not have the particular problem facing the Reformed Epistemologist of how to assure that belief in God, not based on evidence, is a proper function of our cognitive system. For on my account, belief as a result of rational reliances, proceeding from the targeted finality of our cognitive system, is exactly what the system is designed for.

Although I introduced, as a central notion, the idea that rational convictions come about through the targeted finality of the will (in the absence of compelling evidence), I have to stop without discussing what further distinguishes convictions that amount to knowledge (but fall short of conviction compelled by the evidence), from those that are just true beliefs, and those that are just "warranted" by the cognitive system even though not true. And important as the matter is, it is beside the main point here that convictions arising from (properly restrained) willing reliances on expected goods are paradigmatically "rational," that is, "in accord with the original design of humans" for arriving at truth as to survival, animal flourishing, and rational fulfillment.

NOTES

1. Alvin Plantinga, "Advice to Christian Philosophers," *Faith and Philosophy* 1, no. 3 (July 1984), pp. 253–271. See also the following works by Plantinga: "The Foundations of Theism: A Reply," *Faith and Philosophy* 3, no. 3 (July 1986), pp. 298–313; "On Taking Belief in God as Basic," in *Religious Experience and Religious Belief: Essays in the Epistemology of Religion*, ed. Joseph Runzo and Craig Ihara (New York: University Press of America, 1986), p. 307; "Justification and Theism," *Faith and Philosophy* 4, no. 4 (October 1987), pp. 403–426; "Positive Epistemic Status and Proper Function," in *Philosophical Perspectives*, vol. 2: *Epistemology*, ed. by James Tomberlin (Atascadero, Calif.: Ridgeview Press, 1988); "Reason and Belief in God," in *Faith and Rationality*, ed. by Alvin Plantinga and Nicholas Wolterstorff (Notre Dame, Ind.: University of Notre Dame Press, 1983). And see William Alston, essays collected in *Epistemic Justification: Essays in the Theory of Knowledge* (Ithaca: Cornell University Press, 1989); "Christian Experience and Christian Belief," in *Faith and Rationality*, pp. 103–134; "Religious Diversity and Perceptual Knowledge of God," *Faith and Philosophy* 5, no. 4 (October 1988), pp. 433–488; "A 'Doxastic Practice' Approach to Epistemology," in *Knowledge and Skepticism*, ed. by Marjorie Clay and Keith Lehrer (Boulder: Westview Press, 1989), pp. 1–29.

2. I develop these notions at some length in a separate paper: "Musical Standards as Function of Musical Accomplishment," which

takes up, in effect, how music-making makes the standards of music; the essay appears in *The Interpretation of Music: Philosophical Essays,* ed. by Michael Krausz (Oxford: Oxford University Press, forthcoming 1992). I also argue that each of the arts is an epistemic circle entered by initiation and discipleship, mastered by competition, and preserved by dedication and love, with no stable evaluation from outside the craft. See also William Alston, "A 'Doxastic Practice'."

3. Nietzsche's contempt for Christian love ("virtues of the herd") as a means used by the weak to control the strong not only refutes itself by allowing that love as an inspiration may be stronger than force and willfulness but also testifies that the only escape from the internal rationality of Judeo-Christian faith and living that warrants itself is to adopt a wholly different set of goals and values for humanity, as he did—a transvaluation of values under the ideal of the Herrenmensch who is rapacious by instinct and a law to himself, not the sort of person one would like for a neighbor.

4. . . . whether coronation as Roman Emporer, or martyrdom in the rising tide in sixteenth-century Japan, or transformation of a Jesuit missionary into a Mandarin (S. Endo, *Silence*), or even monastic purity or being crippled from birth or being a homeless derelict now.

5. The fact that similar "satisfaction" can be claimed by competing religions or sects (Mormons, Moslems, Baptists, and Quakers, for example) does not undercut the rationality of the personal commitments insofar as they meet that test. It only reminds us that rational belief is not the same as truth.

6. Traditional evidentialism, in which neither deduction nor induction could be justified and religious faith seemed a stepchild with no merit at all, turns out to have everything upside down. The Reformed Epistemologists have not stepped out of that topsy-turvy world, so they have tried to reform it.

7. The fact that Protestant tradition attributes greater distortion of understanding to the disordered will should make epistemologists in that tradition even more sensitive to the cognitive functions of the will.

8. Plantinga does not say exactly this; but he does say that if there is no satisfactory non-theistic *analysis* or *account* of properly functioning cognitive capacities, then we are "in the neighborhood of a theistic argument." If properly functioning cognitive capacities require that the will be aimed at our *real* good, as I argue, and if our real good is supernatural life with God, then, of course, there will be no religiously neutral analysis or account of properly functioning cognitive powers.

9. One would expect Reformed Epistemologists to be less enthusiastic about rational inquiries in support and explanation of their faith, and even to be more skeptical about the proper functioning of the cognitive powers and the results of science than I am, and to expect less from natural theology than I do.

10. See my other papers on "Aquinas on Belief and Knowledge," in *Essays Honoring B. Wolter,* pp. 243–269; on Augustine in "Unless You Believe You Will Not Understand," in *Experience, Reason, and God,* ed. by Eugene Thomas Long (Washington: The Catholic University of America Press, 1980), pp. 113–128; "Reason and Reliance," in *Prospects for Natural Theology,* ed. by Eugene Thomas Long (Washington: The Catholic University of America Press, 1990); "Rational Reliance" (forthcoming); and "Believing for Profit," in *The Ethics of Belief Debate,* ed. by Gerald D. McCarthy, pp. 221–235, AAR Studies in Religion 41 (Atlanta: Scholars Press, 1986) (on Augustine, Aquinas, and John Henry Newman. In fact, the central role of the will in our original design leads to a different account.

11. See my "Rational Reliance" and "Reason and Reliance"; see also my "Wisdom and Ways," *Monist* (forthcoming 1992), issue on Christian philosophy.

12. By "compelling evidence" I mean everything from self-evidence, through what Aquinas called "the manifest vision of truth" to evidence that eliminates all competitors and evidence that makes one's view more likely than any alternative. Any of those may leave one with nothing to choose about believing or not. Thus, if you were falling from an airplane, it would be pathological (though possibly helpful, as for the skydiver who fell 10,000 feet after her parachute failed, losing awareness as she neared a swamp—and survived) to exercise your will and refuse to believe that you were falling.

13. . . . though terms of moral appraisal eventually have to apply to our habits of belief.

14. Beliefs as philosophers usually talk of them are just slices off the seamless stream of our commitments, made to match the linguistic form (sentences) that we use to express them. But our real commitments are broader and vaguer and often inarticulate, for instance, that things are mostly as they seem to be, or that material things persist unless destroyed or corrupted.

15. For more on this, see my "Believing for Profit."

16. In the absence of compelling evidence, and of compelling want, the will is the cause of assent, of commitment. Such commitments are, largely, habitual, rarely deliberate. Sometimes our reliance on logic and induction is no different in cognitive form than our re-

liance on loved ones or on the good to be gained from believing. In fact, just because deduction and induction lack an evidential justification, the rationality of our reliance on such processes must lie in something that does not require an evidential grounding.

17. This is called "assent" in Aquinas's texts and "belief" in contemporary writings. I tend to replace "belief," both as noun and verb, chiefly because "commitment" is not so closely associated with sentential formulations and can include things we are not even aware of, some of which we come to realize that we accept and even know.

18. "Faith" and "knowledge" are not contraries. "Faith" is a product of reliance and may result in warranted or unwarranted commitment and, under favorable circumstances, in knowledge—as in your knowledge that Julius Caesar was really killed. It can also result in error, warranted or unwarranted. And faith can be induced by divine enablement, enlightenment, and invitation, thus amounting to divine faith, salvific faith, that is, a "certain knowledge" of things unseen. These aspects are examined in the papers cited above (see notes 10 and 11) and in my "Reason and Reliance."

19. See my "Reason and Reliance." I made the point in "Aquinas on Belief and Knowledge" that faith and reason are diverse means to warranted belief, even to knowledge; the notion of *scientia* that Aquinas accepted from Aristotle did not allow that *scientia* result from anything less than "a manifest vision of truth"; however, Thomas's own account of *scientia divina* at the beginning of *Summa theologica* suggests that he glimpsed that the revelation on which theology is based is revealed knowledge attained, by us, by faith.

20. I do not think that is regarded as an adequate interpretation of Hume nowadays.

21. Some might argue that compatibility with divine grace is not a condition on warranted commitment arising from the will. But the cognitive powers of humans are functioning with integrity only when their mode of function (not necessarily their content) is compatible with the operations of grace to bring about salvation. For if one's good is misapprehended or sought with impulses opposed to salvation, then the cognitive system is misguided.

22. I set aside the intricate dispute over whether it can ever be good for us to believe what is not true, though I think it obvious that it can be. First, notice that it can be for our good to believe what we do not know, e.g., that a certain person is telling the truth. Secondly, if we believe some placebo is helping us, sometimes there is a genuine improvement and sometimes without the bad side-effects of the authentic medicine.

23. I have to bypass the discussion of how the cognitive aim of humans toward well being also aims the understanding toward the truth. Basically, because what is real causally impacts on us, it is for our well being, both our bodily and our rational well being, as well as our ultimate well being—eternal life—to take things to be as they are, i.e., to commit to the truth, though that aim still leaves warranted much that is not the truth and certainly does not assure access to the whole of what is real. Thus we have to allow that by natural faith, unbelief in God may be warranted as well; otherwise, it would be unreasonable for a child to trust his or her parents who are mistaken on the matter.

24. The marks of mad, irrational belief are that it is willful and compulsive, out of touch with the conditions of environment and the *aims* of our cognitive systems.

25. By the "form" of reliance, here, I mean the "inner mechanism," the working structure. Enjoyment, "liking it," is an example: it explains what we are doing. It can be "low level" as well as intense. As Aquinas said, "delectation is the form of faith." For Aquinas, "form" in this context means "the first act," that is, the activity exercised. See my discussion in "Believing for Profit."

26. This structure, based on how we are taught and treated, can "warrant" not only a Christlike love of others regardless of how they behave, and a child's love of a parent (no matter how cruelly the parent behaves), but a universal distrust of others that involves a component conviction that is untrue. Such extremes form the basis of cognitive therapy as a method of treatment.

27. . . . by "gravity," whatever that is, and turning on its axis at 1,000 miles an hour while gliding in orbit at 32,000 miles an hour, slowly and erratically wobbling like an unstable top.

28. I, of course, think there can be natural faith, even in supernatural truths. For it is no harder for a child to take his mother's word for the fact that Jesus is the Son of God than for the fact that the world is made by a God who cannot be seen.

29. For the possibilities of error are not as extensive as skeptics think, because in the case of much we know that is naturally necessary, the actual exhausts the relevant possibilities with content. See my *Truth and Impossibility* (forthcoming).

30. A novel began with a bright seven-year-old's hearing whispered intense talk, reverential awe, angry disputes, contented possessiveness, recriminations, and apologies—all done secretly—between her parents. The talk was so intense, secret, serious, and sincere that

she thought they were talking all the time about God. Eventually, she found out they were talking about money.

31. "Act rightly," "Act as you like, but don't disgrace us," similarly, "God will punish you" may have far more force than "God loves us"; or "God loves us" may be tied to "will give us what we want," like coaches having teams pray to win a ball game. With others, the love is tied to "will give us what God wants, which is for the best for us, however it appears." Those are immense differences.

32. Nor do I regard such metaphors lightly because, like a Greek Orthodox writer I heard about, I think with deepening realization, "Belief descends from the head to the heart," only I think that it can go deeper and that we have feelings that are *located* in different places that indicate the depth of conviction. So, as we get older, "I am going to die" deepens its threat.

33. See my "Mindful of Man" (forthcoming), which explains "freedom" as the ability to attain life with God, a gift of grace; and "Christians Get the Best of Evolution," in *Evolution and Creation,* ed. by Ernan McMullin (Notre Dame, Ind.: University of Notre Dame Press, 1985), pp. 223–251.

34. Apparently Shakespeare, with the lines about "man's glassy essence" (*Measure for Measure* II iii 11), had expressed that idea fifty years before Descartes made his ever so certain mistake.

35. That, of course, does not mean any human evolved, but that the material organization for humans came about by evolution.

36. See my "Mindful of Man." See also "Christians Get the Best of Evolution," pp. 223–251; and "Eschatological Pragmatism," in *Philosophy and the Christian Faith,* ed. by Thomas Morris (Notre Dame, Ind.: University of Notre Dame Press, 1988), pp. 279–300.

9. Reflections on Christian Philosophy

Ralph McInerny

The topic of Christian philosophy, thanks to the Society of Christian Philosophers and such notables as Alvin Plantinga, has become a commonplace in recent years. Just as in an earlier day the Metaphysical Society of America was founded to provide a haven for philosophers suffocating in the atmosphere of logical positivism, so more recently Christian philosophers have organized meetings where meatier matters than proofs for the existence of God and the possibility of religious language are discussed. The intrepid metaphysicians referred to above did not think themselves less philosophers than the positivists; indeed, they considered themselves to have a solider claim on the title, and time has proved them correct. No more do contemporary Christian philosophers think of themselves as a breed deficient in appreciation of the rigors and criteria of philosophizing. Rather, they find the ambience of secular philosophizing *philosophically* harmful and stultifying. Christian philosophers do not propose a new logic, the epistemological equivalent of a secret handshake, a method out of the reach of others, but wish to expand the range of topics and issues available to philosophical reflection.

Getting a perspective on the present is difficult, not unlike detecting a hum in the ears that has always been there. Recent discussions of Christian philosophy have a largely Protestant

256

provenance though of course this is not to say that Catholics are absent from the movement. In any case, in this paper I propose to say some things about discussions of Christian philosophy that began among Catholic philosophers, almost all Thomists, in the early 1930s, and which, with exceptions here and there, may be said to have run their course. Certainly the main lines of the argument have not changed much since the heyday of the discussion. Indeed, in glancing at those exchanges between Thomists and their critics, and among Thomists themselves, one is visited by thoughts of *plus ça change*, etc. Accordingly, at a given point I will break off my account of the past and turn to some recent suggestions of Plantinga that amount to a continuation of the earlier discussion. No doubt this is true in part at least because of Plantinga's awareness of the earlier disputes. More importantly, he has made what he calls an irenic suggestion on how the Augustinian and the Thomist, as who should say the Christian Reformed and the Catholic, may reconcile their differences.

1. THE BREHIER BROUHAHA

When F. M. Cornford called his account of the pre-Socratics *From Religion to Philosophy*[1] he was, however unconsciously, seeing the beginning of philosophy through very twentieth-century eyes, the same eyes that saw the *Theaetetus* through the lens of Bertrand Russell.[2] The past, looked at from the vantagepoint of the presumed heights of the present, is scarcely the past at all. Marvin O'Connell once told me that when I read Gibbon I was learning as much about the eighteenth century historian as I was about Rome and its empire. Cornford's title suggests the otherness, if not enmity, of philosophy and religion and, further, sees philosophy as an advance on and replacement for religion. Shades of Hegel. The historian who sees the rise of Greek philosophy as the progressive shuffling off of the immortal coil of religion and myth will have problems with the bulk of Western history, and his account of the history of philosophy promises to be odd.

If Thales is located in the sixth century B.C. and Socrates, Plato, and Aristotle flourish in the fourth century B.C., there is only a brief period when what may presumably be regarded as real philosophy on the Cornford hypothesis is going on. The lights are due to go out shortly when the pale Galilean casts his chilling shadow over the minds of men. The continuation of pagan philosophy into the Christian era has few champions. What professional philosopher nowadays ever took or offered a course on the philosophy of Cicero? As for the Neoplatonists, such anti-Christians as Porphyry are embarrassingly religious in their dissent.

The phrases "Dark Ages" and "Middle Ages" may suggest to ordinary folk inadequate plumbing and the absence of pasteurized beer and reliable contraceptives, but intellectuals understand the phrases to refer to a time when the light of reason all but went out. These are the ages of faith, of authority, of superstition. And they went on and on and on. The light at the end of that benighted tunnel was precisely the Enlightenment, *l'âge des lumières*, the time of the *illuministi*. Modern philosophy sees itself not as a continuation but as a beginning, a beginning which gets relocated progressively. Once it was Descartes. When I was a graduate student we read books like Hans Reichenbach's *The Rise of Scientific Philosophy*, in which the discipline begins with Kant. But A. J. Ayer's delightfully bumptious little book, *Language, Truth, and Logic* (1935) suggested it all began when the twenty-five year old author was an undergraduate. The anthology of Feigl and Sellars disseminated with calm triumphalism this confidence that now we can begin. Rorty's *The Linguistic Turn* was a late entry, but the song was by now familiar.

It was not only the lapsed Catholic Will Durant's one-time bestseller *The Story of Philosophy* that found no philosophy going on for the thousand years or more that make up the Middle Ages. Bertrand Russell, not often thought of as an historian of philosophy, put it succinctly:

> In Graeco-Roman times, as today, philosophy was in the main, independent from religion. Philosophers might, of course, ask questions that would be of interest to those who were concerned with religious matters. But priestly organizations had no influ-

ence on, or power over, the thinkers of those times. The intervening period from the fall of Rome to the end of the Middle Ages differs in this respect from both the preceding and subsequent eras.[3]

If the tone is different in Antony Flew's *An Introduction to Western Philosophy* (1971), this is in large part due to the fact that Flew mines ancient and medieval philosophy for texts that enable him to discuss problems he might have discussed without having recourse to them. But he too seems visibly relieved when he gets to Descartes. Flew finds no reason to doubt the sincerity of Descartes's Catholic faith—philosophical tourists may visit his tomb in Saint-Germain-des-Pres—nonetheless "his own dominant intellectual interests were in sharp contrast with those of his Scholastic predecessors and contemporaries. His main personal involvement was not with religion and theology but with science and mathematics. The method which he sought, and thought that he had found, was the method for extending and vindicating these kinds of knowledge."[4] The method of course was that of Reason.

Like a hum in the ear, these assumptions go as unnoticed in current philosophy as the air we breathe. To philosophize is to free oneself from the baleful influence of religious faith, to follow the argument wherever it goes, untrammeled by prejudice or prior commitment. Philosophy is by definition a secular discipline. A believing philosopher must accordingly be schizophrenic, a fideist, or simply confused.

If it took a remarkable time for such assumptions to be challenged among us, in France sixty years ago they were taken to be fighting words when Emile Bréhier, a historian of philosophy not unknown among us, his multi-volumed account having been translated into English, posed a question. In 1931, Bréhier wrote an article which asked Is there any such thing as Christian philosophy?[5] At the outset, in the Fathers, Bréhier professed to see an adoption of pagan philosophy and engagement in it, but, to the degree this was done by, say, Pseudo-Dionysius, it was indistinguishable from the way his pagan contemporary Damascus did it. The trouble begins with

Thomas Aquinas and his teaching on the relation between faith and reason. With Thomas, faith becomes the measure of reason and, Bréhier asks, "if faith is thus the measure of truth, how can we speak any more of the autonomy of reason?"[6] What strikes Bréhier is that the believing philosopher, in Thomas's understanding of him, is committed to truths that have been revealed and reason's role is simply to be at the service of these truths or, negatively, is the search for the refutation of positions in conflict with the faith.

> Once faith has spoken, philosophy is as it were bound to seek, in the supposed proof, some sophism or paralogism hitherto hidden there. Consequently, Thomism always supposes that reason is incapable of finding in itself its proper measure and rule.[7]

Bréhier notes with relief the return in Descartes of reason as possessing a source of certitude in itself, no longer the feeble slave of revelation.

To say that Bréhier's article elicited a response would be an understatement. In the very year his article appeared, replies came from Marcel De Corte,[8] Etienne Gilson.[9] During the next several years the bibliography on the subject grew like the French equivalent of Topsy. A high point of the Catholic response came in the Juvisy meeting.

2. LA PHILOSOPHIE CHRETIENNE

On 11 September 1933, the French Thomistic Society held its second conference on the theme of Christian philosophy. Two principal papers were commissioned for the occasion, one by Aimée Forest on the historical problem of Christian philosophy, the other by the Dominican A.-R. Motte on the doctrinal solution to the problem of Christian philosophy. The day was opened by M. D. Chenu and each paper was discussed in a lively fashion. All this, together with a bibliography up to the end of 1933, is conveyed in the printed proceedings of the day.[10] The reader is struck by the caliber of the participants in the discussion: Bruno de Solages, Father Festugière, Régis Jolivet, Father Mandonnet, Etienne Gilson, Monsignor Masnovo from Milan, and Joseph Dopp from Louvain along with

Fernand van Steenberghen. The proceedings contain as well communications from Jacques Maritain and Roland-Gosselin. Then and future stellar Thomists were involved.

Gilson's *The Spirit of Medieval Philosophy* had anticipated the discussion, but he soon weighed in with a book on the subject.[11] Maritain, who missed the meeting, also devoted a book to Christian philosophy.[12] There were to be many others heard from as time went on, and just as at the Juvisy conference itself, it was clear that Thomists were not of a single mind on the subject of Christian philosophy.[13] The exchanges between Mandonnet and Gilson, two giants in the development of medieval studies, were particularly sharp, Mandonnet finding the phrase "Christian philosophy" unacceptable, Gilson embracing it with gusto. What general pros and cons emerge from this meeting?

Philosophy and Theology

There was no disagreement among the participants as to the formal difference between philosophy and theology, between philosophical and theological discourse. They are all guided by St. Thomas on the matter. At the very outset of the *Summa theologiae,* Thomas asks what need there is for any sciences other than those the philosophers have recognized. There seems to be a discipline to cover every kind of being and what is there beside being? Nor, an objector is imagined to say, echoing Scripture, should we seek things beyond reason[14]— the suggestion being that to be grasped by reason and to fall to philosophy coincide. On the contrary, Thomas replies, we are assured by St. Paul that all divinely inspired Scripture is useful for teaching, arguing, correcting, and instructing to justice. (2 Timothy 3.16) But divinely inspired Scripture is not relevant to philosophical disciplines, which are discovered by human reason. There is then another kind of knowledge, divinely inspired, beyond the philosophical disciplines.

Indeed such knowledge is necessary for human salvation. We are destined for God, an end that exceeds the grasp of reason, but we cannot direct ourselves to what we do not know. Thus it was necessary for our salvation that certain things be made known to us through divine revelation because they exceed human reason. The necessity is of course hypothetical; God acted under no constraint other than his own will in revealing himself.[15]

If philosophical discourse relies only on what is in principle accessible to any human knower, on the assumption that disagreements can either be settled or shown to be reasonable by appeal to latent agreements, however difficult such a reduction may practically prove to be, it is otherwise with theological discourse.[16]

But there is more. Not only have truths we humans could not otherwise have known been revealed, but also naturally knowable truths, the kind that have or could show up in philosophical discourse, have been revealed.

> It was also necessary that man be instructed by divine revelation about things which can be investigated by human reason, because truth concerning God, as investigated by reason, is achieved only by a few, after a long time and then with much error included, yet the whole of human salvation, which lies in God, depends on knowledge of such truth. Thus, in order that human salvation might more certainly and fittingly come about, it was necessary that we be instructed concerning divine things by divine revelation.[17]

We have here what Thomas calls elsewhere and earlier[18] the "preambles of faith" (*praeambula fidei*). Among the things God has revealed about himself, some are such that we could not have come to know them from the things we know about the world and ourselves: these are the "mysteries of faith" (*mysteria fidei*). But God has also revealed truths about himself that we are capable of coming to know, but for the reasons Thomas gives, these too have been revealed: these are the preambles of faith. A consequence of this doctrine is that believers can be certain of truths which are susceptible of demonstration—and thus fall to philosophy in the broad sense of the term Thomas employs—without having the relevant demonstrations or proofs. Moreover, if a believer finds a philosopher teaching something in conflict with the faith, the believer is certain there is something wrong with the argument advanced in favor of the philosophical teaching. This is, in effect, just what led Bréhier to conclude that Christians could not do philosophy. Unlike their atheistic and agnostic contemporaries, they brought antecedent beliefs and convictions to their philosophizing and this, he suggested, vitiated the effort.

The Debate

If the participants in the 1933 Juvisy conference were as one concerning the distinction between theology and philosophy, they differed markedly on the matter of Christian philosophy. There was general agreement that the philosophy engaged in during the Christian era might appropriately be denominated Christian, but many warned that this must not be misunderstood. Such extrinsic denomination is also involved in talk of American philosophy or Indian philosophy, of ancient and modern philosophy: the nature of philosophy, it was urged, cannot be said to alter under different temporal or geographical conditions. Thus, the substantive disagreement had to do with the theoretical question. Is there a *tertium quid* called Christian philosophy that can be situated between "pure" philosophy and theology proper, a philosophy called Christian not simply by extrinsic denomination, as a *per accidens* claim—some philosophers happen to be Christian, some philosophy happened to be done in the Christian era—but rather because philosophy itself is altered by the adjective.[19]

Père Festugière argued that Christianity can be seen as bringing to completion the aspiration of Greek philosophy, an aspiration incapable of realization without grace and revelation. Régis Jolivet reminded Festugière that Plotinus, in *Against the Gnostics,* seemed sufficiently aware of the Christian remedy to reject it violently. Versions of Festugière's claim that the notion of personality, divine and human, was discovered under the aegis of Christianity are often heard. Under the pressure of seeking to get clear about certain dogmas, the Christian thinker acquired an understanding of the nature of person hitherto unrecognized. Yet, what is then said of person is intelligible quite apart from the dogmatic context that occasioned it. In short, this would be a philosophical advance unthinkable apart from Christianity. Other examples often proposed are the real distinction between essence and existence in all creatures and the

concept of creation, the total dependence in being of everything other than the First Cause on the First Cause.

Mandonnet, obviously irked by all this, called his colleagues to order by suggesting that the hybrid "Christian philosophy" had to be broken into its components and clarity
gotten about them. What would be the upshot?

> There have been Christian philosophers, or better, Christians
> who do philosophy, and in that sense they can be said to do
> Christian philosophy. But that is a purely personal matter. They
> have their reasons when they philosophize; they have their rea-
> sons for being Christians; the unity is in the subject who is both
> a believer and a philosopher, but not in the thing they do.[20]

If one argues from and on the basis of faith, then one is doing
theology, not philosophy. For Mandonnet, the phrase Christian
philosophy is an accidental unity, in somewhat the same way as
Christian golf would be.

Although Gilson professed to be in argument with Mandonnet, his intervention made it clear that he had something
more in mind in speaking of Christian philosophy than an accidental conjunction. He invited his listeners to imagine themselves preparing a course in medieval philosophy. They would
want, at the outset, to take note of how the practice of the discipline alters in the Christian dispensation: philosophy now accepts the regulative role of Christian dogma.[21] He further
means by it the enrichment of Greek philosophy by the Christian contribution. He adds an anecdote. As professor of medieval philosophy at the Sorbonne he did not for years insist upon
the reading of St. Thomas. Why? Because he thought of
Thomas as simply Aristotle plus a theology. On the philosophical level, Aristotle and Thomas were interchangeable. But the
time came when he saw that this equation was not true. When
he did offer a course on the philosophy of Thomas, he taught
the things in Thomas that were not to be found in Aristotle.[22]
And then Gilson put his finger on what distinguishes proponents and opponents of the notion of Christian philosophy.
There is a fundamental disagreement between those who admit
and those who deny the influence of Christian revelation on

the exercise of reason. On the other hand, those who accept this influence can disagree about the acceptability of the phrase "Christian philosophy." Gilson does not care about the phrase so much as about the fact of the influence of revelation.[23]

The Upshot

One could of course go on, but perhaps this will suffice to have before us the essentials of the debate. Let us enumerate common as well as controverted points. (1) There is general agreement that the believing philosopher will conduct himself differently in doing philosophy than does his non-believing counterpart. (2) Thomists all agree that there is a formal distinction between knowledge and faith and, derivatively, between philosophy and theology. (3) This distinction is taken by some, e.g., Mandonnet, to render the phrase "Christian philosophy" misleading: it suggests a combination in discourse that is impossible. (4) Yet there seems to be general agreement that there are notions which de facto come into the philosophical realm from Christian belief, notions such as person and creation. Still, as philosophical doctrines, the Christian provenance of these notions is no part of their intelligibility. (5) I will mention, though I cannot discuss it here,[24] Jacques Maritain's controversial notion of "moral philosophy adequately considered."[25] The moral philosopher cannot know, on the basis of natural reason, the actual condition of human beings and their destiny; therefore, in order for his prescriptive discourse to be adequate, it must be subalternated to moral theology and the belief in sin and redemption. It is significant that the usual objection to this doctrine of Maritain is that it fudges the distinction between philosophy and theology.

It is easily enough seen that, when philosophical and theological arguments are formally distinguished in the manner indicated, a suggestion is created that, in the realm of philosophizing, everything proceeds nicely, that nothing put forward in any way betrays whether the speaker is a believer or not. That is, the reverse side of the recognition that the presence of Christian beliefs influences one's philosophizing is that its absence also does. This is so because it is wrong to think of unbelief as a simple negation, as if removing belief simply leaves pure reason, which is moved always and only by evidence available to all. And it may seem to be just this unimaginable situation that the distinction between philosophical argument and theological argument presupposes: if reasoning is not influenced by faith, it is not influenced at all, it takes place in an existential vacuum. No one can read *Aeterni Patris* and think that this was the view of Leo XIII. Is there a name for what very likely influences the non-believing philosopher and leads him along paths unlike those pursued by the believing philosopher? Plantinga has proposed not just one name, but two: Perennial Naturalism and Creative Anti-Realism.[26] The naturalist is one who interprets human beings and their destiny on the assumption that human beings are merely natural things among natural things and what generally serves to explain other natural things will explain human beings. But the naturalist rejects the need to introduce God as an explanation of nature. The consequences for Christianity are clear. Of course the naturalist will interpret the believer's negative attitude toward naturalism as a disinclination to follow reason wherever it leads. The creative anti-realist reads nature through the lens of the forms of sensibility and reason and the human being is the measure of nature rather than the reverse. Now if either of these two is permitted to define philosophy in such a way that anti-Christian components become part of what philosophy is, then of course Christian philosophy is impossible. Indeed, the Christian ought not engage in an activity the presupposition of which is that his faith is nonsense. One can see how discussions of Christian philosophy have as much to do with rescuing philosophy as they do with defending the faith.

Plantinga's point is made somewhat differently by Alasdair MacIntyre, who tells us of three rival versions of moral enquiry, each representing a tradition that colors and guides the views held within it.[27] Both of my colleagues thus dispute the assumption that philosophizing, when it is not influenced by Christian belief, is influenced by nothing at all. Plantinga goes on from this to develop an account that he sees as an alternative to Thomism but then strikes an irenic note and proposes ways of reconciling Thomist and non-Thomist, that is, Thomist and Augustinian, views. MacIntyre develops what he regards as a version of Thomism to deal with the rivalry he lays out in a masterly fashion. In what follows, for obvious contextual reasons, I am concerned only with what Plantinga has to say.

3. GOODNIGHT IRENISM?

Plantinga, in his Stob Lectures, delivered at Calvin College in 1989 and 1990, presents a defense of Christian scholarship in the teeth of Thomistic obstacles to his task. This is the most refined presentation of Christian philosophy Plantinga has given to date and it repays close consideration. Moreover, it considerably simplifies the task of comparing Thomistic and Plantingian doctrine since it incorporates an effort to do this.

In the first lecture, Plantinga has reminded his audience that there is a great deal of implicit and explicit hostility to Christianity in much of what passes for scholarship today and this requires the believer to be on his critical toes lest he take Naturalism and Creative Anti-Realism to be neutral stances rather than antitheses to the faith. Since he has taught generations how to alvanize holders of such views, the first lecture may seem to the superficial reader to be largely *déjà poopooh*. On the contrary, it is remarkably astute and profound. The second lecture seeks to develop a positive sense of Christian scholarship as a lively alternative to the two views critically discussed in the first. In doing this, however, Plantinga encounters difficulties arising from sources that might be expected to be friendly to his project.

His project in a nutshell is to foster scholarly efforts which will bring to bear on the various sciences the resources of Christian truth. But there are believers who will say that to proceed in this way cannot be productive of scholarship. Their position is that scholarship is a matter of knowledge or reason, and faith is distinct from reason and that, accordingly, to make a scholarly effort depend on Christian belief is to rob it of the name of scholarship.

Plantinga counters this objection coming from Thomists with (1) the claim that far from being opposed to knowledge, faith is a kind of knowledge and with (2) an irenic proposal directed at the objection that discourse or inquiry essentially dependent on faith is theology and not philosophy, psychology, sociology, etc.

Faith and Reason

A quick way of dealing with the problem is simply to question the distinction between faith and knowledge and to assert that faith is a kind of knowledge. Plantinga finds support for this in Calvin and of course could find it in Aquinas as well. Knowledge involves thinking something or other true which is true and having a warrant for doing so. After Plantinga has examined fulfilling one's epistemic obligations and coherence as providing the needed warrant and found them wanting, Plantinga turns to warrant as reliability. Plantinga's full-blown study of warrant has yet to appear. Here he puts forward as a first approximation to a better view of warrant this, that a belief has a warrant for a person only if his faculties are working properly. Calvin provides Plantinga with a way of saying that there are two belief-producing systems with respect to truths about God, one of which is natural, involving only reason, the other of which is faith. The mechanism that produces beliefs of the first kind is called the *Sensus Divinitatis,* the knowledge of God that we have because it is just part of our created nature. As it happens, this knowledge has been spoiled, suppressed, and damaged by sin, and is not salvific. In the believer this natural knowledge is qualified and corrected by faith, is absorbed and taken up into faith. Thanks to faith the believer knows vastly more about God than the *Sensus Divinitatis* delivers or could have delivered even if humankind had not sinned. Just as the *Sensus Divinitatis* is the source of natural knowledge of God, so the testimony of the Holy Spirit persuades us that the prophets faithfully proclaim what has been divinely commanded.[28]

On the basis of this, short shrift can be made of the objection that if you begin with faith you cannot end with knowledge. If faith counts as knowledge, a scholarly enterprise that takes off from faith can be productive of knowledge.

The *Sensus Divinitatis* and the Testimony of the Holy Spirit are, of course, sources of belief, belief producing processes or mechanisms, as we might say; in this regard they are just like memory, perception and other belief producing systems. Their purpose is to enable us to form true beliefs we wouldn't otherwise form.[29]

What further implications might be drawn from the distinction between the *Sensus Divinitatis* and the Testimony of the Holy Spirit? If both are productive of beliefs about God and both are called knowledge, how are they distinguished as knowledge? Would Calvin say that anyone, despite sin and apart from those further beliefs about God produced by the Testimony of the Spirit, has or can have the knowledge of God based on the *Sensus,* and that another, who has both the knowledge of God based on the *Sensus* as well as that due to the Holy Spirit, can talk with the first on the common basis? Can they for example discuss how God's workmanship tells us of God?[30] If any human being in virtue of his created nature could be presumed to have some knowledge of God, this is by definition not the case of the further truths about God, belief in which is produced in us by the Testimony of the Holy Spirit.

Even if it be granted that faith is a form of knowledge, it thus seems to be significantly different, not only from such belief-producing systems as psychology and sociology, but also from the *Sensus Divinitatis;* so different that, absent the Testimony of the Holy Spirit in all parties, a commonly relevant scholarship could not be engaged in with regard to it. It is because faith is a knowledge stemming from such a special source that it cannot be assumed to be present in just any interlocutor.

The *Sensus Divinitatis* and the Testimony of the Holy Spirit can both be distinguished from memory and perception as belief-producing systems in that they produce beliefs about God but they differ from one another in their respective sources. An objector might accordingly say that Plantinga, far from calling into question the distinction between faith and reason, has rather provided an elegant restatement of it. As it stands, Plantinga's proposal could seem disingenuous, and an objector might say, "I see what you mean by calling faith knowledge, but since it can't be hooked up with the other belief-producing systems you mention—memory and perception, for example—in such a way that it could be acquired by one not having it, let's continue to distinguish faith as knowledge from all the other kinds of knowledge. Natural knowledge of God, on the other hand, as you have described it, triggered by seeing God's workmanship in the world around, is knowledge in pretty much the same sense as the other kinds."

Theology and Philosophy

What now of the claim that any scholarly inquiry that begins from what is known by faith will result in theology rather than philosophy or psychology or sociology? In framing the issue, Plantinga uses "theology" and "theological convictions" both for the starting point and the result of a scholarly undertaking. Since faith is knowledge of God, that is understandable, but perhaps something would be gained by employing "faith" for the knowledge of God caused by the Testimony of the Holy Spirit and using "theology" to name a scholarly inquiry and/or its conclusions. The position Plantinga is considering would then be summed up as "Faith in, theology out." He asks why the Thomist thinks it desirable to have a philosophy or psychology or whatever unspotted by theology.

He takes the Thomistic answer to be that what we know by way of reason has an epistemic advantage over what we know by faith. What we know by faith, we know by testimony, and that is epistemically lower than knowing on one's own. Plantinga uses examples from mathematics and logic. If I accept the Pythagorean theorem, or the proposition that there is no set of all sets, or Goedel's Theorem on the say-so of some mathematician, this is on the epistemic scale lower than accepting any of those because I grasp them, understand the proofs of them, and see by myself that they are true.

While Plantinga thinks this distinction has merit, he doubts that it has much applicability beyond mathematics and logic. I accept as true, claims in physics, such as the speed of light, yet I myself never make the measurements on which the claim is based. Even the professional scientist accepts most of what he holds to be true in his science on the say-so of colleagues. Indeed, those who make the measurements on which the speed of light is based, in that very experiment accept some things as true only on the basis of the say-so of others. From this Plantinga concludes that the difference the Thomist wants to see between theology and the non-theological sciences actually "applies very narrowly—only to elementary mathematics and logic, and perhaps to such obvious perceptual beliefs as that, e.g., the pointer is now between the 4 and the 5 on the dial" (pp. 59–60). Theology is taken to be a lot more like other sciences than the Thomist thinks and his insistence on its uniqueness an overstatement.

In my taking the word of the physicist on the speed of light and in any physicist's taking the word of colleagues on most of the things he holds to be true in physics, this kind of faith or trust seems *toto coelo* different from divine faith. The essential claim of science is that anyone making the requisite measurements or performing the experiment will get the same results. That I myself do not do this is quite accidental to the nature of those claims—that is, they do not intrinsically depend on most people just taking them on trust. So too, while it may be practically impossible for the scientist to verify *every* claim even in his own science, he can verify *any* of them.

That other disciplines fall away from mathematics in rigor and certainty seems irrevelant to the point Plantinga wants to make. The distinction obtains even in the case of taking someone's word for an opinion when the opinion is supported by considerations anyone can check out. One might come to reject on the basis of his own inquiry an opinion he previously held on another's say-so, just as he might come to hold it on his own rather than on trust in another's word. It is because the objects of divine faith (the *mysteria fidei* in Thomas's phrase) can only be held on the basis of authority that they differ so markedly from matters which, while they might be believed, need not be. That not everything that God has revealed about himself is of this kind, some revealed truths being in principle knowable (the *praeambula fidei*), makes an inquiry into truths about God a possible common scholarly inquiry of believers and non-believers.[31]

If Plantinga's questioning of the distinction of faith and reason and of the distinction between theology and the non-theological sciences is subject to such demurs as these, there remains his irenic proposal. The proposal is intended to effect a peaceful resolution of the differences between the Augustinian and the Thomist. While the latter distinguishes between theology and philosophy, the former is in favor of using all that we know, including what we know by faith and revelation, and not bothering about labels. Plantinga, on the basis of what we have just looked at, favors the Augustinian stance. But he is more interested in reconciling than choosing between the two traditions. He observes that both Thomist and Augustinian agree that the Christian community needs fuller understanding of all the sciences and of the way they relate to the faith.

Here is the proposal. Let *F* stand for the deliverances of faith. "There is also the result of thinking about the subject matter of science, appealing to the deliverances of faith as well as to the deliverances of reason: call that 'FS' " (p. 60). Thomist and Augustinian agree that we need *FS*, but the Thomist calls it theology rather than sociology or psychology or whatever.

> But now consider the conditional or hypothetical proposition *if F then FS;* the proposition that says what the implications of faith *are* for the discipline in question. Perhaps this proposition *if F then FS* is best thought of as a large number of propositions, each explicating the bearing of the faith on some part of the discipline in question—or perhaps we should think of it as one enormously long proposition. Either way, both parties to the discussion will agree that this proposition is not *itself* among the deliverances of faith; we learn it, or know it, by reason, not by faith. (Pp. 60–61)

Seeing the implications of the faith for psychology, say the implications of the scriptural teachings about love, sin, or repentance on psychology or sociology is a matter of reason, not faith. What the Thomist holds, and the Augustinian does not, is that when we assert the consequents of such conditionals we are doing theology. Plantinga suggests that the Augustinian concede this point. Maybe it does not matter whether we call asserting those consequents theology or call it psychology or philosophy or economics or whatever. What the Thomist is asked to concede in turn (he is taken already to have conceded it) is that the formation of such conditions, quite apart from asserting their consequents, is a work of reason, is non-theological, is the work of the one best trained to formulate them—the psychologist, historian, biologist, economist, literary critic, and so on.

This is an ingenious and welcome proposal. I take Plantinga to mean not simply that it is important for the Christian community that such implications be spelled out (though this is of course his chief concern), but that such hypotheticals can be acknowledged by others doing the sciences in question. Thus, if in a given phase of its ongoing history, philosophy of mind puts forth the thesis that human action is determined and thus not free and responsible, it will be a simple work of reason to point out that this tenet is in conflict with Christian faith. So too with the cosmologist who speaks of the universe, not simply by omitting talk of a creator, but insisting that what we know precludes such talk, it is a simple matter of reason to show that such a stance is incompatible with Christian belief. And so on.

One need only imagine such hypotheticals to predict the result of formulating them. A certain kind of non-believer will conclude from them that Christianity has thus been discredited by science. Plantinga has another outcome in mind. I take him to be suggesting that the believing scientist will be guided by his faith to see that certain theories are false and this will suggest a research project that would minimally show that the theory in question is unproven. But to show this will require work that relies on the methods and criteria of that science. And this suggests that the role of faith remains extrinsic to the practice of the science itself. And that is why a Thomist can agree with Plantinga's proposal. Perhaps the conditional should be reformulated as *if F then S*, such that the *assertion of the consequent* is a move in the science itself, not in theology. The faith does not provide one with a biological theory but it suggests research projects which must be carried out within biology. I conclude that Plantinga has provided powerful support for the view that Christian philosophy or Christian science draws attention to extra-philosophical or extra-scientific advantages that believers have over non-believers in pursuing philosophy and science.

Moreover, he enables us to see that the difference between the Christian and the non-Christian is pre-scientific, so to speak, or on the level of research projects. What seems clearly to motivate many "evolutionists" is to make biology unsafe for Christianity. There is an antecedent disposition to do biology in such a way that God could never enter the picture. The believer, on the other hand, believing what he believes to be true, is antecedently committed to the falsehood of whatever contradicts his beliefs. These antecedent attitudes can lead people to think they have proofs or disproofs when they do not.[32] Plantinga himself, taking note of the evolutionist's argument for the common origin of life (something a believer would expect to emerge), comments that he does not think the argument conclusive. The Thomist will be reminded of his mentor's discussion of the eternity of the world, a doctrine of Aristotle. Thomas believes that time and change had a beginning; thus he believes that Aristotle is wrong. Faith thus dictates the search for a disproof of the eternity of the world and a proof of its non-eternity. Thomas does not think either can be found. Bonaventure, on the standard interpretation of his thought sought to reject Aristotle by arguing that an eternal world is a self-contradictory notion, presupposing a greatest number to which units are continually being added. Thomas rebuts Bonaventure's refutation, argues that God could have created an eternal world and, if it is false to say that he did, we know this, not through reason, but through faith. Aristotle's position is therefore intelligible and lays out a possibility that could have been realized. Because it has not been, Aristotle's arguments for the eternity of the world cannot be conclusive. But it is a task to show this. Simply to say *if F then FS* seems to suggest that revealed truths become components of the science, but that would seem to be the complement of the perennial naturalist's attempting to make his predilections part of philosophy such that to be a philosopher entails being a perennial naturalist. Surely we do not want to suggest that being a biologist entails being a Christian. As Plantinga observes, the relation between what one believes and the upshot of research projects suggested by faith is a very complicated one. But it does not seem to me complicated in the way *FS* suggests, if that symbol is meant to suggest an amalgam of believed truths and scientific truths. Whatever our pre-philosophical or pre-scientific convictions, our philosophical and/or scientific positions are not as such in essential dependence upon them.

By way of conclusion, I suggest that Plantinga's formula *if F, then FS* conveniently expresses the procedure of theology. Faith in, faith out, so to say. The theological project begins from revealed truth as from its principles, and concludes to an account of them the truth of which continues to depend on the truth of revelation. *If F, then S,* on the other hand, can be taken to express the nature of Christian philosophizing. The Christian faith of the thinker will prompt him to undertake certain research projects in a given science. Reading what is said about evolutionary theory by those who take it to rule out the dependence of the process on God, the believer will be prompted to look into evolution. If he eventually proposes an interpretation which does not collide with his faith, his proposal has to commend itself in terms of procedures appropriate to the science in question. In the same way, a refutation of the interpretation inimical to faith must be in terms of the procedure of the science. Thus, Christian philosophizing does not result in an amalgam of faith and knowledge, but in a gain in knowledge that might never have been made without the prompting of faith.

NOTES

1. Francis MacDonald Cornford, *From Religion to Philosophy* (Cambridge, 1912; New York: Harper, 1952). See as well his *Principium Sapientiae: A Study of the Origins of Greek Philosophical Thought* (Cambridge, 1952).

2. See Francis MacDonald Cornford, *Plato's Theory of Knowledge,* Library of Liberal Arts (New York, 1957), p. 311.

3. Bertrand Russell, *The Wisdom of the West,* ed. Paul Foulkes (New York: Crescent Books, 1989), p. 122. This is a coffee-table edition, replete with lovely illustrations, of a book that first appeared in 1959.

4. Antony Flew, *An Introduction to Western Philosophy: Ideas and Argument from Plato to Sartre* (Indianapolis, Ind.: Bobbs-Merrill, 1971), p. 275.

5. Emile Bréhier, "Y a-t-il une philosophie chrétienne?" *Revue de la métaphysique et la morale* 38 (1931), pp. 133–162.

6. " . . . si la foi est ainsi la mesure de la vérité, comment parler encore de l'autonomie de la raison?" (Bréhier, "Y a-t-il une philosophie chrétienne?" p. 144).

7. "Des que la foi a parlé le philosophie est pour ainsi diré tenu à chercher, dans sa prétendue démonstration, quelque sophisme ou paralogisme jusqu'ici caché. Par conséquent, le thomisme supposé toujours que la raison est incapable de trouver en elle-même sa propre mesure et sa propre règle" (Bréhier, "Y a-t-il une philosophie chrétienne?" p. 147).

8. Marcel De Corte, "Sur la notion de 'philosophie chrétienne,' " *Revue catholique des idées et des faits* (27 March 1931).

9. Etienne Gilson, "La problème de la philosophie chrétienne," *Vie intellectuelle* 12 (September 1931), pp. 214–232.

10. *La philosophie chrétienne,* Journées d'Etudes de la Société Thomiste (Juvisy: Les Editions du Cerf, 1934).

11. Gilson's Gifford lectures became *The Spirit of Medieval Philosophy* (New York: Scribner's, 1936), reprint ed. (Notre Dame, Ind.: University of Notre Dame Press, 1991). See Etienne Gilson, *Christianisme et philosophie* (Paris: Vrin, 1936).

12. Jacques Maritain, *De la philosophie chrétienne* (Paris: Desclée, 1933), English trans. by Edward H. Flannery (New York: The Philosophical Library, 1955).

13. This is noted by Edith Stein, who develops her own version of Christian philosophy that in her estimation owes much to Jacques Maritain. Cf. her *Endliches und ewiges Sein: Versuch eines Austiegs zum Sinn des Seins* (Freiburg, Basel, and Vienna, 1986), pp. 12–30.

14. In the little work, attributed to Thomas, *De modo studendi*, the sixteenth maxim is precisely "Altiora te ne quaesieris," drawn from Ecclesiasticus 3.22. The interesting commentary of Nazarius on this work, and on this particular maxim, can be found in *D. Thomae Aquinatis Monita et Preces,* ed. Thomas Esser (Paderborn, 1890).

15. I am paraphrasing here the two objections and the first part of the response of *Summa theologiae,* Ia, q.1, a.1.

16. Thomas adopts what he takes to be the Aristotelian position that there are certain principles or starting points in both the theoretical order and the practical order that are knowable to all, not that they are chronologically first, but rather that they are latent in whatever we say. Thus, while it is scarcely necessary to state at the outset of practical reasoning that the good is what we seek and evil what we wish to avoid, that is the latent assumption of all such discourse. Nor need we, by way of getting started, remind one another explicitly that $-(p. -p)$, but anything we do say involves the common recognition of it. It is at first surprising to see starting points treated as points of arrival, but outside of mathematics that is what they are. Under the pressure of disagreement, we seek common ground with our interloc-

utor and may be driven as to a last recourse to cry out, "But $-(p.-p)$!"
Of course, the laying bare of such latent fundamental supports of
practical and theoretical discourse does not entail that one and only
one more particular statement is compatible with them. This is true
when the analysis is apodictic, but by and large we find that neither of
the contradictories is so grounded in the latent principles that the
other must be rejected on penalty of incoherence. In any case, it is
such common principles, considered as in the public domain, that
characterize and regulate philosophical discourse. They are not the
last word in the case of theological discourse. What play the role of
principles there are the truths God has revealed. Thus, while the
theologian is of course interested to show that the doctrine of a trinity
of persons in one divine nature does not violate the principle of contradiction, that scarcely establishes the truth of the dogma. It is accepted as true on the authority of revelation.

17. "Ad ea etiam quae de Deo ratione humana investigari pos-
sunt, necessarium fuit hominem instrui revelatione divina. Quae ver-
itas de Deo, per rationem investigata, a paucis, et per longum
tempus, et cum admixtione multorum errorum, homini proveniret: a
cuius tamen veritatis cognitione dependet tota hominis salus, quae in
Deo est. Ut igitur salus hominibus et convenientius et certius prove-
niat, necessarium fuit quod de divinis per divinam revelationem in-
struantor" (*Summa theologiae.* Ia, q.1, a.1).

18. E.g., in his commentary on Boethius's *De trinitate,* q.2, a.3.

19. M. D. Chenu put it with elegant clarity thus: "Il ne s'agit pas
seulement d'une étiquette à trouver, chronologique ou géographique,
comme il en serait des qualifications de philosophie kantienne. Il
s'agit d'enregistrer dans un vocable, et donc, pour que ce vocable soit
sensé, d'énoncer dans un concept, l'émergence et la croissance, en
terre et méthode rationelles, de vérités d'origins révélée, qui en fait
commanderent le développement de la pensée philosophique et l'en-
richerent de données jusqu'alors inuoïes. Implication par l'intérieur
donc, qui, soit dans les apports objectifs, soit dans les confortations
subjectifs, laisserait intacte devant l'esprit la différence des 'objets
formels' entre philosophie et théologie, mais aussi dépasserait la coincidence fortuite de deux données totalement hétérogènes. Sans
quoi, le mot n'exprimerait qu'une observation de fait, non une con-
nexion intelligible, et serait dépourvu de valeur philosophique. Autonomie de la méthode rationelle des sa première démarche, par
conséquent, mais non pas discipline imperméable et à jamais close
dans la loi de son objet. Liaison donc, et liaison intrinsèque, entre *philosophie* et *chrétienne;* une 'état' chrétien de la philosophie, comme dit

M. Maritain; sous peine de traiter le fait observé par l'historien comme une recontre de hasard, un accident sans 'raison' " (*La philosophie chrétienne*, Journées d'Etudes de la Société Thomiste [Juvisy: Les Editions du Cerf, 1934], p. 14).

20. "Il y a eu des philosophes chrétiens, ou mieux des chrétiens qui faisaient de la philosophie: en ce sens, ils font de la philosophie chrétienne. Mais c'est là affaire purement personelle. Ils ont leurs raisons quand ils philosophent; ils ont leurs raisons d'être chrétiens; l'unité est dans le sujet, qui se trouve être un croyant et un philosophe; elle n'est pas dans l'ouvrage qu'ils font" (*La philosophie chrétienne*, Journées d'Etudes de la Société Thomiste [Juvisy: Les Editions du Cerf, 1934], p. 63).

21. Noting that he had used the phrase already in his Gifford lectures, Gilson said he had done so without any sense of innovation. The phrase is common. "On la trouve, notamment, dans le titre ajouté à L'Encyclique *Aeterni Patris* et elle y a exactement le sens que je lui donne: la philosophie qui accepté l'action régulatrice du dogme chrétiens" (*La philosophie chrétienne*, Journées d'Etudes de la Société Thomiste [Juvisy: Les Editions du Cerf, 1934], p. 64). *Aeterni Patris* is the encyclycal in which Leo XII urged Catholics to turn to Thomas Aquinas as a principal exponent of Christian philosophy.

22. Gilson, in *La philosophie chrétienne*, Journées d'Etudes de la Société Thomiste (Juvisy, Les Editions du Cerf, 1934), p. 66. This approach to Thomas, Thomistic philosophy being what is peculiar to Thomas, has, in the minds of critics like myself, fateful consequences for Gilson's account of the philosophy of St. Thomas.

23. Ibid., p. 67.

24. I have done so in my McGivney Lectures, *The Question of Christian Ethics*, delivered at the John Paul II Institute, Washington, D.C., fall 1990. These will be published by The Catholic University of America Press in 1992.

25. Jacques Maritain, *Science and Wisdom* (London, 1940), part 2, p. 137ff.

26. See Alvin Plantinga, *The Twin Pillars of Christian Scholarship*, the Stob Lectures, delivered at Calvin College and Seminary, 1989–1990 (Grand Rapids, Mich.: Calvin College and Seminary, 1990).

27. Alasdair MacIntyre, *Three Rival Versions of Moral Enquiry* (Notre Dame, Ind.: University of Notre Dame Press, 1990).

28. To make these points, Plantinga quotes generously from John Calvin, *Institutes of the Christian Religion*, English trans. by Ford Lewis Battles (Philadelphia: Westminster Press, 1960).

29. Plantinga, *Twin Pillars*, p. 56.

30. I am thinking of the remark of Calvin that Plantinga quotes in his *Twin Pillars*, p. 53: "Lest anyone, then, be excluded from access to happiness, he not only sowed in men's minds that seed of religion of which we have spoken, but revealed himself and daily discloses himself in the whole workmanship of the universe. As a consequence, men cannot open their eyes without being compelled to see him."

31. Plantinga has noted that faith is not productive of opinion but of maximally certain knowledge. If certainty and evidence are components of knowledge, faith could be called knowledge because it is most certain—Thomas even suggests that we are more certain of the faith than of self-evident principles of reason—but weak in evidence, while mathematics is ranked epistemically high when it is taken to excel in both certainty and evidence.

32. One of the great merits of Plantinga's approach is that he emphasizes that both non-believer and believer have antecedent attitudes. What the Christian's antecedent attitude is, is easily seen: he holds all kinds of things as true on the basis of revelation. The antecedent attitudes of the non-believer often pass themselves off as mere common sense. Plantinga, by assigning them labels—Perennial Naturalism, Creative Anti-Realism—smokes them out and alerts Christians to their all but pervasive presences. Years ago I said some things about such antecedent attitudes to philosophizing in my *Thomism in an Age of Renewal* (New York: Doubleday, 1965).

Bibliography on Reformed
Epistemology

Abraham, William J. 1985. *An Introduction to the Philosophy of Religion.*
Chapters 7, 8, 9, and 10. Englewood Cliffs, N.J.: Prentice-Hall.

Alston, William P. 1981. "The Christian Language-Game." In *The Autonomy of Religious Belief*, ed. F. J. Crosson. Notre Dame, Ind.:
University of Notre Dame Press.

———. 1982. "Religious Experience and Religious Belief." *Nous* 16:
3–12.

———. 1983. "Christian Experience and Christian Belief." In Plantinga and Wolterstorff (1983), 103–134.

———. 1985. "Plantinga's Epistemology of Religious Belief." In
Tomberlin and Van Inwagen (1985), 289–311.

———. 1986a. "Is Religious Belief Rational?" In *The Life of Religion*,
ed. S. M. Harrison and R. C. Taylor. Lanham, Md.: University
Press of America.

———. 1986b. "Perceiving God." *Journal of Philosophy* 83: 655–665.

———. 1986c. "Religious Experience as a Ground of Religious Belief." In Runzo and Ihara (1986).

———. 1988a. "The Perception of God." *Philosophical Topics* 16:
23–52.

———. 1988b. "Religious Diversity and Perceptual Knowledge of
God." *Faith and Philosophy* 5 (October): 433–448.

———. 1989a. "A 'Doxastic Practice' Approach to Epistemology." In
Knowledge and Skepticism, ed. Marjorie Clay and Keith Lehrer, 1–
29. Boulder: Westview Press.

———. 1989b. *Epistemic Justification: Essays in the Theory of Knowledge.*
Ithaca: Cornell University Press.

———. 1991a. "Knowledge of God." In *Faith, Reason, and Skepticism*,
ed. M. Hester. Philadelphia: Temple University Press.

281

————. 1991b. *Perceiving God*. Ithaca: Cornell University Press.

Appleby, Peter C. 1985. "Reformed Epistemology, Rationality, and Belief in God." *International Journal for the Philosophy of Religion* 24 (November): 129–144.

Askew, Richard. 1988. "On Fideism and Alvin Plantinga." *International Journal for the Philosophy of Religion* 23: 3–16.

Audi, Robert. 1986. "Direct Justification, Evidential Dependence, and Theistic Belief." In Audi and Wainwright (1986).

————. 1991. "Faith, Belief, and Rationality." In Tomberlin (1991).

Audi, Robert, and William J. Wainwright, eds. 1986. *Rationality, Religious Belief, and Moral Commitment: New Essays in the Philosophy of Religion*. Ithaca: Cornell University Press.

Basinger, David. 1988. "Hick's Religious Pluralism and Reformed Epistemology: A Middle Ground." *Faith and Philosophy* 4 (October): 421–432.

Beversluis, J. 1985. *C. S. Lewis and the Search for Rational Religion*. Grand Rapids: Eerdmans.

Boyle, Joseph. 1988. "Is 'God Exists' a Properly Basic Belief?: A Consideration of Alvin Plantinga's Argument." In Kennedy (1988), 169–184.

Boyle, Joseph, J. Hubbard, and Thomas Sullivan. 1982. "The Reformed Objection to Natural Theology: A Catholic Perspective." *Christian Scholar's Review* 11: 199–211.

Clifford, W. K. 1987. "The Ethics of Belief." In Pojman (1987b), 383–387.

Cornman, James W. 1978. "Foundational versus Non-Foundational Theories of Empirical Justification." In *Essays on Knowledge and Justification*, ed. George Pappas and Marshall Swain. Ithaca: Cornell University Press.

Daniels, Charles B. 1989. "Experiencing God." *Philosophical Phenomenological Research* 49 (March): 487–499.

Davies, Brian. 1987. "Faith, Objectivity, and Historical Falsifiability." In *Language, Meaning, and God*. London: Geoffrey Chapman.

Davis, Caroline Franks. 1989. *The Evidential Force of Religious Experience*. Oxford: Clarendon Press.

Donagan, Alan. 1990. "Can Anybody in a Post-Christian Culture Rationally Believe in the Nicene Creed?" In *Christian Philosophy*, ed. Thomas P. Flint. Notre Dame, Ind.: University of Notre Dame Press.

Dowey, Edward A. 1952. *The Knowledge of God in Calvin's Theology*. New York: Columbia University Press.

Evans, Stephen C. 1985. *Philosophy of Religion: Thinking about Faith*. Chapter 1. Downers Grove, Ill.: InterVarsity Press.

———. 1988. "Kierkegaard and Plantinga on Belief in God: Subjectivity as the Ground of Properly Basic Religious Beliefs." *Faith and Philosophy* 5 (January): 25–39.

———. 1991. "The Epistemological Significance of Transformative Religious Experiences: A Kierkegaardian Exploration." *Faith and Philosophy* 8 (April): 180–193.

Feenstra, Ronald J. 1988. "Natural Theology, Epistemic Parity, and Unbelief." *Modern Theology* 5 (October): 1–12.

Ferre, Frederick. 1986. "Contemporaneity, Knowledge, and God." In *Physics and the Ultimate Significance of Time*, ed. David R. Griffin. Albany: State University of New York Press.

Flint, Thomas P., ed. 1990. *Christian Philosophy.* Notre Dame, Ind.: University of Notre Dame Press.

Goetz, Stewart C. 1983. "Belief in God Is Not Properly Basic." *Religious Studies* 19: 475–484.

Grigg, Richard. 1983. "Theism and Proper Basicality: A Response to Plantinga." *International Journal for the Philosophy of Religion* 14: 123–127.

———. 1990. "The Crucial Disanalogies between Properly Basic Belief and Belief in God." *Religious Studies* 26 (September): 389–401.

Gutting, Gary. 1982. *Religious Belief and Religious Skepticism.* Notre Dame, Ind.: University of Notre Dame Press.

———. 1985. "The Catholic and the Calvinist: A Dialogue on Faith and Reason." *Faith and Philosophy* 2 (July): 236–256.

———. 1987a. "A Dialogue on Wittgenstein Fideism." In *Philosophy of Religion*, 430–440. Belmont, Calif.: Wadsworth.

———. 1987b. Review of Nicholas Wolterstorff: *Reason within the Bounds of Religion. Faith and Philosophy* 4 (April): 225–229.

Hanink, James G. 1987. "Some Questions about Proper Basicality." *Faith and Philosophy* 4 (January): 13–25.

Hart, H. J., Van der Hoeven, and N. Wolterstorff, eds. 1983. *Rationality in the Calvinian Tradition.* Lanham, Md.: University Press of America.

Hasker, William. 1986. "On Justifying the Christian Practice." *The New Scholasticism* 60 (Spring): 129–144.

Hatcher, Donald. 1986. "Plantinga and Reformed Epistemology: A Critique." *Philosophy and Theology* 1 (Fall): 84–95.

Herbert, R. T. 1991. "Is Coming to Believe in God Reasonable Or Unreasonable?" *Faith and Philosophy* 8 (January): 36–50.

Hick, John. 1966. *Faith and Knowledge.* 2d ed. Ithaca: Cornell University Press.

———. 1971. *Rational Theistic Belief without Proof.* London and Basingstoke: Macmillan.

Hoitenga, J. Dewey, Jr. 1983. "Faith and Reason in Calvin's Doctrine of the Knowledge of God." In Hart, Van der Hoeven, and Wolterstorff (1983).

———. 1991a. *Faith and Reason from Plato to Plantinga: An Introduction to Reformed Epistemology.* Albany: State University of New York Press.

———. 1991b. "Knowledge, Belief, and Revelation: A Reply to Patrick Lee." *Faith and Philosophy* 8 (April): 244–251.

Hustwit, Ronald E. 1988. "Professor Plantinga on Belief in God." In *The Grammar of the Heart,* ed. Richard H. Bell. San Francisco: Harper and Row.

Jantzen, Grace. 1987. "Epistemology, Religious Belief, and Religious Experience." *Modern Theology* 3 (January): 189–192.

Johnson, Bredo C. 1986. "Basic Theistic Belief." *Canadian Journal of Philosophy* 16 (September): 455–465.

Kaufman, Gordon D. 1989. "Evidentialism: A Theologian's Response." *Faith and Philosophy* 6 (January): 35–46.

Kellenberger, J. 1990. Review of D. Z. Phillips: "Faith after Foundationalism." *Faith and Philosophy* 7 (July): 351–356.

Keller, James A. 1988a. "Reflections on a Methodology for Christian Philosophers." *Faith and Philosophy* 5 (April): 144–158.

———. 1988b. "Response to Plantinga." *Faith and Philosophy* 5 (April): 165–168.

———. 1989. "Accepting the Authority of the Bible: Is It Rationally Justified?" *Faith and Philosophy* 6 (October): 378–398.

Kennedy, Leonard A., ed. 1988. *Thomistic Papers* 4. Houston: Center for Thomistic Studies.

Kenny, Anthony. 1983. *Faith and Reason.* New York: Columbia University Press.

Konyndyk, Kenneth. 1986. "Faith and Evidentialism." In Audi and Wainwright (1986), 82–108.

———. 1990. "The Rationality of Religious Belief." *Faith and Philosophy* 7 (July): 347–351.

Kretzmann, Norman. 1990. "Faith Seeks, Understanding Finds: Augustine's Charter for Christian Philosophy." In Flint (1990), 1–36.

———. "Evidence against Anti-Evidentialism." Unpublished.

Lee, Patrick. 1986. "Aquinas on Knowledge of Truth and Existence." *New Scholasticism* 40: 46–71.

———. 1989. "Reasons and Religious Belief." *Faith and Philosophy* 6 (January): 19–34.

Levine, Michael P. 1990. "If There Is a God, Any Experience Which

Seems to Be of God Will Be Genuine." *Religious Studies* 26 (June): 207–217.

Lewis, C. S. "Obstinacy in Belief." In Pojman (1987b).

Long, Eugene Thomas, ed. 1980. *Experience, Reason, and God.* Washington, D.C.: The Catholic University of America Press.

Long, Eugene Thomas, ed. 1992. *Prospects for Natural Theology.* Washington, D.C.: The Catholic University of America Press.

McCarthy, Gerald D., ed. 1986. *The Ethics of Belief Debate.* AAR Studies in Religion 41. Atlanta: Scholars Press.

McInerny, Dennis Q. 1988. "Some Considerations Concerning Perceptual Practice and Christian Practice." In Kennedy (1988).

McInerny, Ralph. 1980. "On Behalf of Natural Theology." In *Proceedings of the American Catholic Philosophical Association* 54: 63–73.

———. 1986. "Analogy and Foundationalism in Thomas Aquinas." In Audi and Wainwright (1986), 271–288.

McKim, Robert. 1989. "Theism and Proper Basicality." *International Journal for the Philosophy of Religion* 26 (August): 29–56.

McLeod, Mark S. 1988. "Can Belief in God Be Confirmed?" *Religious Studies* 24: 311–323.

Maitzen, Stephen. 1991. "Swinburne and Credal Belief." *International Journal for the Philosophy of Religion* 29 (June): 143–157.

Malcolm, Norman. 1987. "The Groundlessness of Belief." In Pojman (1987b).

Malino, Jonathan. 1985. "Comments on Quinn." *Faith and Philosophy* 2 (October): 487–492.

Markham, Ian. 1991. "Faith and Reason: Reflections on MacIntyre's Tradition-Constituted Enquiry." *Religious Studies* 27 (June): 259–267.

Mavrodes, George. 1970. *Belief in God.* New York: Random House.

———. 1982. "Belief, Proportionality, and Probability." In *Reason and Decision,* ed. Michael Bradie and Kenneth Sayre. Bowling Green, Ohio: Applied Philosophy Program.

———. 1983. "The Stranger." In Plantinga and Wolterstorff (1983).

———. 1984. Review of Gary Gutting: *Religious Belief and Religious Skepticism. Faith and Philosophy* 1 (October): 440–442.

———. 1988. *Revelation in Religious Belief.* Philadelphia: Temple University Press.

———. 1989a. "Enthusiasm." *International Journal for the Philosophy of Religion* 25: 171–186.

———. 1989b. "Revelation and the Bible." *Faith and Philosophy* 6 (October): 398–411.

———. Response to Stephen Wykstra's "Until Calvin and Evidentialism Embrace." Unpublished.

Mitchell, Basil. 1981. *The Justification of Religious Belief*. Oxford: Oxford University Press.

Moser, Paul. 1989. *Knowledge without Evidence*. Cambridge: Cambridge University Press.

Nielsen, Kai. 1985. "God and Coherence: On the Epistemological Foundations of Religious Belief." In *Knowing Religiously*, ed. Leroy Rouner. Notre Dame, Ind.: University of Notre Dame Press.

———. 1988. "Belief, Unbelief, and the Parity of Argument." *Sophia* 27 (October): 2–12.

Pargetter, Robert. 1990. "Experience, Proper Basicality, and Belief in God." *International Journal for the Philosophy of Religion* 27: 141–163.

Parsons, Keith M. 1989. *God and the Burden of Proof: Plantinga, Swinburne, and the Analytic Defense of Theism*. Buffalo: Prometheus.

Penelhum, Terence. 1983. *God and Skepticism*. Dordrecht: Reidel.

Phillips, D. Z. 1988. "Faith after Foundationalism." New York: Croon Helm.

Plantinga, Alvin. 1967. *God and Other Minds: A Study of the Rational Justification of Belief in God*. Ithaca: Cornell University Press.

———. 1979. "Is Belief in God Rational?" In *Rationality and Religious Belief*, ed. C. F. Delaney. Notre Dame, Ind.: University of Notre Dame Press.

———. 1980. "The Reformed Objection to Natural Theology." In *Proceedings of the American Catholic Philosophical Association* 54.

———. 1981. "Is Belief in God Properly Basic?" *Nous* 15: 41–51.

———. 1982a. "On Reformed Epistemology." *The Reformed Journal* 32 (January): 13–17.

———. 1982b. "Rationality and Religious Belief." In *Contemporary Philosophy of Religion*, ed. Steven M. Cahn and David Shatz. New York: Oxford University Press.

———. 1982c. "The Reformed Objection to Natural Theology." *Christian Scholar's Review* 11: 187–198. Reprinted in Hart, Van der Hoeven, and Wolterstorff (1983), 363–383.

———. 1983. "Reason and Belief in God." In Plantinga and Wolterstorff (1983), 16–93.

———. 1984. "Advice to Christian Philosophers." *Faith and Philosophy* 1 (July): 253–271.

———. 1985a. "Alvin Plantinga: Self-Profile." In Tomberlin and Van Inwagen (1985), 3–97.

———. 1985b. "Replies to Articles." In Tomberlin and Van Inwagen (1985).

———. 1986a. "Coherentism and the Evidentialist Objection to Belief in God." In Audi and Wainwright (1986).

———. 1986b. "Epistemic Justification." *Nous* 20 (March): 3–18.

———. 1986c. "The Foundations of Theism: A Reply." *Faith and Philosophy* 3 (July): 298–313.

———. 1986d. "On Taking Belief in God as Basic." In Runzo and Ihara (1986).

———. 1987. "Justification and Theism." *Faith and Philosophy* 4 (October): 403–426.

———. 1988a. "Positive Epistemic Status and Proper Function." In *Philosophical Perspectives* 2: *Epistemology,* ed. James Tomberlin. Atascadero, Calif.: Ridgeview Press.

———. 1988b. "Response to Keller." *Faith and Philosophy* 5 (April): 159–164.

———. 1990a. "Justification in the 20th Century." *Philosophy and Phenomenological Research* 50, supplement (Fall).

———. 1990b. *The Twin Pillars of Christian Scholarship.* The Stob Lectures, delivered at Calvin College, 1989–1990. Grand Rapids: Calvin College and Seminary.

———. 1991. "The Prospects for Natural Theology." In Tomberlin (1991), 287–316.

———. 1992a. *Warrant and Proper Function.* New York: Oxford University Press.

———. 1992b. *Warrant: The Current Debate.* New York: Oxford University Press.

Plantinga, Alvin, and Nicholas Wolterstorff, eds. 1983. *Faith and Rationality: Reason and Belief in God.* Notre Dame, Ind.: University of Notre Dame Press.

Pojman, Louis. 1987a. "Can Religious Belief Be Rational?" In *Philosophy of Religion,* 441–490. Belmont, Calif.: Wadsworth.

Pojman, Louis P., ed. 1987b. *Philosophy of Religion: An Anthology.* Belmont, Calif.: Wadsworth.

Quinn, Philip. 1985. "In Search of the Foundations of Theism." *Faith and Philosophy* 2 (October): 469–486.

———. 1991. "Epistemic Parity and Religious Argument." In Tomberlin (1991).

Robbins, J. Wesley. 1985. "Does Belief in God Need Proof?" *Faith and Philosophy* 2 (July): 272–286.

Ross, James F. 1986a. "Aquinas on Belief and Knowledge." In McCarthy (1986).

————. 1986b. "Believing for Profit." In McCarthy (1986), 221–235.

————. 1986c. "Unless You Believe You Will Not Understand." In McCarthy (1986).

————. 1988. "Eschatological Pragmatism." In *Philosophy and the Christian Faith*, ed. Thomas Morris. Notre Dame, Ind.: University of Notre Dame Press.

————. 1992. "Reason and Reliance: The Cognitive Functions of Feeling." In Long (1992).

Runzo, Joseph, and Craig Ihara, eds. 1986. *Religious Experience and Religious Belief: Essays in the Epistemology of Religion.* New York: University Press of America.

Russman, Thomas. 1988. "Reformed Epistemology." In Kennedy (1988), 185–205.

————. 1990. "A Faith of True Proportions: Reply to Sullivan." *Thomistic Papers* 5, ed. Thomas Russman, 81–91. Houston: Center for Thomistic Studies.

Schlesinger, George N. 1984. "The Availability of Evidence in Support of Religious Belief." *Faith and Philosophy* 1 (October): 421–436.

Smith, Stephen G. 1988. "Trying to Believe and the Ethics of Belief." *Religious Studies* 24 (December): 439–449.

Sparrow, M. F. 1991. "The Proofs of Natural Theology and the Unbeliever." *American Catholic Philosophical Quarterly* 65, 2 (Spring): 129–141.

Sullivan, Thomas D. 1988. "Adequate Evidence for Religious Assent." In Kennedy (1988), 73–100.

Swinburne, Richard. 1979. *The Existence of God.* Oxford: Clarendon Press.

————. 1981. *Faith and Reason.* Oxford: Oxford University Press.

Talbot, Mark R. 1985. " 'Self-Profile': Replies." In Tomberlin and Van Inwagen (1985).

————. 1989. "Is It Natural to Believe in God?" *Faith and Philosophy* 6 (April): 155–171.

Tilley, Terrence W. 1990. "Reformed Epistemology and Religious Fundamentalism: How Basic Are Our Basic Beliefs?" *Modern Theology* 6 (April): 237–257.

Tomberlin, James, ed. 1988. *Philosophical Perspectives 2: Epistemology.* Atascadero, Calif.: Ridgeview Press.

Tomberlin, James, ed. 1991. *Philosophical Perspectives 5: Philosophy of Religion.* Atascadero, Calif.: Ridgeview Press.

Tomberlin, James, and Peter Van Inwagen, eds. 1985. *Alvin Plantinga.* Dordrecht: Reidel.

Van Hook, Jay M. 1981. "Knowledge, Belief, and Reformed Epistemology." *The Reformed Journal* 31 (July): 12–15.

Vos, Arvin. 1985. *Aquinas, Calvin, and Contemporary Thought.* Washington, D.C.: Christian University Press.

———. 1986. Review of Hart, Van der Hoeven, and Wolterstorff, eds.: *Rationality in the Calvinian Tradition. Faith and Philosophy* 3 (July): 324–327.

Ward, William G. 1878. "The Reasonable Basis of Certitude." Reprinted in McCarthy (1986).

Watts, Fraser, and Mark Williams. 1988. *The Psychology of Religious Knowing.* Cambridge: Cambridge University Press.

Wippel, John F. 1984. "The Possibility of a Christian Philosophy: A Thomistic Perspective." *Faith and Philosophy* 1 (July): 272–290.

Wisdo, David. 1988. "The Fragility of Faith: Toward a Critique of Reformed Epistemology." *Religious Studies* 24 (September): 365–374.

Wittgenstein, Ludwig. "A Lecture on Religious Belief." In Pojman (1987b), 418–421.

Wolterstorff, Nicholas. 1976. *Reason within the Bounds of Religion.* Grand Rapids: Eerdmans. 2d ed. Grand Rapids: Eerdmans, 1984.

———. 1981. "Is Reason Enough?" *Reformed Journal* 31.

———. 1983a. "Can Belief in God Be Rational If It Has No Foundations?" In Plantinga and Wolterstorff (1983), 135–186.

———. 1983b. "Thomas Reid on Rationality." In Hart, Van der Hoeven, and Wolterstorff (1983).

———. 1986. "The Migration of Theistic Arguments: From Natural Theology to Evidentialist Apologetics." In Audi and Wainwright (1986), 38–81.

———. 1988. "Once Again, Evidentialism—This Time Social." *Philosophical Topics* 16: 53–74.

———. 1989. "Evidence, Entitled Belief, and the Gospels." *Faith and Philosophy* 6 (October): 429–444.

———. 1990. "The Assurance of Faith." *Faith and Philosophy* 7 (October): 396–417.

Wykstra, Stephen J. 1986. Review of Plantinga and Wolterstorff, eds.: *Faith and Rationality: Reason and Belief in God. Faith and Philosophy* 3 (April): 206–213.

———. 1989. "Toward a Sensible Evidentialism: On the Notion of 'Needing Evidence'." In *Philosophy of Religion: Selected Readings,* ed. W. L. Rowe and W. J. Wainwright. 2d ed. New York: Harcourt Brace Jovanovitch.

Zeis, John. 1990. "A Critique of Plantinga's Theological Foundationalism." *International Journal for the Philosophy of Religion* 28 (December): 173–189.

DATE DUE
